BLUE BOOK OF BROWNING FIREARMS & VALUES
by S.P. Fjestad

Publisher's Suggested List Price
$14.95

BLUE BOOK POCKET GUIDE FOR BROWNING/FN FIREARMS & VALUES

This book is the result of nonstop and continuous firearms research obtained by attending and/or participating in trade shows, gun shows, auctions, and also communicating with contributing editors, gun dealers, collectors, company historians, and other knowledgeable industry professionals worldwide each year. This book represents an analysis of prices for which collectible firearms have actually been selling during that period at an average retail level. Although every reasonable effort has been made to compile an accurate and reliable guide, gun prices may vary significantly (especially auction prices) depending on such factors as the locality of the sale, the number of sales we were able to consider, and economic conditions. Accordingly, no representation can be made that the guns listed may be bought or sold at prices indicated, nor shall the author or publisher be responsible for any error made in compiling and recording such prices and related information.

All Rights Reserved
Copyright 2013
Second printing 2013

Blue Book Publications, Inc.
8009 34th Avenue South, Suite 250
Minneapolis, MN 55425 U.S.A.

Orders Only: 800-877-4867, ext. 3 (domestic only)
Phone No.: 952-854-5229
Fax No.: 952-853-1486
General Email: support@bluebookinc.com
Web site: www.bluebookofgunvalues.com
Published and printed in the United States of America

ISBN 10: 1-936120-30-5
ISBN 13: 978-1-936120-30-7

Distributed in part to the book trade by Ingram Book Company and Baker & Taylor.
Distributed throughout Europe by:

Visier GmbH
Wipsch 1
Bad Ems, Germany D-56130
www.vsmedien.de

Deutsches Waffen Journal
Rudolf-Diesel-Strasse 46
Blaufelden, D-74572 Germany
Website: www.dwj.de

No part of this publication may be reproduced in any form whatsoever, by photograph, mimeograph, fax transmission or any other mechanical or electronic means. Nor can it be broadcast or transmitted, by translation into any language, nor by electronic recording or otherwise, without the express written permission from the publisher – except by a reviewer, who may quote brief passages for critical articles and/or reviews.

The percentage breakdown by firearms condition factor with respective values per condition and the Photo Percentage Grading System™ (PPGS) are copyrighted by Blue Book Publications, Inc. Any unauthorized usage of these systems for the evaluation of firearms values and color photo percentage breakdown is expressly forbidden by the publisher.

Table of Contents

Title Page 1

Publisher's Note/Copyright 2

Table of Contents 3

Acknowledgements/Credits 4

How to Use This Book 5-7

Grading Criteria 8

NRA Condition Standards 9

Browning Information/Values 10-125

Fabrique Nationale Information/Values 127-134

FNH USA Information/Values 135-140

Abbreviations 142-146

Contact Information 146

Browning Serialization 148-157

Serialization Index 159

Index 160

ACKNOWLEDGEMENTS/CREDITS

The author/publisher would like to thank the following individuals and companies for their contributions to this *Blue Book Pocket Guide for Browning/FN Firearms & Values*:

Glen Jensen, Jackie Love, and Paul Thompson – Browning

Rodney Herrmann

Gary Chatham

Anthony Vanderlinden

Bruce Hart

Glen Nilson

David Babcock – Jaqua's

Orvin Olson

Richard "Doc" Desira

Mike Vertesch

Harold Pedersen

John Lacy

Richard Spurzem

Jim King

Bert O'Neill, Jr.

ABOUT THE FRONT COVER:
Engraved Belgian Baby Browning pistol manufactured during 1960 with original black leatherette case.

ABOUT THE BACK COVER:
Belgian Browning Diana Grade Superposed Broadway Trap Model shotgun manufactured in 1968.

DEDICATION:
This book is dedicated to Mr. Glen Jensen, Browning's long-time historian and is a fully licensed Gunocologist – one of only two. Anyone who has ever had a question on an older Browning firearm has probably talked to Glen, and we are all extremely thankful for the help, knowledge, enthusiasm, and humor he has provided us over the years.

CREDITS:
Cover photography and some information courtesy of Rock Island Auctions (RIA) – www.rockislandauction.com

Cover artwork: Clint H. Schmidt

Printing: POD by RR Donnelley

How to Use This Book 5

The values listed in this *Blue Book Pocket Guide for Browning/FN Firearms & Values* are based on national average retail prices for both modern and antique firearms, and some accessories/accoutrements. This is not a firearms wholesale pricing guide. More importantly, do not expect to walk into a gun/pawn shop or gun show and think that the proprietor/dealer/collector should pay you the retail values listed within this text for your gun(s). Resale offers on many models could be anywhere from near retail to 20%-50% less than the values listed, depending upon locality, desirability, dealer inventory, and profitability. In other words, if you want to receive 100% of the retail value, then you have to do 100% of the work (become the retailer, which also includes assuming 100% of the risk).

Percentages of original condition (with corresponding values) are listed between 60%-100% on most modern firearms since condition below 60% is seldom encountered (or purchased). Please consult our revised Photo Percentage Grading System™ (PPGS) available on our website: www.bluebookofgunvalues.com to learn more about the condition of your firearm(s). Since condition is the overriding factor in price evaluation, study these photos and captions carefully to learn more about the condition of your specimen(s).

NRA condition standards and grading criteria have been included to make the conversion to percentages easier (see pages 8-9).

To find a model in this text, first look under the name of the manufacturer, either Browning or Fabrique Nationale. Next, find the correct category name(s) (Commemoratives, Pistols, Rifles, Shotguns, etc.). When applicable, antiques will appear before modern guns, and are typically listed in chronological sequence.

Trademarks are listed alphabetically in uppercase bold typeface, like this:

BROWNING, FABRIQUE NATIONALE (F.N.), FNH

Manufacturer/trademark information is listed directly beneath the trademark heading:

Current manufacturer located in Herstal, near Liege, Belgium. The current company name is "Group Herstal", however, the company is better known by "Fabrique Nationale" or "Fabrique Nationale d'Armes de Guerre". FN entered into their first contract with John M. Browning in 1897 for the manufacture of their first pistol, the FN 1899 Model.

Manufacturer notes may appear next under individual heading descriptions and can be differentiated by the following typeface:

> Also see: Browning Arms under Rifles, Shotguns, and Pistols, and FNH USA for current offerings in the U.S.

The next classification is the category name (normally, in alphabetical sequence) in uppercase lettering (inside a screened gray box) which primarily refers to a firearm's configuration. Category names include:

CARBINES: SEMI-AUTO, PISTOLS: SEMI-AUTO, REVOLVERS,
RIFLES: BOLT ACTION, SHOTGUNS: O/U

A further sub-classification may appear under a category name, as depicted below. These are sub-categories of a major category name, appear in both upper and lower case type, and typically appear in alphabetical order. Examples include:

Pistols: Semi-Auto

Following a category or sub-category name, a category note may follow to help explain

HOW TO USE THIS BOOK

the category, and/or provide limited information on the models and values listed within the category. This appears as follows:

For FN Models 1899, 1900, 1903, 1905, 1910, 1922 (10/22), Baby Model, Model 10/71, and BAC marked Hi-Powers (post 1954 mfg.), please refer to the Browning Pistol section in this text.

Model names appear flush left, are bold faced, and are in uppercase lettering either in chronological order (normally) or alphabetical order (sometimes, the previous model name and/or close sub-variation will appear at the end in parentheses) and are listed under the individual category and sub-category names. Examples include:

RENAISSANCE HI-POWER, PS90, FN SIDELOCK STANDARD GRADE

Model descriptions are denoted by the following typeface and usually include the following information:

– calibers, gauges/bore, action type, barrel length(s), finish(es), weight, and other descriptive data are provided adjacent to model names in this typeface. This is where most of the information is listed for each specific model, including identifiable features and possibly some production data, including quantity, date of manufacture, and discontinuance date, if known.

Variations (and possible production periods) within a model appear as sub-models - they are differentiated from model names by an artistic icon * prefix, are italicized and indented, and appear in upper and lowercase type, as follows:

* *WWII Production: Waffenampt Proofed Type I, A-Bolt Grade I .22 LR cal., FNP-45 Tactical*

This is usually followed by a short description of that sub-model. These sub-model descriptions have the same typeface as the model descriptions:

– additional sub-model information could include finishes, calibers, barrel lengths, special order features, or other production data specific for that sub-model.

Also included is yet another layer of model/information nomenclature differentiating sub-models from variations of sub-models or a lower hierarchy of sub-model information. These items are indented from the sub-models, and have the icon graphic », for example:

» *Model 585 Sporting Clays Set, Citori Superlight Grade I Earlier Mfg. without Invector Choking*

A description for this level of sub-model information may appear next to the sub-entry, and uses the same typeface as model and sub-model descriptions shown above.

Model notes and information appear in smaller type, generally after the price line, and should be read since they contain important, critical, and interesting facts/information. In some cases, factory recalls (some include serialization) are also provided. Examples include:

Original buttplates with unaltered (uncut) stock are very important to collectors for this period of Superposed manufacture.

Extra features/special orders which can add or subtract value are placed either under category names, model/sub-model descriptions, or pricing lines. On current models that don't have a price line, the MSR will also appear in this typeface, in addition to

HOW TO USE THIS BOOK

other pricing information regarding that model. These individual lines appear bolder than other descriptive typeface, such as the following:

Add 10% for NIB condition.
Subtract 20% for blued receiver.
Current MSR on this model is $2,384.

On many discontinued models/variations after 1985, the following line may appear under the price line, indicating the last manufacturer's suggested retail price flush right on the page, like this:

Last MSR was $1,495.
Last MSR in 2006 was $7,500.

Grading lines normally appear at the top of each page, and in the middle if price lines change. If you are uncertain as to how to properly grade a particular firearm, please refer to the digital color Photo Percentage Grading System (PPGS) at www.bluebookofgunvalues.com for more assistance. The most commonly encountered grading line (shown with a typical price line underneath) in this text is for 100%-60% condition factors:

MSR	100%	98%	95%	90%	80%	70%	60%

Price line formats are as follows - when the price line shown below (with proper grading line) is encountered, it automatically indicates the gun is currently manufactured, and the MSR is shown left of the 100% column. Following this are the 100%-60% values. This 100% value is the national average price a consumer will typically expect to pay for that model in NIB unfired condition. 100% specimens without boxes, warranties, etc., which are currently manufactured may be discounted (5%-20%, depending on the desirability of make and model). This 100% price on currently manufactured guns also assumes not previously sold at retail.

MSR $1,150	$925	$795	$675	$600	$475	$375	$325
	$895	$775	$675	$575	$500	$450	$400
	$2,050	$1,795	$1,550	N/A	N/A	N/A	N/A

When "N/A" (Not Applicable) is listed instead of a value, this indicates that this particular model is not encountered enough in those condition factors to warrant a value - especially true on antiques in upper condition factors and with commemoratives and special/limited editions under 95%.

Values for conditions under 60% will typically be no less than 50% (1/2) of the 60% price, unless the gun has been shot to a point where the action may be loose or questionable. Obviously, no "MSR" will appear in the left margin, but a last manufacturer's suggested retail price may appear flush right below the price line, automatically indicating a discontinued gun, like this:

Last MSR was $675.

Some antiques listed will not have price lines, but rather value ranges for Above Average, Average, and Below Average condition factors. These value range price lines with corresponding grading lines will appear as follows:

Above Average	Average	Below Average
$80,000 - $120,000	$35,000 - $80,000	$20,000 - $35,000

Additionally, you might want to refer to the Index on page 160 for an alphabetical listing of all category names. Abbreviations listings are on pages 142-146 and company contact information is also listed on page 146 for Browning, Fabrique Nationale, and FNH USA. You will also find Serialization on pages 148-157 and the Serialization Index on page 159.

GRADING CRITERIA

Most dealers and collectors are now utilizing what is essentially an objective method for deciding the condition of a gun: THE PERCENTAGE OF ORIGINAL FACTORY FINISH(ES) REMAINING ON THE GUN. After looking critically at a variety of firearms and carefully studying the Photo Percentage Grading System™ (available online at www.bluebookofgunvalues.com), it will soon become evident if a specific gun has 98%, 90%, 70% or less finish remaining. Remember, sometimes an older unfired gun described as NIB can actually be 98% or less condition, simply because of the wear accumulated by taking it in and out of the box and excessive handling. Commemoratives are especially prone to this problem. Of course, factors such as quality of finish(es), engraving (and other embellishments), special orders/features, historical significance and/or provenance, etc. can and do affect prices immensely. Also, it seems that every year bore condition (especially on antiques) becomes more important in the overall grading factor (and price) of both collectible and desirable Browning and FN models. Because of this, bore condition must be listed separately for those guns where it makes a difference in value.

Every gun's unique condition factor – and therefore the price – is best determined by the percentage of original finish(es) remaining, with the key consideration being the overall frame/receiver finish. The key word here is "original", for if anyone other than the factory has refinished the gun, its value as a collector's item has been diminished. The exceptions would be rare and historical guns that have been properly restored. Every year, top quality restorations have become more accepted, and prices have gone up proportionately with the quality of the workmanship. Also popular now are antique finishes, and a new question has come up, "What is 100% antique finish on new reproductions?" Answer – a gun that started out as new, and then has been aged to a lower condition factor to duplicate natural wear and tear.

When examining a gun's condition, note where the finishes of a firearm typically wear off first. These are usually places where the gun accumulates wear from holster/case rubbing, and contact with the hands or body over an extended period of time.

It should be noted that the older a collectible firearm is, the smaller the percentage of original finish one can expect to find. Some very old and/or very rare firearms are sought by collectors in almost any condition!

PHOTO PERCENTAGE GRADING SYSTEM CONVERSION GUIDELINES

New/Perfect – 100% condition with or without box. 100% on currently manufactured firearms assumes NIB (New In Box) condition and not sold previously at retail.

Mint – typically 98%-99% condition with almost no observable wear. Probably sold previously at retail, and may have been shot occasionally.

Excellent – 95%+ - 98% condition.

Very Good – 80% - 95% condition (all parts/finish should be original).

Good - 60% – 80% condition (all parts/finish should be original).

Fair – 20% - 60% condition (all parts/finish may or may not be original, but must function properly and shoot).

Poor – under 20% condition (shooting not a factor).

NRA CONDITION STANDARDS

The NRA conditions listed below have been provided as guidelines to assist the reader in converting and comparing condition factors. Once the gun's condition has been accurately assessed, only then can values be accurately ascertained. Please refer to the Photo Percentage Grading System (PPGS) available online at www.bluebookofgunvalues.com to learn more about condition factors. Why guess when you can be sure?

NRA MODERN CONDITION DESCRIPTIONS

New – not previously sold at retail, in same condition as current factory production.

Perfect – in new condition in every respect, may have previously been sold at retail.

Excellent – near new condition, used but little, no noticeable marring of wood or metal, bluing near perfect (except at muzzle or sharp edges).

Very Good – in perfect working condition, no appreciable wear on working surfaces, no corrosion or pitting, only minor surface dents or scratches.

Good – in safe working condition, minor wear on working surfaces, no broken parts, no corrosion or pitting that will interfere with proper functioning.

Fair – in safe working condition, but well worn, perhaps requiring replacement of minor parts or adjustments which should be indicated in advertisement, no rust, but may have corrosion pits which do not render article unsafe or inoperable.

NRA ANTIQUE CONDITION DESCRIPTIONS

Factory New – all original parts; 100% original finish; in perfect condition in every respect, inside and out.

Excellent – all original parts; over 80% original finish; sharp lettering, numerals and design on metal and wood; unmarred wood; fine bore.

Fine – all original parts; over 30% original finish; sharp lettering, numerals and design on metal and wood; minor marks in wood; good bore.

Very Good – all original parts; none to 30% original finish; original metal surfaces smooth with all edges sharp; clear lettering, numerals and design on metal; wood slightly scratched or bruised; bore disregarded for collectors firearms.

Good – less than 20% original finish, some minor replacement parts; metal smoothly rusted or lightly pitted in places, cleaned or reblued; principal lettering, numerals and design on metal legible; wood refinished, scratched, bruised or minor cracks repaired; in good working order.

Fair – less than 10% original finish, some major parts replaced; minor replacement parts may be required; metal rusted, may be lightly pitted all over, vigorously cleaned or reblued; rounded edges of metal and wood; principal lettering, numerals and design on metal partly obliterated; wood scratched, bruised, cracked or repaired where broken; in fair working order or can be easily repaired and placed in working order.

Poor – little or no original finish remaining, major and minor parts replaced; major replacement parts required and extensive restoration needed; metal deeply pitted; principal lettering, numerals and design obliterated, wood badly scratched, bruised, cracked or broken; mechanically inoperative, generally undesirable as a collector's firearm.

BROWNING

Current manufacturer with U.S. headquarters located in Morgan, UT. Browning guns originally were manufactured in Ogden, UT, circa 1880. Browning firearms are manufactured by Fabrique Nationale in Herstal and Liège, Belgium. Beginning 1976, Browning also contracted with Miroku of Japan and A.T.I. in Salt Lake City, UT to manufacture both long arms and handguns. In 1992, Browning (including F.N.) was acquired by GIAT of France. During late 1997, the French government received $82 million for the sale of F.N. Herstal from the Walloon business region surrounding Fabrique Nationale in Belgium.

The category names within the Browning section have been arranged in an alphabetical format: - PISTOLS (& variations), RIFLES (& variations), SHOTGUNS (& variations), SPECIAL EDITIONS, COMMEMORATIVES & LIMITED MFG.

The author would like to express his sincere thanks to the Browning Collector's Association, including members Rodney Herrmann, Richard Spurzem, Jim King, Bert O'Neill, Jr., Anthony Vanderlinden, Richard Desira, Gary Chatham, Bruce Hart, and Glen Nilson for continuing to make their important contributions to the Browning section.

In addition to the models listed within this section, Browning also offered various models/variations that were available only at the annual SHOT SHOW beginning 2004. More research is underway to identify these models, in addition to their original MSRs (if listed).

BROWNING HISTORY

The Browning firm, first known as J.M. Browning & Bro., was established in Ogden, Utah about 1880. Later known as Browning Brothers and Browning Arms Company (BAC), the firm actually manufactured only one gun - the Model 1878 Single Shot which was John M.'s first patent. Winchester bought the production and distribution rights to this gun in 1883, bringing it out as the Winchester M1885. From that time until 1900, Mr. Browning sold Winchester the exclusive rights to 31 rifles and 13 shotguns, of which Winchester produced only 7 rifles (M1885SS: the lever actions M1886, 1892, 1894 and 1895: and the slide action .22s M1890 and 1906) and 3 shotguns (M1887, M1893 and M1897). The other models were bought from Browning simply to keep them out of the hands of other arms makers.

John M. Browning, perhaps the greatest firearms inventor the world has ever known, was directly responsible for an estimated 80 separate firearms that evolved from his 128 patents. During his most prolific period from 1894 to 1910, Browning sold the rights to his rifles, semi-auto pistols, shotguns and machine guns to Winchester, Remington, Colt and Stevens in this country and to Fabrique Nationale (Belgium) for sale outside the U.S. Every Colt and F.N. semi-auto pistol is based on a Browning patent. In 1902, Browning broke off relations with Winchester when the company refused to negotiate a royalty arrangement for his new semi-auto shotgun (A-5). Browning took the prototype to F.N. Since 1902, F.N. has produced numerous automatic pistols, 3 rifles and 2 shotguns designed by John M. Browning and is still a major producer of arms sold by Browning in the U.S. and by F.N. distributors worldwide.

Our American military was armed for many years with Browning designed weaponry, not the least of which is the venerable "Old Slabside" 1911 Govt. Model .45 ACP. Today, the firm that bears the Browning name still stands at the forefront with the other makers of fine sporting firearms.

BROWNING FACTS

Note: Between 1966-1971 Browning used a salt-curing process on some of its raw wood to speed the drying time needed to produce its walnut stock blanks. Unfortunately, the salt would be released from the wood and oxidize (rust) the metal surface(s) after a period of time. Although not all Browning guns were salty, those affected guns, especially bolt action rifles in all grades, some BARs, Superposed shotguns, and T-bolt models should be examined carefully around where the metal contacts with the wood for signs of freckling and rust. Discount values on guns which show tell-tale characteristics of salt corrosion range from 25%-40%, depending on how severe the rust damage is. Check all screws which have direct contact with wood and the wood under the buttplate as well. Original Superposed owners of salt wood guns who still have their original owner's warranty card are still eligible for Browning factory refurbishing of affected parts only without charge. Otherwise, Browning has a standardized repair charge for each model.

Since the inception and standardization of steel shot for hunting purposes, the desirability factor of shotguns has changed considerably. On newer manufacture, most shooters/buyers now expect choke tubes, and shotguns without choke tubes must be discounted somewhat. Browning does not recommend using steel shot in any Superposed (B-25) or older Belgian Auto-5 barrels.

Browning's Miroku plant in Japan, in addition to making models specifically for the Browning Arms Company (BAC) in the U.S., also makes a wide variety of makes and models specifically for European sale. These models are normally not imported into the U.S., and because of this, they are not included in this section. You may be able to find more information on the current European models by visiting Browning's international website: www.browningint.com.

BROWNING VALUES INFORMATION

Editor's Note: It is important to note the differences in values of Browning firearms manufactured in Belgium by F.N. and those made recently in Japan by Miroku. We feel that these values are somewhat higher because of collector interest in Belgian guns, and not as the result of any inferiority of the quality of Browning guns made anywhere else.

AS A FINAL NOTE: Most post-war Brownings are collectible only if in 95% or better condition as most models have relatively high mfg. and are not that old. Condition under 95% is normally very shootable, but not as collectible and values for 95% or less condition could be lower than shown in some areas.

All add-ons or deductions on Browning's currently manufactured models reflect retail pricing without any discounting. On higher grade Browning firearms that are engraved, signed specimens by FN's master engravers Funken, J. Baerten, Vrancken, and Watrin will command premiums over the values listed.

BROWNING SERIALIZATION

In addition to the Belgian Browning serialization listed in the back of this text, the following codes will determine the year and origin of those guns made from 1975 to date. The 2 letters in the middle of the serial number are the code designations for year of manufacture. They represent the following: RV - 1975, RT - 1976, RR - 1977, RP - 1978,

BROWNING CUSTOM SHOP

MSR	100%	98%	95%	90%	80%	70%	60%

RN - 1979, PM - 1980, PZ - 1981, PY - 1982, PX - 1983, PW - 1984, PV - 1985, PT - 1986, PR - 1987, PP - 1988, PN - 1989, NM - 1990, NZ - 1991, NY - 1992, NX - 1993, NW - 1994, NV - 1995, NT - 1996, NR - 1997, NP - 1998, NN - 1999, MM - 2000, MZ - 2001, MY - 2002, MX - 2003, MW - 2004, MV - 2005, MU - 2006, MT - 2007, MS - 2008, MN - 2009, ZM - 2010, ZZ - 2011, ZY-2012, ZX-2013, ZW-2014.

Since most recently manufactured Browning's use a 3-digit model identification code with the two-letter date code in the serial number (appearing before the year code on European and U.S. mfg. guns, and after the year code on Japanese mfg.) the configuration of a model can also be determined. For example, S/N 611RP2785 would be a Model B-2000 made in 1978 with 2785 being the shotgun's number. S/N 01001NY873 would be the first production example of a Citori Grade III 28 gauge Lightning Model shotgun manufactured in 1992. Refer to Browning Serialization in the back of this text of additional information on Browning model codes.

BROWNING CUSTOM SHOP

Browning's Custom Shop in Herstal, Belgium, continues to make a wide variety of firearms, a number of which have limited importation into the U.S. Current Custom Shop Superposed prices and model information have been provided in the Superposed section. For more information on the Browning Custom Shop's additional offerings, please look under the various category names for availability and current pricing. Please refer to Browning's web site at www.browning.com for more information on the wide variety of firearms available from the Browning Custom Shop in Belgium, or contact Browning directly.

PISTOLS: SEMI-AUTO, CENTERFIRE, F.N. PRODUCTION UNLESS OTHERWISE NOTED

MODEL 1899-FN – 7.65mm cal., first Belgian Browning, 4 in. barrel, similar to later M-1900 but w/o safety markings or lanyard ring, almost 15,000 mfg. 1899-1901.

$1,850 $1,500 $1,250 $1,000 $750 $600 $550

Add 15% for guns manufactured in 1899 (ser. nos. 1-3900, without "A" prefix or suffix).
Add 50% for factory nickel finish (nickel finish with blue trigger and blue safety lever) - if 95% condition or better.
Add $800 for factory presentation case with accessories.

MODEL 1900-FN – 7.65mm cal., 4 in. barrel, standard safety markings are in French: Feu and Sur. 724,500 mfg. 1900-1914.

$1,200 $1,050 $900 $800 $600 $500 $350

Add 50% for factory nickel finish (nickel finish with blue trigger and safety lever) - if 95% condition or better.
Add $800 for factory presentation case with accessories.
Add $750 for Imperial Russian contract (crossed rifles marking on blue or nickel guns).
Add $100 for Imperial German contracts with German safety markings (Feuer & Sicher).
Add $100 minimum for special contract or retailer markings.

MODEL 1903-FN – 9mm Browning Long cal., 5 in. barrel. 58,400 mfg. 1903-1927.

$2,000 $1,750 $1,500 $1,250 $1,000 $800 $600

| MSR | 100% | 98% | 95% | 90% | 80% | 70% | 60% |

Add 100% if slotted to accept shoulder stock - beware of fakes.

Add $150 minimum for special contract or retailers markings.

This variation was also manufactured with a detachable shoulder stock. This accessory is rare and can add $1,500-$2,500 (shoulder stock w/o extended magazine) or $2,000-$3,000 (shoulder stock with extended magazine and cleaning rod) to the values listed.

MODEL 1905-FN (VEST POCKET) – 6.35mm cal. (.25 ACP), 6 shot mag. dubbed "Vest Pocket" model, 2 in. barrel, manufactured by Fabrique Nationale, Herstal, Belgium. 1,086,133, mfg. 1906 to circa 1949.

* *Model 1905-FN First Variation* – no slide lock/safety lever.

| | $600 | $475 | $375 | $325 | $275 | $225 | $175 |

Add 50% for factory nickel finish (nickel finish with blue trigger and blue safety lever) - if 95% condition or better.

Add $500 for factory presentation case.

Add $750 for Imperial Russian contract (crossed rifles marking on blue or nickel guns).

Add $150 minumum for special contract or retailers markings.

* *Model 1905-FN Second Variation* – post 1908, with slide lock/safety lever.

| | $550 | $425 | $325 | $275 | $225 | $175 | $125 |

Add 50% for factory nickel finish (nickel finish with blue trigger and blue safety lever) - if 95% condition or better.

Add $500 for factory presentation case.

Add $750 for Imperial Russian contract (crossed rifles marking on blue or nickel guns).

Add $150 minimum for special contract or retailers markings.

MODEL 1907 HUSQVARNA MFG. – 9mm Browning Long cal., identical to FN Browning 1903, mfg. by Husqvarna in Sweden to supply the Swedish military. Mfg. started in 1917 because the FN Browning 1903 was not available from Belgium during WWI, produced 1917-1942. Most were arsenal refinished in Sweden featuring a dull blue finish over sandblasted metal. Many were imported into the U.S. and converted to .380 ACP cal. in the U.S.

| | $1,000 | $900 | $800 | $750 | $650 | $550 | $450 |

Add 50% for original early factory high polish blue finish.

Add 20% for early "Browning's Patent" slide legend.

Add 10% for "System Browning" slide legend.

Subtract 20% for .380 ACP conversion.

MODEL 1910-FN (MODEL 1955) – 7.65mm (.32 ACP) or Browning 9mm short (.380 ACP) cal., 3 7/16 in. barrel. FN manufacture. 701,266 mfg. 1912-1983.

| | $625 | $475 | $325 | $275 | $250 | $195 | $150 |

Add 20% if BAC marked and 7.65mm cal., or if FN marked and .380 ACP cal.

Add $100 minimum for special contract or retailer markings.

This model is also referred to as the Model 1910/55. BAC marked pistols were imported 1954-1968. Importation ceased after the 1968 GCA.

PISTOLS: SEMI-AUTO, CENTERFIRE, F.N. PRODUCTION UNLESS OTHERWISE NOTED

MSR	100%	98%	95%	90%	80%	70%	60%

* ***Model 1955 Renaissance*** – Renaissance engraved model. Most often encountered with BAC slide legend, rarely encountered in the U.S. with "Fabrique Nationale" slide legend.

$2,950 $2,375 $1,800 $1,400 $1,000 $850 $700

Add $100 for original Browning case.

MODEL 1922 OR 10/22 FN – 7.65mm (.32 ACP) or .380 ACP cal., 4 1/2 in. barrel, Model 10/22 and 1922 are the same. The Model 1910 was modified by FN technicians for sale to the Yugoslav military in 1922, includes a longer barrel, larger frame and magazine. Made primarily for police and military contracts, it was also sold in France, Holland, Greece, Germany, Turkey, and many other nations. Several hundred thousand were mfg. during the Nazi occupation of FN during 1940-44. Most common variations are wartime "WaA140" marked pistols.

$525 $425 $375 $325 $275 $225 $200

Add 150% if .380 ACP and WaA613 marked on trigger guard.
Add 100% if .32 ACP and WaA613 marked.
Add 30% if WaA103 marked.
Add 30% if Wartime commercial Eagle N marked.
Add 25% for post liberation "A" prefix ser. no.
Add at least $100 for special prewar contract markings.
Subtract 10% for common WaA140 wartime marked pistols.

FN "BABY" MODEL – 6.35mm (.25 ACP) cal., 6 shot mag., 2 in. barrel, w/o grip safety or slide lock lever, imported under BAC trademark from 1954-68+ in standard blue finish, lightweight nickel and alumnium frame, and engraved Renaissance models. Over 510,000 mfg. 1931-83. Reintroduced during the 1990s for the European market.

* ***FN "Baby" Model: FN Marked*** – slide marked "Fabrique Nationale", blue finish standard.

$775 $600 $475 $425 $350 $300 $225

Add 20% for pre-war production (ser. no. 1-50140).
Add $100 for original cardboard or plastic box with extras.
Add $700 for pre-war factory presentation case.
Add $150 minimum for special contract or retailers markings.

* ***FN "Baby" Model: BAC Marked*** – slide marked "Browning Arms Co.", blue finish standard.

$550 $475 $400 $350 $250 $200 $150

Add $50-$100 for original box and manual, or $25-$50 for original BAC pouch and manual.

* ***FN "Baby" Model: Lightweight Model*** – nickel or aluminum (introduced 1954) frame, with pearl grips.

$625 $525 $425 $375 $275 $225 $200

* ***FN "Baby" Model: Renaissance Model*** – engraved, satin grey finish.

$2,400 $1,800 $1,500 $1,200 $900 $800 $600

PISTOLS: SEMI-AUTO, CENTERFIRE, F.N. PRODUCTION UNLESS OTHERWISE NOTED 15

MSR	100%	98%	95%	90%	80%	70%	60%

FN/BROWNING MODEL 10/71 – .380 ACP cal., 4 1/2 in. barrel, modified version of Model 1922 (10/22), grip safety, includes target sights and grips in addition to incorporating a magazine finger tip extension designed to comply with GCA of 1968. Sold in U.S. by BAC 1970-1974 as the "Standard .380," still mfg. by FN as Model 125.

| | $595 | $500 | $450 | $400 | $375 | $350 | $300 |

* *FN/Browning Model 10/71 Renaissance Model*

| | $2,250 | $1,900 | $1,500 | $1,300 | $1,150 | $925 | $700 |

MODEL 1935 HI-POWER (HP) – 9mm Para. cal., 13 shot mag., 4 21/32 in. barrel, John M. Browning's last pistol design, mfg. 1935 to date in variations for commercial, military, and police use in over 68 countries, first imported under BAC trademark in 1954.

Please refer to the Fabrique Nationale section of this book for pre-1954 variations (including pre-WWII, WWII, and earlier commercial models), as well as contemporary production of those variations not imported by BAC.

HI-POWER: POST-1954 MFG. – 9mm Para. or .40 S&W (mfg. 1995-2010) cal., similar to FN model 1935, has BAC slide marking, 10 (C/B 1994) or 13* shot mag., 4 5/8 in. barrel, polished blue finish, checkered walnut grips, fixed sights, molded grips were introduced in 1986 (disc. in 2000), ambidextrous safety was added to all models in 1989, approx. 32 (9mm Para.) or 35 (.40 S&W) oz., mfg. by FN in Belgium, imported 1954-2000, reintroduced 2002.

* *Hi-Power Standard - Polished Blue Finish (Imported 1954-2000)* – 9mm Para. or .40 S&W (new 1995-) cal., includes fixed front and lateral adj. rear sight, 32 or 35 oz.

| | $875 | $700 | $550 | $475 | $425 | $350 | $325 |

Add 50% for ring hammer and internal extractor.
Add 20% for ring hammer and external extractor (post 1962 mfg.).
Add 30% for thumb print feature.
Add 15% for T-prefix serial number.
Older specimens in original dark green, maroon, or red/black plastic boxes were mfg. 1954-1965 and are scarce - add $100+ in value. Black pouches (circa 1965-1968, especially with gold metal zipper) will also command a $25-$50 premium, depending on condition.

Major identifying factors of the Hi-Power are as follows: the "Thumb-Print" feature was mfg. from the beginning through 1958. Old style internal extractor was mfg. from the beginning through 1962, the "T" SN prefix (T-Series start visible extractor) was mfg. 1963-mid-1970s for all U.S. imports by BAC, 69C through 77C S/N prefixes were mfg. 1969-1977. Rounded type Ring Hammers with new external extractor were mfg. from 1962-1972 (for U.S. imports by BAC, much later on FN marked pistols). Spur Hammers have been mfg. 1972-present, and the "245" S/N prefix has been mfg. 1977-present. During 2010, all Hi-Powers featured a 75th Anniversary logo etched onto the top of the slide.

MSR	100%	98%	95%	90%	80%	70%	60%

* **Hi-Power Standard - Polished Blue Finish (Imported 2002-Current)** – 9mm Para. or .40 S&W (mfg. 1995-2010) cal., includes fixed front and lateral adj. rear sight, 32 or 35 oz.

  MSR $1,070 $850 $685 $535 $465 $415 $350 $325

* **Hi-Power Standard with Adj. Rear Sight** – 9mm Para. or .40 S&W cal. (disc. 2010), similar to Hi-Power Standard blue, except has adj. rear sight.

  MSR $1,150 $900 $715 $585 $485 $425 $385 $350

* **Hi-Power Standard - Polished Blue Finish 75th Anniversary Edition** – 9mm Para. cal. only, similar to Hi-Power Standard Polished Blue Finish, except has "75 years 1935-2010" etched on the top of slide. Limited production 2011 only.

     $850 $685 $535 $450 $400 $350 $325

  Last MSR was $1,030.

  Add $70 for adj. rear sight.

* **Hi-Power Mark III** – 9mm Para. or .40 S&W (mfg. 1994-2000, reintroduced 2003-2010) cal., non-glare matte blue (disc. 2005) or black epoxy (new 2006) finish, ambidextrous safety, tapered dovetail rear fixed sight, two-piece molded grips, Mark III designation became standard in 1994, approx. 35 oz. Imported 1985-2000, reintroduced 2002.

  MSR $1,060 $845 $585 $485 $425 $365 $335 $300

  This model's finish may be confused with some other recent imports which have a "black" painted finish. These black finish guns are painted rather than blue, and some parties have been selling them as original military FNs.

  » **Hi-Power Mark III 75th Anniversary Edition** – 9mm Para. cal. only, features "75th year" logo etched on top of slide. Limited production 2011 only.

     $825 $675 $525 $450 $400 $350 $325

  Last MSR was $1,030.

* **Hi-Power Silver Chrome Finish** – 9mm Para. or .40 S&W (new 1995) cal., entire gun finished in silver chrome, includes adj. sights and Pachmayr rubber grips, 36 (9mm Para.) or 39 (.40 S&W) oz. Assembled in Portugal, and imported 1991-2000.

     $795 $675 $550 $500 $425 $400 $375

  Last MSR was $718.

  Add 50% for circa 1980 Belgian model marked "Made in Belgium."

* **Hi-Power Practical Model** – 9mm Para. or .40 S&W (new 1995) cal., features blue (disc. 2005) or black epoxy slide, silver-chromed frame finish, wraparound Pachmayr rubber grips, round style serrated hammer, and choice of adj. sights (mfg. 1993-2000) or removable front sight, 36 (9mm Para.) or 39 (.40 S&W) oz. Imported 1990-2000, reintroduced 2002-2006.

     $725 $600 $525 $450 $425 $400 $375

  Last MSR was $863.

  Add $58 for adj. sights (disc. 2000).

MSR	100%	98%	95%	90%	80%	70%	60%

* ***Hi-Power Nickel/Silver Chrome Finish*** – not to be confused with stainless steel (never offered in the Hi-Power), this nickel/silver chrome finish is different from the silver chrome finish released in 1991, gold trigger, checkered walnut grips. Approx. 11,609 mfg. 1980-85.

$795 $675 $550 $500 $425 $400 $375

Last MSR was $525.

Add 50% for circa 1980 Belgian model marked "Made in Belgium."

* ***Hi-Power .30 Luger cal.*** – .30 Luger cal., mfg. for European sales (most are marked BAC on slide), approx. 1,500 imported late 1986-89, similar specifications as 9mm Para. model.

$925 $775 $625 $550 $450 $425 $375

This model was never cataloged for sale by BAC in the U.S. A few earlier specimens have been noted with F.N. markings and ring hammer.

* ***Hi-Power GP Competition*** – 9mm Para. cal., competition model with 6 in. barrel, detent adj. rear sight, rubber wraparound grips, front counterweight, improved barrel bushing, decreased trigger pull, approx. 36 1/2 oz.

$995 $895 $725 $600 $550 $500 $450

The original GP Competition came in a black plastic case w/ accessories and is more desirable than later imported specimens which were computer serial numbered and came in a styrofoam box. Above prices are for older models - subtract 10% if newer model (computer serial numbered). This model was never cataloged for sale by BAC in the U.S., and it is not serviced by Browning.

* ***Hi-Power Tangent Rear Sight*** – 9mm Para. cal., manufactured from 1965-1978. 50-500 meter tangent sight. A total of approx. 7,000 were imported by Browning Arms Co. Early pistols are designated by "T" prefix and were mfg. 1964-69, later pistols mfg. 1972-76, had spur hammers and followed the 69C-76C ser. no. prefixes.

$1,150 $975 $825 $600 $475 $400 $375

Add $100 for "T" prefix.
Add $50 for original pouch and instruction manual.

* ***Hi-Power Tangent Capitan Polished Blue Finish*** – 9mm Para. cal., features 50-500 meter tangent rear sight, blue finish with walnut grips, slide is marked "Made in Belgium, Assembled in Portugal", 32 oz. Imported 1993-2000.

$925 $750 $600 $500 $400 $350 $300

Last MSR was $764.

* ***Hi-Power Tangent Rear Sight & Slotted*** – 9mm Para. cal., variation with grip strap slotted to accommodate shoulder stock. Early pistols had "T"

prefixes. Later pistols had spur hammers and are in the serial range 73CXXXX-74CXXXX.

MSR	100%	98%	95%	90%	80%	70%	60%
	$1,550	$1,300	$1,100	$900	$775	$650	$525

Add $200 if with "T" prefix.
Add $50 for original pouch and instruction booklet.

This variation will command a premium; beware of fakes, however (carefully examine slot milling and look for ser. no. in 3 places).

Vektor Arms in N. Salt Lake, UT, imported this model again in limited quantities circa 2004 with both the "245" and seldom seen "511" (includes wide trigger, loaded chamber indicator and external extractor) ser. no. prefixes. These guns are not arsenal refinished or refurbished, and were sold in NIB condition, with two 13 shot mags. Original pricing was $895 for the "245" prefix, and $995 for the "511" prefix.

BCA EDITION HI-POWER – 9mm Para. cal., limited edition made specifically for the Browning Collectors Association in 1980, approx. 100 were delivered.

	$950	$750	$575	N/A	N/A	N/A	N/A

GOLD LINE HI-POWER – 9mm Para. cal., blue finish with gold line perimeter engraving.

	$5,250	$4,500	$3,750	N/A	N/A	N/A	N/A

Check this model carefully for factory originality - including the ring hammer, engraving and bluing, as most models encountered are reproductions.

RENAISSANCE HI-POWER – 9mm Para. cal., extensive scroll engraving on grey silver slide and frame, synthetic pearl grips, gold plated trigger. Disc. approx. 1978.

	MSR	100%	98%	95%	90%	80%	70%
Round Hammer/fixed sights	$3,795	$3,250	$2,950	N/A	N/A	N/A	N/A
Spur Hammer/fixed sights	$3,250	$2,750	$2,250	N/A	N/A	N/A	N/A

Add $100 for internal extractor (pre-1962 mfg.)
Add $100 for "Thumb Print."
Add $50 for original pouch and booklet.
Add $600 for older individual blue leatherette European case.
Add $300-$500 for hi-polished silver finish, depending on condition.

Target sights do not affect the value of this model significantly.

Currently, the Browning Custom Shop in Belgium is making the following Renaissance models: Dore ($7,406 MSR), Nickele ($7,323 MSR), L1 ($4,377 MSR), I1 ($6,581 MSR), and the B2 ($4,571 MSR).

HI-POWER: CUSTOM SHOP MODELS

Currently, the Browning Custom Shop in Belgium is making the following Hi-Power custom shop models: 75th Anniversary Model ($6,971 MSR), Renaissance "Dore" or Gold ($6,247 MSR),

MSR	100%	98%	95%	90%	80%	70%	60%

Renaissance Nickele ($6,185 MSR), L1 ($4,089 MSR), I1 ($5,225 MSR), and B2 ($4,089 MSR).

CASED RENAISSANCE SET – one pistol each in .25 ACP, .380 ACP (rarest cal. of the three), and 9mm Para. cal., Hi-Power Renaissance models in walnut or black vinyl case, ser. no. not related to other calibers. Offered 1954-1969.

	$9,500	$8,250	$5,700	N/A	N/A	N/A	N/A

Add 30% for coin finish/high polish in early walnut case.
Add $100 for "St. Louis" slide address.
Add $150 for old style Hi-Power extractor.

All original Renaissance cased sets had 9mm Para. Hi-Powers with Ring Hammers. The .380 ACP cal. is the rarest of this set, and will bring $2,500 if new.

CASED GRADE I (BLUE) SET – one pistol each in .25 ACP, .380 ACP, and 9mm Para. cal., Hi-Power Grade I Models in walnut or black vinyl case, ser. no. not related to other calibers.

	$2,500	$2,100	$1,700	N/A	N/A	N/A	N/A

Add $100 for walnut presentation case.
Add $100 for thumbprint.
Add $100 for "St. Louis" slide address.
Add $100 for old style Hi-Power extractor.

All original Grade I blue cased sets had 9mm Para. Hi-Powers with Ring Hammers.

CENTENNIAL MODEL HI-POWER – similar to fixed sight Hi-Power, chrome plated with inscription "Browning Centennial/1878-1978", engraved on side, checkered walnut grips with "B" in circle, cased, 3,500 mfg. in 1978. Original issue price was $495.

	$1,100	$900	$750	N/A	N/A	N/A	N/A

CENTENAIRRE MODEL HI-POWER 1 OF 100 – 9mm Para. cal., unique pattern chemically etched, signed by the engraver, checkered walnut grips with border. 100 mfg. during 1989 - approx. half were sold in U.S., the other half in Europe.

	$5,000	$4,000	$3,250	N/A	N/A	N/A	N/A

LOUIS XVI MODEL – 9mm Para., chemically etched throughout in leaf scroll patterns, satin finish, checkered grips, walnut case. Disc. 1984.

	$1,900	$1,600	$1,100	N/A	N/A	N/A	N/A

CLASSIC HI-POWER SERIES – 9mm Para. cal., less than 2,500 manufactured in Classic model and under 350 manufactured in Gold Classic. Both editions feature multiple engraved scenes, and a special silver grey finish, presentation grips, cased. Mfg. 1984-86.

	$1,925	$1,700	$1,200	N/A	N/A	N/A	N/A

Last MSR was $1,000.

MSR	100%	98%	95%	90%	80%	70%	60%

* ***Gold Classic Hi-Power*** – 5 gold inlays, select walnut grips are both checkered and carved. Less than 350 mfg. 1984-1986.

	$4,250	$3,700	$2,950	N/A	N/A	N/A	N/A

Last MSR was $2,000.

125th ANNIVERSARY HI-POWER – 9mm Para. cal., silver nitride finish with scroll engraving, gold enhanced 125th Browning Anniversary logo with image of John M. Browning in gold on slide, 10 shot mag., fixed sights, smooth oil finished walnut grips. 125 mfg. 2003-2004 only.

	$1,900	$1,600	$1,100	N/A	N/A	N/A	N/A

Last MSR was $1,516.

BROWNING DOUBLE ACTION – this model was first listed in the Browning catalog in 1985 but was never imported commercially. The advertised 1985 retail price was $494.

BDM/BPM/BRM SINGLE/DOUBLE ACTION – 9mm Para. cal., double mode design featuring slide selector allowing choice between pistol (true double action operation) or revolver mode (full hammer decocking after each shot), available in double mode, single mode (BPM-D decocker, mfg. 1997), or double action only (BRM-DAO, mfg. 1997), dual purpose decocking lever/safety, 4.73 in. barrel, 10 (C/B 1994) or 15* shot mag., matte blue finish, black molded wraparound grips, unique breech block allows visible cartridge inspection, adj. rear sight, 31 oz. Mfg. in U.S. 1991-1997.

	$600	$450	$400	$350	$300	$280	$260

Last MSR was $551.

This model features hammer block and firing pin block safeties.

* ***BDM Practical*** – similar to Standard BDM, except has matte blue slide and silver chrome frame. Mfg. 1997-98.

	$600	$450	$400	$350	$300	$280	$260

Last MSR was $571.

* ***BDM Silver Chrome*** – similar to Standard BDM, except has silver chrome finish. Only 119 mfg. in 1997 only.

	$650	$500	$400	$350	$300	$280	$260

Last MSR was $571.

FN DA 9 – 9mm Para. cal., choice of double action or double action only, 4 5/8 in. barrel, molded rubber grips, 10 shot mag., 31 oz. Mfg. by FN. **The retail price on this model was listed at $613.**

While advertised in 1996, this model was never imported commercially.

PRO-9/PRO-40 – 9mm Para. or .40 S&W cal., single/double action, 4 in. barrel, 10, 14 (.40 S&W cal. only), or 16 (9mm Para. cal. only) shot mag., ambidextrous decocking and safety, black polymer frame with satin stainless steel slide, under barrel accessory rail, interchangeable backstrap inserts, fixed sights only, 30 (9mm Para.) or 33 oz. Mfg. in the U.S. by FNH USA 2003-2006.

	$525	$430	$370	$350	$315	$295	$260

Last MSR was $641.

Please refer to FNH USA handgun listing for current manufacture.

BDA-380 – .380 ACP cal., double action, 10 (C/B 1994) or 14* shot, 3 13/16 in. barrel, fixed sights, smooth walnut grips, 23 oz., introduced 1978 - later production was by Beretta. Disc. 1997.

Blue finish	$595	$525	$450	$395	$325	$275	$225
Nickel finish	$675	$595	$495	$450	$350	$295	$250

Last MSR was $564 and $607 for Nickel finish.

BDA MODEL – 9mm Para. (9 shot, 2,740 mfg.), .38 Super (752 mfg.), or .45 ACP (7 shot) cal., mfg. from 1977-80 by Sig-Sauer of W. Germany (same as Sig-Sauer 220).

9mm Para.	$600	$550	$450	$375	$295	$250	$225
.38 Super	$795	$675	$600	$500	$450	$390	$350
.45 ACP	$650	$575	$500	$400	$325	$275	$250

PISTOLS: SEMI-AUTO, .22 CAL. RIMFIRE

NOMAD MODEL – .22 LR cal., 10 shot, 4 1/2 and 6 3/4 in. barrels, steel or alloy frame, adj. sights, blue finish, black plastic grips. Mfg. 1961-1974 by FN.

	$475	$400	$325	$300	$225	$200	$175

Add 10% for alloy frame.

CHALLENGER MODEL – .22 LR cal., 10 shot, 4 1/2 and 6 3/4 in. barrels, steel frame, adj. sights, checkered walnut or plastic (mfg. 1974 only) wraparound grips, gold plated trigger. Mfg. 1962-1975 by FN.

	$650	$575	$550	$500	$475	$400	$350

* *Challenger Renaissance* – engraved satin nickel finish, 437 mfg. total (121 with 4 1/2 in. barrel, and 316 with 6 3/4 in. barrel).

	$3,150	$2,350	$1,700	N/A	N/A	N/A	N/A

* *Challenger Gold Line* – blue finish, gold line border on perimeter of frame surfaces, 293 mfg. total (147 with 4 1/2 in. barrel, and 146 with 6 3/4 in. barrel).

	$3,250	$2,400	$1,750	N/A	N/A	N/A	N/A

CHALLENGER II – .22 LR cal., Salt Lake City mfg., 6 3/4 in. barrel, steel frame, plastic impregnated hardwood grips, 38 oz. Mfg. 1975-82.

	$350	$300	$275	$250	$200	$175	$150

CHALLENGER III – .22 LR cal., Salt Lake City mfg., 5 1/2 in. bull barrel, 11 shot, alloy frame, adj. sights, 35 oz. Mfg. 1982-85.

	$295	$250	$200	$150	$135	$120	$110

Last MSR was $240.

MSR	100%	98%	95%	90%	80%	70%	60%

* ***Challenger III BCA Commemorative*** – .22 LR cal., mfg. to commemorate BCA's fourth anniversary.

$500 $450 $400 N/A N/A N/A N/A

CHALLENGER III SPORTER – .22 LR cal., similar to Challenger III, except has 6 3/4 in. round barrel, wide trigger, 29 oz. Mfg. 1983-1985.

$295 $250 $200 $150 $135 $120 $110

Last MSR was $240.

MEDALIST MODEL – .22 LR cal., 6 3/4 in. barrel, vent. rib, adj. target sights and barrel weights (3 supplied), blue finish, target walnut grips with thumbrest, dry-fire mechanism, 46 oz., black case with red cloth interior. 24,001 mfg. 1962-1976 by FN.

$1,500 $1,300 $1,100 $950 $825 $725 $625

Subtract 20%-30% if without case and accessories, depending on condition.

The following is a breakdown on how many USA Medalists were manufactured per year: 1962 - 1,068, 1963 - 4,661, 1964 - 1,666, 1965 - 1,170, 1966 - 1,400, 1967 - 2,631, 1968 - 3,039, 1969 - 2,897, 1970 - 1,131, 1971 - 425, 1972 - 1507, 1973 - 708, 1974 - 906, 1975 - 792, 1976-10 (no case or accessories).

* ***Medalist Gold Line*** – 407 mfg. 1962-1975.

$3,900 $3,150 $2,500 N/A N/A N/A N/A

* ***Medalist Renaissance Model*** – 11 pistols were mfg. 1962-1967 with full coverage engraving, and 382 were mfg. 1970-1975 w/o full coverage engraving, early production guns were coin finished and later ones were satin chrome. Mfg. by FN 1964-1975.

$4,200 $3,500 $2,750 N/A N/A N/A N/A

* ***Medalist BCA Engraved Edition*** – this BAC edition was a special order (not regular production), featured full coverage engraving. 60 mfg. 1986 only.

$5,250 $4,250 $3,150 N/A N/A N/A N/A

The BCA Medalist features full coverage engraving (similar to 1962-67 Renaissance mfg.), and has a finish similar to 1970-75 Renaissance production.

INTERNATIONAL MEDALIST – target variation model manufactured 1971, 1974, and 1977-1980 (late model), 5 7/8 (early model) or flatsided 5 15/16 (late model, no production statistics) in. barrel, dull black finish, however 681 were mfg. with BCA markings and blue finish. Recently manufactured by FN in the parkerized international configuration.

Late Model	$850	$750	$600	$500	$400	$350	$325
Early Model	$1,250	$1,050	$825	$725	$600	$525	$400

BUCK MARK STANDARD URX – .22 LR cal., 10 shot mag., 5 1/2 in. bull barrel, aluminum frame, composite grips with skipline checkering (disc. 1990), molded rubber grips (mfg. 1991-2006), or URX grips

PISTOLS: SEMI-AUTO, .22 CAL. RIMFIRE

MSR	100%	98%	95%	90%	80%	70%	60%

(ambidextrous with finger grooves, new 2006, became standard during 2007), adj. sights, gold trigger, matte blue finish, 34-36 oz. New 1985.

MSR $460 $375 $295 $250 $200 $150 $125 $110

Add $58 for nickel finish (mfg. 1991-2005).
Subtract approx. 10% for composite or molded rubber grips.

Buck Mark models are manufactured in Salt Lake City, UT.

* *Buck Mark Standard Stainless URX* - similar to Buck Mark Standard, except stainless steel, 34 oz. New 2005.

MSR $500 $395 $325 $275 $225 $175 $150 $125

Subtract 10% for molded rubber grips (mfg. 2005-2006).

BUCK MARK MICRO STANDARD URX - similar to Buck Mark Standard, except has 4 in. barrel, choice of standard or nickel finish, URX grips became standard 2007, 32 oz. New 1992.

MSR $460 $375 $295 $250 $200 $150 $125 $110

Add $58 for nickel finish (disc. 2005).
Subtract approx. 10% for composite or molded grips.

* *Buck Mark Micro Standard Stainless URX* - similar to Buck Mark Micro Standard, except stainless steel, URX grips became standard 2007, 34 oz. Mfg. 2005-2010.

                $375 $295 $250 $200 $170 $145 $125

Last MSR was $469.

* *Buck Mark Micro Plus* - similar to Micro Buck Mark, except has ambidextrous contoured laminated wood grips, nickel (new 1996) or blue finish. Disc. 2001.

                $325 $275 $225 $200 $170 $145 $125

Last MSR was $350.

Add $33 for nickel finish.

BUCK MARK CHALLENGE - .22 LR cal., features smaller grip circumference for smaller hands, smooth (disc.) or checkered walnut grips with medallions, matte blue finish, 5 1/2 in. lightweight barrel, Pro-Target sights, 25 oz. Mfg. 1999-2010.

                $350 $295 $225 $175 $150 $125 $110

Last MSR was $429.

* *Buck Mark Micro Challenge* - similar to Buck Mark Challenge, except has 4 in. barrel. 23 oz. Mfg. 1999-2000.

                $295 $240 $200 $175 $150 $125 $110

Last MSR was $311.

BUCK MARK CAMPER - .22 LR cal., features 5 1/2 in. heavy barrel, ambidextrous molded black composite grips, matte blue or satin nickel finish, Pro-Target sights, 34 oz. Mfg. 1999-2012.

                $290 $225 $175 $125 $100 $95 $85

Last MSR was $380.

Add $33 for satin nickel finish (disc. 2005).

* **_Buck Mark Camper Stainless_** – similar to Buck Mark Camper, except stainless steel, 34 oz. Mfg. 2005-2012.

    $315 $240 $190 $145 $110 $95 $75

    Last MSR was $420.

* **_Buck Mark Camper Stainless URX Field_** – .22 LR cal., alloy receiver, 5 1/2 in. stainless tapered bull barrel, ambidextrous Ultragrip RX grips, matte blued finish, Pro-Target adj. rear sight, Truglo/Marbles fiber optic front sight, 34 oz. Available from Full Line Browning dealers only. New 2008.

    MSR $430 $325 $250 $195 $150 $115 $100 $80

BUCK MARK CAMPER UFX – .22 LR cal., alloy frame, matte blue finish, tapered bull 5 1/2 in. barrel, 10 shot mag., Pro-Target adj. sights, ambidextrous overmolded black/grey UFX grips, 34 oz. New 2013.

MSR $380 $295 $235 $185 $135 $110 $100 $90

* **_Buck Mark Camper Stainless UFX_** – similar to Buck Mark Camper UFX, except has satin finished stainless steel barrel and slide assembly, 34 oz. New 2013.

    MSR $420 $325 $245 $190 $150 $115 $100 $85

BUCK MARK HUNTER – .22 LR cal., features 7 1/4 in. round heavy barrel with integral scope base, Truglo front sight, smooth cocobolo target grips, matte blue finish, 38 oz. New 2005.

MSR $480 $370 $275 $210 $145 $110 $100 $90

BUCK MARK PLUS UDX – similar to Buck Mark Standard, except has uncheckered laminated wood (disc. 2006) grips, or walnut ambidextrous DX Ultragrips (new 2007), Tru-Glo Marble front sight (new 2002), and choice of high polish blue or nickel (mfg. 1996-2006), 34 oz. Mfg. 1987-2007, reintroduced 2010.

MSR $520 $390 $290 $225 $170 $135 $120 $110

Add approx. 10% for nickel finish (disc. 2006).

* **_Buck Mark Field Plus UDX (Classic Plus)_** – similar to Buck Mark Plus, except has rosewood grips (disc. 2006, reintroduced 2010) or DX Ultragrips (mfg. 2007), and Tru-Glo Marble front sight. Mfg. 2002-2007, reintroduced 2010.

    MSR $520 $395 $295 $225 $165 $135 $120 $110

    This model is available from Full-Line dealers only.

* **_Buck Mark Plus Stainless UDX_** – similar to Buck Mark Plus, except has stainless steel barrel/slide, choice of black or brown (disc. 2010) UDX laminate grips, 34 oz. Mfg. 2007, reintroduced 2010.

    MSR $560 $450 $375 $295 $220 $190 $165 $150

    Subtract $35 for brown laminate grips.

BUCK MARK BULLSEYE TARGET – .22 LR cal., Bullseye model featuring 16 click per turn Pro-Target rear sight, 7 1/4 in. fluted barrel, matte blue

MSR	100%	98%	95%	90%	80%	70%	60%

finish, adj. trigger pull, contoured rosewood target or wraparound finger groove (disc.) grips, 10 shot mag., 36 oz. Mfg. 1996-2005.

	$495	$395	$295	$225	$190	$165	$150

Last MSR was $604.

* *Buck Mark Bullseye Target Stainless* – similar to Buck Mark Bullseye Target, except is stainless steel and has laminated rosewood grips, 39 oz. Mfg. 2006-2011.

	$595	$475	$350	$285	$225	$175	$150

Last MSR was $759.

* *Buck Mark Bullseye Standard* – similar to Buck Mark Bullseye Target, except has molded composite ambidextrous grips, 36 oz. Mfg. 1996-2006.

	$375	$295	$250	$200	$160	$145	$125

Last MSR was $468.

BUCK MARK BULLSEYE URX – .22 LR cal., 7 1/4 in. fluted barrel, matte blue finish, URX ambidextrous grips with finger grooves, 39 oz. Mfg. 2006-2010.

	$460	$375	$300	$230	$190	$165	$150

Last MSR was $579.

BUCK MARK 5.5 TARGET – .22 LR cal., same action as Buck Mark, 5 1/2 in. barrel with serrated top rib allowing adj. sight positioning, target sights, matte blue or nickel (mfg. 1994-2000) finish, choice of contoured walnut (disc. 2004), cocobolo (became standard 2005), or walnut wraparound finger groove grips (new 1992-disc.), 35 oz. Mfg. 1990-2009.

	$440	$350	$285	$225	$190	$170	$135

Last MSR was $579.

Add $54 for nickel finish (mfg. 1994-2000).

* *Buck Mark 5.5 Gold Target* – similar to 5.5 Target, except has gold anodized frame and top rib. Mfg. 1991-99.

	$375	$295	$250	$200	$160	$145	$125

Last MSR was $477.

BUCK MARK 5.5 FIELD – same action and barrel as the Target 5.5, except sights are designed for field use, anodized blue finish, choice of contoured walnut, cocobolo (became standard 2005), or walnut wraparound finger groove grips (new 1992-disc.), 35 1/2 oz. Mfg. 1991-2011.

	$450	$350	$295	$230	$190	$170	$135

Last MSR was $619.

BUCK MARK LITE GREEN/GRAY – features alloy matte green or gray receiver, fluted alloy sleeved 5 1/2 or 7 1/4 (mfg. 2010 only) in. barrel, blowback action, Ultragrip RX ambidextrous grips, Pro-Target adj. rear sight and TruGlo/Marble's fiber optic front sight, 28-30 oz. New 2010.

MSR $560	$435	$350	$280	$220	$190	$165	$150

Add $20 for 7 1/4 in. barrel (disc. 2010).

PISTOLS: SEMI-AUTO, .22 CAL. RIMFIRE

MSR	100%	98%	95%	90%	80%	70%	60%

BUCK MARK LITE SPLASH URX – .22 LR cal., 5 1/2 or 7 1/4 in. round barrel, aluminum barrel and receiver feature gold splash annodizing, URX grips standard, adj. sights with TruGlo fiber optic front sight, 28 or 30 oz. Mfg. 2006-2009.

	$370	$290	$230	$180	$150	$135	$120

Last MSR was $489.

Add $20 for 7 1/4 in. barrel.

BUCK MARK CONTOUR URX – .22 LR cal., 5 1/2 or 7 1/4 in. specially contoured steel or alloy (Lite) sleeved barrel with full length scope base, matte blue finish, URX grips, adj. rear sight, 28-36 oz. (Contour Lite variation is 8 oz. less than standard). New 2006.

MSR $540	$395	$300	$225	$170	$135	$120	$110

Add $10 for 7 1/4 in. barrel.

Add $50 for Contour Lite variation (alloy sleeved barrel, 8 oz. less than steel, disc. 2010).

BUCK MARK PRACTICAL URX – features alloy matte gray finished receiver, tapered 5 1/2 in. bull barrel, matte blue finish, Ultragrip RX ambidextrous grips, Pro-Target adj. rear sight, TruGlo/Marble's fiber optic front sight, 34 oz. New 2010.

MSR $430	$320	$235	$185	$140	$110	$95	$75

BUCK MARK VARMINT – .22 LR cal., same action as Buck Mark, 9 7/8 in. barrel with serrated top rib allowing adj. sight positioning, laminated wood grips, choice of contoured walnut or walnut wraparound finger groove grips (new 1992), optional detachable forearm, matte blue, 48 oz. Mfg. 1987-99.

	$375	$300	$225	$175	$155	$135	$120

Last MSR was $403.

BUCK MARK SILHOUETTE – .22 LR cal., silhouette variation of the Buck Mark, 9 7/8 in. bull barrel with serrated top rib allowing adj. sight positioning, hooded target sights, laminated wood stocks and forearm, choice of contoured walnut or walnut wraparound finger groove grips (new 1992), matte blue, 53 oz. Mfg. 1987-99.

	$395	$325	$250	$195	$170	$150	$135

Last MSR was $448.

* *Buck Mark Unlimited Silhouette (Match)* – similar to Silhouette Model featuring 14 in. barrel with set back front sight, choice of contoured walnut or walnut wraparound finger groove grips (new 1992), 64 oz. Mfg. 1991-99.

	$495	$400	$350	$250	$195	$170	$150

Last MSR was $536.

BUCK MARK COMMEMORATIVE – features 6 3/4 in. Challenger style tapered barrel, white bonded ivory grips with scrimshaw style patterning including "1 of 1,000 Commemorative Model" on sides, matte blue

MSR	100%	98%	95%	90%	80%	70%	60%

finish, gold trigger, 30 1/2 oz. 1,000 mfg. 2001 only.

	$395	$315	$250	N/A	N/A	N/A	N/A

Last MSR was $437.

1911-22 – .22 LR cal., patterned after the Colt Model 1911-A1 .22 LR cal. Ace pistol, choice of 3 5/8 (Compact Model) or 4 1/4 (A1 Model) in. barrel, alloy frame and slide, matte black finish, fixed sights, checkered brown composite grips, 10 shot mag., approx. 15 oz. Mfg. in the USA beginning 2011.

MSR $600	$525	$450	$415	$385	$360	$340	$325

Pistols made during 2011 include a limited edition canvas and leather zippered commemorative case, plus a collector's certificate.

1911-22 BCA EDITION – .22 LR cal., special 1911 Anniversary Edition, "BCA" is incorporated into the serial number, only 100 mfg. during 2011-2012.

	$925	$825	$725	N/A	N/A	N/A	N/A

Last MSR was $850.

RIFLES: BOLT ACTION

MODEL 52 LIMITED EDITION – .22 LR cal., virtually identical to the original Winchester Model 52C Sporter, except for minor safety enhancements, bolt action, 24 in. drilled and tapped barrel, 5 shot detachable mag., pistol grip walnut stock with oil style finish, deep blue finish, adj. trigger, two-position safety, 7 lbs. 5,000 mfg. 1991-92.

	$950	$850	$700	N/A	N/A	N/A	N/A

Last MSR was $500.

MODEL BBR – .25-06 Rem., .270 Win., .30-06, 7mm Mag., .300 Win. Mag. or .338 Win. Mag. cal., short action available in .22-250 Rem., 243 Win., 257 Roberts, 7mm-08 Rem., or 308 Win. cal., 24 in. standard or heavy barrel, 60 degree bolt throw, fluted bolt, adj. trigger, hidden detachable mag., no sights, checkered pistol grip, Monte Carlo stock. Mfg. 1978-84 by Miroku.

	$695	$600	$475	$400	$325	$250	$200

Some rare production calibers will add premiums to the values listed (i.e., add 50% for .243 Win. cal.).

BBR RIFLE ELK ISSUE – 7mm Rem. Mag. cal., deeply blued receiver which has multiple animals gold inlaid, high grade walnut stock and forearm feature skipline checkering. 1,000 mfg. Disc. 1986.

	$1,800	$1,500	$1,100	N/A	N/A	N/A	N/A

Last MSR was $1,395.

T-BOLT SPORTER/TARGET (NEW MFG.) – .17 HMR (new 2008), .22 LR, or .22 WMR (new 2008) cal., original straight pull action with enlarged bolt handle, 22 in. free floating medium sporter or heavy target barrel, 10 shot double helix rotary mag., blued steel receiver, satin finish

MSR	100%	98%	95%	90%	80%	70%	60%

sporter or target (w/cheekpiece) walnut stock with cut checkering, sling studs, gold trigger, no sights, top tang safety, right or left-hand (new 2009) action, 4 lbs., 14 oz. (sporter) or 5 1/2 (target) lbs. New 2006.

MSR $750 $615 $515 $435 $380 $325 $250 $195

Add $30 for Target/Varmint configuration (new 2007).

Add $40 for .17 HMR or .22 WMR cal. in sporter configuration, or $20 for same cals. in Target/Varmint configuration.

Add $10 for left-hand.

* ***T-Bolt Composite Sporter/Target (New Mfg.)*** – similar to T-Bolt Sporter/Target, except has matte black composite stock, includes sling swivels, choice of 22 in. medium (Sporter) or heavy target (Target/Varmint) barrel, right or left-hand (new 2009) action, approx. 4 1/2 (Sporter) or 5 lbs. 2 oz. (Target/Varmint). New 2008.

MSR $750 $615 $515 $435 $380 $325 $250 $195

Add $30 for Target/Varmint configuration (new 2007).

Add $40 for .17 HMR or .22 WMR cal. in sporter configuration, or $20 for same cals. in Target/Varmint configuration.

Add $10 for left hand.

T-BOLT T-1 – .22 LR cal., straight pull bolt action, 5 shot mag., 22 in. barrel, adj. rear sight, 5 1/2 lbs., plain pistol grip stock. Mfg. 1965-1974 by FN.

             $600 $525 $450 $410 $330 $270 $210

Add 10%-15% for left-hand model (mfg. 1967-1974 only).

An aperture rear sight was standard for the first nine years of production.

Watch for salt wood.

T-BOLT T-2 – similar to T-1, only with select checkered walnut stock (lacquer finished), pinned front sight blade, 24 in. barrel, 6 lbs.

       $875 $765 $655 $595 $480 $395 $305

Add 10%-15% for left-hand model (mfg. 1969-74 only).

Watch for salt wood.

* ***T-Bolt T-2 Late Production*** – features oil finished stock, press fit plastic front sight, and Browning computerized serialization.

       $600 $525 $435 $375 $305 $250 $195

FN HIGH-POWER MODEL – .222 Rem. (Sako action), .222 Rem. Mag. (Sako action), .22-250 Rem. (Sako action), .243 Win., .257 Roberts, .264 Win. Mag., .270 Win., .284 Win. (Sako action), .30-06, .308 Win. 7mm Mag., .300 Win. Mag., .308 Norma Mag., .300 H&H, .338 Win. Mag., .375 H&H, or .458 Win. Mag. cal., standard Mauser type action with either short or long (more desirable) extractor, 22 or 24 in. (heavy available) barrel, folding leaf sight, checkered pistol grip stock. Mfg 1960-1974 by FN.

RIFLES: BOLT ACTION

MSR	100%	98%	95%	90%	80%	70%	60%

The .243 Win. and .308 Win. cals. were built on the small ring Mauser action prior to using the Sako medium action.

Note: Grades differ in engraving, finish, checkering, and grade of wood. It should be noted that the salt wood problem is more common in these high powered models. Guns should be checked carefully for rust below wood surfaces.

* ***FN High-Power Safari Grade Basic Model*** – basic model with blue finish.

Standard cals.	$1,675	$1,475	$1,275	$1,175	$995	$850	$550
Mag. cals.	$1,850	$1,650	$1,425	$1,275	$1,075	$900	$650
.257 Roberts	$2,825	$2,500	$2,150	$1,875	$1,500	$1,250	$1,150
.308 Norma Mag.	$2,250	$1,950	$1,550	$1,375	$1,250	$1,050	$975
.338 Win. Mag.	$1,995	$1,750	$1,400	$1,250	$1,050	$900	$800
.375 H&H	$2,195	$1,850	$1,500	$1,350	$1,150	$1,000	$900

Add 15% for Magnum long extractor models.

Between 1963 and 1974, Browning also offered short and medium barrelled actions in the Safari, Medallion and Olympian Grades. These models have Sako barrelled actions and were stocked by FN. Medium weight barrels could also be ordered.

* ***FN High-Power Safari Grade Short Sako Action*** – .222 Rem. or .222 Rem. Mag. cal., short action.

$1,675 $1,475 $1,275 $1,175 $995 $850 $695

* ***FN High-Power Safari Grade Medium Sako Action*** – .22-250 Rem., .243 Win., .284 Win. or .308 Win. cal., medium action.

$1,595 $1,375 $1,175 $1,050 $900 $750 $550

Add 75% for .284 Win. cal. (mfg. 1965-76).

In .284 Win. cal., only 162 rifles were mfg. in Safari Grade, 29 in Medallion Grade, and 10 in Olympian Grade.

* ***FN High-Power Medallion Grade*** – features select figured walnut with skipline checkering, rosewood grip and forearm caps, blue/black lustre bluing, receiver and barrel portion scroll engraved, ram's head engraved on floor plate.

$3,250 $2,950 $2,500 $2,200 $1,850 $1,500 $1,200

Add 20%-60% for rare calibers, depending on rarity.
Add 15% for Mag. cals. with long extractor.

Caliber rarity is as follows: .30-06 (least rare), .300 H&H, .375 H&H long extractor, .264 Win. Mag., .222 Rem./.222 Rem. Mag., .284 Win. (rarest).

This model was also available with a Sako short or medium action - cals. are the same as listed for the Sako Safari.

* ***FN High-Power Olympian Grade*** – top-of-the-line model featuring highly figured walnut stock that is both checkered and carved. Receiver,

| MSR | 100% | 98% | 95% | 90% | 80% | 70% | 60% |

floor plate, and trigger guard are chrome plated in a satin finish that has deep relief animal scenes engraved, as well as deep scroll work on other metal parts.

$9,250 $8,000 $6,850 $6,200 $5,200 $4,400 $3,850

Add 20%-60% for rare calibers, depending on the rarity.

Add 15% for Mag. cals. with long extractor.

Caliber rarity is as follows: .30-06 (least rare), .308 Norm. Mag., .300 H&H, .375 H&H long extractor, .264 Win. Mag., .222 Rem./.222 Rem. Mag., .284 Win. (rarest).

This model was also available with a Sako short or medium action - cals. are the same as listed for the Sako Safari.

ACERA MODEL – .30-06 or .300 Win. Mag. cal., features straight pull action, Teflon coated breech block face, 7 lug bolt, 22 or 24 (.300 Win. Mag.) in. barrel, available w/o sights, with sights (disc. 1999), or with BOSS, detachable box mag., checkered walnut stock, gloss metal finish, 7 lbs. 3 oz. - 7 lbs. 9 oz. Mfg. 1999-2000, reintroduced during 2002 only.

$895 $800 $650 $575 $475 $375 $285

Last MSR was $896.

Add $34 for .300 Win. Mag. cal.
Add $24 for iron sights (disc. 1999).
Add $80 for barrel BOSS (.30-06 cal. mfg. 2002 only).

RIFLES: BOLT ACTION, CENTERFIRE A-BOLT I SERIES

A-BOLT HUNTER MODEL I – available in .25-06 Rem., .270 Win., .280 Rem. (new 1988), .30-06, 7mm Rem. Mag., .300 Win. Mag., or .338 Win. Mag. cal. in long action, short action available in .223 Rem. (new 1988), .22-250 Rem., .243 Win., .257 Roberts, .284 Win. (new 1989) 7mm-08 Rem., or .308 Win. cal., 3 or 4 shot mag., matte blue finish, 3 lug rotary bolt locking, 22 (short action only), 24 in. (disc. 1987), or 26 in. barrel (new 1988 - long action Mag. cals. only), 60 degree bolt throw, adj. trigger, hidden detachable mag., with or without sights, top tang thumb safety, checkered pistol grip stock, 6 lbs. 3 oz. - 7 lbs. 11oz. Mfg. 1985-93 by Miroku. Replaced by A-Bolt Model II in 1994.

$495 $425 $325 $295 $240 $195 $150

Last MSR was $510.

Add $65 for open sights.

* *A-Bolt Hunter Medallion Model* – same A-Bolt specifications, except also available in .375 H&H cal., features better grade walnut stock with rosewood pistol grip and forend cap, synthetic floor plate, high lustre bluing, no sights. Disc. 1993. Replaced by A-Bolt Medallion Model II in 1994.

$625 $525 $425 $355 $290 $235 $185

Last MSR was $592.

Add $25 for left-hand action (avail. in long action cals. only).
Add $100 for .375 H&H cal. (open sights only).

RIFLES: BOLT ACTION, CENTERFIRE A-BOLT I SERIES

MSR	100%	98%	95%	90%	80%	70%	60%

Left-hand action available in .25-06 Rem., .270 Win., .280 Rem., .30-06, 7mm Rem. Mag., .300 Win. Mag., .338 Win. Mag., or .375 H&H cal.

* ***A-Bolt Hunter Micro Medallion Model*** – .223 Rem. (new 1988), .22-250 Rem., .243 Win., .257 Roberts, .284 Win., .308 Win., or 7mm-08 Rem. cal., scaled down variation of the A-Bolt Hunter Model, 20 in. barrel, short action only, 13 5/16 in. LOP, 3 shot mag., no sights, 6 lbs. 3 oz. for short action. Mfg. 1988-93. Replaced by A-Bolt Micro Medallion Model II in 1994.

	$625	$525	$425	$355	$290	$235	$185

Last MSR was $597.

* ***A-Bolt Hunter Gold Medallion Model*** – .270 Win., .30-06, .300 Win. Mag. (new 1993), or 7mm Rem. Mag. cal., similar to Medallion Model, except has extra select walnut stock with continental style cheekpiece, gold lettering and light engraving, no sights. Mfg. 1988-93. Replaced by A-Bolt Gold Medallion Model II in 1994.

	$750	$650	$550	$500	$405	$330	$255

Last MSR was $810.

* ***A-Bolt Hunter Euro-Bolt*** – .22-250 Rem., .243 Win., .270 Win., .30-06, .308 Win., or 7mm Rem. Mag. cal., features European styling including Schnabel style forearm, rounded rear receiver, Mannlicher style bolt, European cheekpiece on satin finished checkered stock, low-lustre bluing, hinged floor plate with removable mag., cocking indicator, upper tang thumb activated safety, 6 lbs. 14 oz. - 7 lbs. 6 oz. (Mag.). Mfg. 1993-96.

	$675	$550	$475	$425	$345	$280	$220

Last MSR was $700.

* ***A-Bolt Hunter Stainless Stalker*** – .22-250 Rem. (left-hand only, new 1993), .25-06 Rem., .270 Win., .280 Rem., .30-06, 7mm Rem. Mag., .300 Win. Mag., .338 Win. Mag. or .375 H&H (new 1990) cal., action and barrel are stainless steel, matte black graphite fiberglass composite stock, dull stainless finish, no sights, 6 lbs. 11 oz. - 7 lbs. 3 oz. Mfg. 1987-93. Replaced by Stainless Stalker II in 1994.

	$625	$525	$450	$410	$330	$270	$210

Last MSR was $665.

Add $100 for .375 H&H cal.
Add $20 for left-hand action.

Originally, this model was offered in .270 Win., .30-06, or 7mm Rem. Mag. cal. only.

* ***A-Bolt Hunter Camo Stalker*** – .270 Win., .30-06, or 7mm Rem. Mag. cal., laminated black and green wood stock, matte finish on metal parts, no sights. Mfg. 1987-89.

	$475	$425	$350	$300	$250	$190	$150

Last MSR was $483.

RIFLES: BOLT ACTION, CENTERFIRE A-BOLT II SERIES

MSR	100%	98%	95%	90%	80%	70%	60%

* ***A-Bolt Hunter Composite Stalker*** – .25-06 Rem., .270 Win., .280 Rem., .30-06, 7mm Rem. Mag., .300 Win. Mag., or .338 Win. Mag. cal., black graphite fiberglass composite stock, matte non-glare metal finish, 6 lbs. 11 oz. - 7 lbs. 3 oz. Mfg. 1988-93. Replaced by Composite Stalker II in 1994.

	$525	$425	$350	$300	$250	$190	$150

Last MSR was $525

A-BOLT BIGHORN SHEEP ISSUE – .270 Win. cal. only, 22 in. barrel, high grade walnut stock with gloss finish and skipline checkering, deep relief engraving on receiver barrel, floorplate, and trigger guard, two 24Kt. inlays depicting bighorn sheep. 600 mfg. 1986-87 only.

	$1,450	$1,100	$950	$850	$725	$550	$500

Last MSR was $1,365

A-BOLT PRONGHORN ISSUE – .243 Win. cal., presentation grade walnut with skipline checkering and pearl borders, receiver and barrel engraving, multiple gold inlays on receiver top and floor plate. 500 mfg. 1987 only.

	$1,450	$1,100	$950	N/A	N/A	N/A	N/A

Last MSR was $1,302

RIFLES: BOLT ACTION, CENTERFIRE A-BOLT II SERIES

The A-Bolt II Series was introduced in 1994, and differs from the original A-Bolt variations (disc. 1993) in that a new anti-bind bolt featuring a non-rotating bolt sleeve has been incorporated in addition to an improved trigger system. Action feeding is similar to A-Bolt I Series, with a hinged floorplate featuring a detachable box magazine. Consumers also may have their name/inscription engraved on the flat bolt-face on any A-Bolt II Series variation for an additional $25. Browning introduced the BOSS (Ballistic Optimizing Shooting System) in 1994 as an option on A-Bolt rifles, except Micro-Medallion models. is a user-adjustable barrel tuning attachment which greatly improves accuracy. The BOSS version has porting, which functions as a muzzle brake and reduces recoil by approx. 30%. The BOSS-CR (Conventional Recoil) is not ported, and does not have the substantially increased noise/muzzle blast of the BOSS.

During 2010, the A-Bolt celebrated its 25th Anniversary, and in commemoration, select A-Bolt rifles have a "25th Anniversary A-Bolt" etched on the floorplate.

A-BOLT HUNTER MODEL II – available in various cals. between .22-250 Rem. - .338 Win. Mag. (disc.), currently available in .270 WSM, 7mm WSM cals. (new 2002), .300 WSM (new 2001), or .325 WSM (new 2005) cal., 22 (disc.), 23 (.300 WSM cal. only), 24, or 26 in. barrel with (disc. 1998) or w/o open sights, walnut stock with gloss finish, top tang safety, low lustre bluing, 60 degree bolt throw, right hand action was disc. during 2007, except for Full Line dealer model, left hand action disc. 2010. 6 lbs. 7 oz. - 7 lbs. 3 oz. Disc. 2012.

	$825	$630	$575	$475	$375	$335	$300

Last MSR was $1,030 (right hand)

RIFLES: BOLT ACTION, CENTERFIRE A-BOLT II SERIES

MSR	100%	98%	95%	90%	80%	70%	60%

Subtract approx. $70 for left hand action (disc. 2010).
Subtract approx. $65 for Mag. cals. on left hand action.
Add approx. $60 for open sights (available in 8 cals., disc. 1998).

Beginning 2007, right hand action in this model was only available through Full Line Browning dealers.

* ***A-Bolt Hunter Model II WSSM*** – .223 WSSM, .25 WSSM (new 2004), or .243 WSSM cal., 3 shot mag., super short action, 21 or 22 (new 2004) in. barrel, walnut stock with satin finish and smaller dimensions, 6 1/4 lbs. Mfg. 2003-2007.

$650	$575	$450	$375	$325	$280	$240

Last MSR was $770.

* ***A-Bolt Hunter Model II with BOSS*** – same cals. as Hunter Model II until 1999, available only in .22-250 Rem., .243 Win., .270 Win., .280 Rem., .30-06, or .308 Win. cal. during 1999, features 22 or 26 (Mag. cals. only, disc. 1998) in. barrel with BOSS. Mfg. 1994-99.

$595	$500	$425	$350	$300	$275	$250

Last MSR was $617.

A-BOLT HUNTER FIELD II (CLASSIC HUNTER) – .270 Win. (disc. 2001), .270 WSM (new 2002), .30-06 (disc. 2001), .300 Win. Mag. (disc. 2001), .300 WSM (new 2002), .325 WSM (new 2005) 7mm Rem. Mag. (disc. 2001), or 7mm WSM (new 2002) cal., 22 (disc. 2001), 23 (new 2002, WSM cals. only), or 26 (disc. 2001) in. barrel, 3-5 shot mag., features low-lustre bluing and select checkered satin finished Monte Carlo walnut stock and forend, approx. 6 1/2 - 7 1/4 lbs. Mfg. 1999-2006.

$695	$595	$475	$395	$325	$275	$250

Last MSR was $808.

This model was available to Full-line and Medallion dealers only.

* ***A-Bolt Hunter Field II WSSM (Classic Hunter)*** – .223 WSSM, .25 WSSM (new 2004), or .243 WSSM cal., 3 shot mag., super short action, 22 in. barrel, satin finished Monte Carlo walnut stock with palm swell and double bordered checkering, low lustre bluing, 6 1/4 lbs. Mfg. 2003-2006.

$725	$600	$500	$400	$350	$300	$275

Last MSR was $829.

This model was available to Full-line and Medallion dealers only.

A-BOLT RMEF SPECIAL HUNTER – .325 WSM cal., similar to Medallion Model II, except has satin finished Monte Carlo stock and special RMEF logo insert on floorplate. Mfg. 2007-2008.

$725	$625	$495	$395	$350	$300	$275

Last MSR was $864.

MSR	100%	98%	95%	90%	80%	70%	60%

A-BOLT NRA WILDLIFE CONSERVATION COLLECTION – .243 Win. cal., 22 in. barrel, blue finish, features NRA Heritage logo laser engraved in satin finished walnut stock, approx. 6 1/2 lbs. Limited mfg. 2006-2007.

	$725	$625	$495	$395	$350	$300	$275

Last MSR was $813.

A-BOLT MICRO HUNTER II – .22 Hornet (only available cal. in right hand action beginning 2009), .22-250 Rem. (disc. 2010), .223 Rem. (mfg. 2000-2005), .243 Win. (disc. 2010), .260 Rem. (disc. 2001), .270 WSM (mfg. 2003-2010), 7mm WSM (mfg. 2003-2010), .300 WSM (mfg. 2003-2010), .325 WSM (mfg. 2005-2010), .308 Win. (disc. 2010), or 7mm-08 Rem. (disc. 2010) cal., 3 shot mag., features shorter LOP and 20 or 22 in. barrel w/o sights, checkered walnut stock and forend, approx. 6 1/4 lbs. Mfg. 1999-2012.

	$675	$500	$385	$335	$285	$250	$225

Last MSR was $870.

Add $60 for Mag. cals. (disc. 2009)
Add $30 for left-hand action (new 2003).

A-BOLT MEDALLION MODEL II – .375 H&H cal., previously available in various cals. between .22-250 Rem. (disc.) - .338 Win. Mag., similar to Medallion Model with A-Bolt II improvements, without sights, except for .375 H&H cal. (open sights standard), gloss finished walnut stock with rosewood grip and forend caps, right hand action w/o BOSS was disc. 2007, 6 lbs. 7 oz. - 7 lbs. 1 oz. Mfg. 1994-2011.

	$775	$625	$525	$400	$350	$295	$275

Last MSR was $990.

Subtract approx. $30 for standard, non-Mag. cals., including WSM.
Subtract approx. $20 for right hand action w/o BOSS (only available in .375 H&H cal. beginning 2007).

* *A-Bolt Medallion Model II WSSM* – .223 WSSM, .25 WSSM (new 2004), or .243 WSSM cal., 3 shot mag., super short action, 22 in. barrel, engraved receiver, Monte Carlo gloss finished walnut stock with rosewood pistol grip and forend caps, palm swell and double bordered checkering, no sights, low lustre bluing, 6 1/4 lbs. Mfg. 2003-2007.

	$695	$575	$475	$425	$385	$365	$335

Last MSR was $872.

* *A-Bolt Medallion Model II with BOSS* – various cals. between .223 WSSM - .375 H&H, similar to Medallion Model II, except has 22, 23 (new 2002, WSM cals. only), or 26 in. BOSS barrel. New 1994.

MSR $1,120	$885	$700	$565	$450	$400	$375	$335

Add $30 for normal Mag. and WSM cals. or $51 for WSSM (disc. 2007) cals.
Add $32 for left-hand action (disc. 2005).

* *A-Bolt Micro Medallion Model II* – .22 Hornet, .22-250 Rem., .223 Rem., .243 Win., 7mm-08 Rem., .284 Win. (disc. 1997), or .308 Win.

MSR	100%	98%	95%	90%	80%	70%	60%

cal., similar to Micro Medallion Model with A-Bolt II improvements, 20 or 22 (.22 Hornet only) in. barrel without sights, 6 lbs. Mfg. 1994-98.

$525 $465 $400 $350 $300 $275 $250

Last MSR was $636.

A-BOLT CUSTOM TROPHY II – .270 Win., .30-06, .300 Win. Mag., or 7mm Rem. Mag. cal., features 24 or 26 (Mag. cals. only) in. octagon barrel with gold band at muzzle, no sights, gold outlines on barrel and receiver, checkered select American walnut stock with shadowline cheekpiece and skeleton pistol grip, approx. 7 1/2 lbs. Mfg. 1998-2000.

$1,150 $925 $800 $660 $525 $450 $375

Last MSR was $1,428.

A-BOLT GOLD MEDALLION MODEL II – .270 Win., .30-06, .300 Win. Mag., or 7mm Rem. Mag. cal., similar to Gold Medallion Model, except has A-Bolt II improvements, 22 or 26 in. barrel, approx. 7 1/2 lbs. Mfg. 1994-98.

$695 $595 $450 $375 $335 $300 $265

Last MSR was $855.

* *A-Bolt Gold Medallion Model II with BOSS* – mfg. 1994-97.

$750 $625 $525 $450 $375 $325 $285

Last MSR was $916.

A-BOLT WHITE GOLD MEDALLION MODEL II – .270 WSM (new 2004), .270 Win., .30-06, .300 Win. Mag., .300 WSM (new 2004), .325 WSM (new 2005), 7mm WSM (new 2004), or 7mm Rem. Mag. cal., stainless steel receiver and 22, 23 (new 2004), or 26 in. barrel, gold engraving, checkered high gloss Monte Carlo walnut stock with rosewood cap on forend and pistol grip, 6 lbs. 6 oz. - 7 lbs. 11 oz. Mfg. 1999-2009.

$1,025 $775 $625 $525 $425 $360 $300

Last MSR was $1,279.

Add $30 for Mag. cals.

* *A-Bolt White Gold Medallion II RMEF* – 7mm Rem. Mag. (disc. 2006) or .325 WSM (new 2007) cal., similar to White Gold Medallion, includes RMEF logo on pistol grip cap, gold engraved, stainless steel receiver and 26 in. barrel, select walnut stock, contrasting spacers and rosewood caps on forend and pistol grip, continental style cheekpiece and sling swivels, 7 lbs., 11 oz. Limited edition 2003-2008.

$1,045 $785 $630 $515 $450 $375 $325

Last MSR was $1,312.

* *A-Bolt White Gold Medallion II with BOSS* – similar to White Gold Medallion, except has barrel with BOSS, and not available in WSM cals. Disc. 2006.

$985 $765 $610 $500 $435 $375 $320

Last MSR was $1,235.

Add $28 for non-WSSM Mag. cals.

RIFLES: BOLT ACTION, CENTERFIRE A-BOLT II SERIES

MSR	100%	98%	95%	90%	80%	70%	60%

A-BOLT ECLIPSE HUNTER II WITH BOSS – .22-250 Rem. (disc. 1999), .243 Win. (disc. 1997), .270 Win., .30-06, .308 Win. (disc. 2000), or 7mm Rem. Mag. cal., features laminated thumbhole wood stock with cheekpiece, long action, 22 or 26 (7mm Rem. Mag. only) in. barrel with BOSS, approx. 7 1/2 lbs. New 1996.

MSR $1,430 $1,100 $850 $650 $550 $425 $350 $325

Add $30 for 7mm Rem. Mag. cal.

* ***A-Bolt Eclipse Varmint II with BOSS*** – .22-250 Rem., .223 Rem., or .308 Win. cal., 24 in. heavy barrel with BOSS, 4 shot mag., otherwise similar to Eclipse Model, approx. 9 lbs. Mfg. 1996-99.

    $810 $655 $535 $455 $375 $325 $285

    Last MSR was $969.

A-BOLT ECLIPSE M-1000 II – .22-250 Rem. (new 2006), .270 WSM, 7mm WSM, .300 WSM, or .308 Win. (new 2006) cal., features 26 in. heavy blue barrel, 3 shot mag., 9 lbs. 14 oz. New 2004.

MSR $1,340 $1,050 $800 $665 $535 $400 $350 $300

Add $20 for WSM cals.

* ***A-Bolt Eclipse M-1000 II with BOSS*** – .22-250 Rem. (new 2006), .300 Win. Mag., .308 Win. (new 2006), .270 WSM (new 2006), 7mm WSM (new 2006), or .300 WSM (new 2006) cal., features special 26 in. heavy target barrel, refined trigger system, 10 lbs.

MSR $1,440 $1,150 $925 $750 $635 $525 $425 $350

Add $30 for Mag. cals.

* ***A-Bolt Eclipse M-1000 II Stainless*** – similar to Eclipse M-1000 II, except features 26 in. stainless bull barrel, 9 lbs., 14 oz. New 2004.

MSR $1,600 $1,325 $1,150 $975 $875 $700 $575 $475

Add $100 for BOSS.
Add $40 for WSM cals.

A-BOLT VARMINT II WITH BOSS – .22-250 Rem., .223 Rem., or .308 Win. (new 1995) cal., features A-Bolt II improvements, 22 in. heavy barrel with BOSS, blue/gloss or satin/matte (new 1995, .223 Rem. disc. 1999) finish, black laminated wood stock with checkering, palm swell and solid recoil pad, without sights, 9 lbs. Mfg. 1994-2000.

$715 $600 $465 $380 $335 $300 $265

Last MSR was $879.

A-BOLT EURO-BOLT II – .243 Win., .270 Win., .30-06, .308 Win., or 7mm Rem. Mag. cal., similar to Euro-Bolt with A-Bolt II improvements, 22 or 26 (7mm Rem. Mag. only) in. barrel w/o sights, 6 lbs. 7 oz. - 7 lbs. 3 oz. (Mag.). Mfg. 1994-96.

$625 $510 $410 $355 $300 $265 $250

Last MSR was $824.

RIFLES: BOLT ACTION, CENTERFIRE A-BOLT II SERIES

MSR	100%	98%	95%	90%	80%	70%	60%

* ***A-Bolt Euro-Bolt II with BOSS*** – .243 Win., .270 Win., or .308 Win. cal., 22 in. barrel with BOSS, 6 lbs. 7 oz.

$725 $600 $500 $425 $350 $325 $295

Last MSR was $922.

A-BOLT STAINLESS STALKER II – similar to Stainless Stalker with A-Bolt improvements, available in various cals, between .22-250 Rem. - .375 H&H, .223 Rem. reintroduced during 2004 in super short action only, no sights, right hand action w/o Boss was disc. 2007, 6 lbs. 1 oz. - 7 lbs. 3 oz. Mfg. 1994-2010.

$885 $625 $450 $375 $325 $275 $250

Last MSR was $1,099.

Add $40 for normal Mag. or WSM cals.
Subtract approx. $20 for right hand action (available in .375 H&H cal. only beginning 2007).

* ***A-Bolt Stainless Stalker II WSSM*** – .223 WSSM, .25 WSSM (new 2004), or .243 WSSM cal., 3 shot mag., super short action, 21 (disc.) or 22 in. barrel, walnut stock with satin finish and smaller dimensions, 6 lbs., 1 oz. Mfg. 2003-2007.

$790 $585 $425 $350 $300 $250 $215

Last MSR was $966.

* ***A-Bolt Stainless Stalker II with BOSS*** – various cals. between .22-250 Rem. and .375 H&H, 22, 23 (new 2002, .300 WSM cal. only), 24 (.375 H&H cal. only) or 26 (Mag. cals. only) in. barrel with BOSS. Approx. 6 1/4 - 7 lbs.

MSR $1,240 $995 $750 $525 $400 $350 $300 $285

Add $30 for normal Mag. or WSM cals., or $51 for WSSM cals. (mfg. 2004-2007).
Add $30 for left-hand action.

A-BOLT CARBON FIBER STAINLESS STALKER II – .22-250 Rem. or .300 Win. Mag. cal., features Christensen lightweight 22 or 26 in. carbon fiber barrel with steel liner, stainless steel action, black synthetic stock, 4 or 5 shot mag., approx. 6 1/4 or 7 1/4 lbs. Mfg. 2000-2001.

$1,475 $1,225 $975 $860 $700 $600 $500

Last MSR was $1,750.

A-BOLT COMPOSITE STALKER II – various cals. between .22-250 Rem. - .338 Win. Mag., similar to Composite Stalker with A-Bolt II improvements, 22, 23 (WSM cals. only), 24, or 26 (Mag. cals. only) in. barrel without sights, 6 lbs. 1 oz. - 7 lbs. 3 oz. Mfg. 1994-2007.

$595 $525 $400 $350 $300 $250 $225

Last MSR was $719.

Add $30 for all Mag. cals.

* ***A-Bolt Composite Stalker II WSSM*** – .223 WSSM, .25 WSSM (new 2004), or .243 WSSM cal., 3 shot mag., super short action, 21 (disc.)

RIFLES: BOLT ACTION, CENTERFIRE A-BOLT II SERIES

MSR	100%	98%	95%	90%	80%	70%	60%

or 22 in. barrel, black composite stock with matte blued metal and smaller dimensions, 6.1 lbs. Mfg. 2003-2007.

$650 $535 $435 $380 $335 $295 $260

Last MSR was $770.

* *A-Bolt Composite Stalker II with BOSS* – various cals., 22, 23 (WSM cals. only), or 26 (Mag. cals. only) in. barrel with BOSS, 6 lbs., 6 oz. - 7 lbs., 3 oz.

MSR $1,000 $815 $625 $525 $425 $350 $300 $275

Add $30 for standard Mag. and WSM cals., or $51 for WSSM cals. (mfg. 2004-2007).

A-BOLT VARMINT STALKER II – .22-250 Rem. or .223 Rem. (SSA only beginning 2004) cal., 24 or 26 (.22-250 Rem. cal. only) in. heavy barrel, features Dura-Touch armor coated composite stock with slight palm swell, matte blue metal, 4 or 6 shot mag., approx. 7 3/4 lbs. Mfg. 2002-2008.

$715 $575 $450 $360 $300 $255 $230

Last MSR was $895.

* *A-Bolt Varmint Stalker II WSSM* – .223 WSSM, .25 WSSM (new 2004), or .243 WSSM cal., 3 shot mag., super short action, 21 (mfg. 2003 only) or 24 (new 2004) in. barrel, features Dura-Touch armor coated composite stock with slight palm swell, matte blue metal, 7 lbs., 13 oz. Mfg. 2003-2007.

$745 $580 $475 $395 $335 $295 $275

Last MSR was $928.

A-BOLT II MOUNTAIN TI – .243 Win. (new 2006), .308 Win. (new 2006), 7mm-08 Rem. (new 2006), .270 WSM, .300 WSM, 7mm WSM, .223 WSSM (mfg. 2005-2010), .243 WSSM (mfg. 2005-2010), .25 WSSM (mfg. 2005-2010), or .325 WSM (new 2006) cal., features titanium short action receiver with composite bolt sleeve and stainless steel 23 in. barrel, fiberglass Bell & Carlson stock with Mossy Oak New Break-Up or Break-Up Infinity (new 2010) camo and Dura-Touch armor coating, Pachmayr Decelerator recoil pad, approx. 5 1/2 lbs. Mfg. 2004-2011.

$1,565 $1,225 $985 $850 $725 $625 $525

Last MSR was $1,960.

Add $30 for WSM cals.

A-BOLT II GREYWOLF – .25-06 Rem., .270 Win., .280 Rem., .30-06, .300 Win. Mag., .338 Win. Mag., or 7mm Rem. Mag. cal., stainless steel, classic sporter with select walnut stock. Limited mfg. during 1994 only.

$850 $675 $595 $525 $450 $400 $350

Last MSR was $935.

A-BOLT TARGET II – .223 Rem., .308 Win., .300 WSM cal., 28 in. heavy contour bull barrel, 4 or 6 shot mag., matte blue finish, satin grey

MSR	100%	98%	95%	90%	80%	70%	60%

checkered laminated wood stock with adj. comb, right-hand palm swell, drilled and tapped, 13 lbs. New 2009.

MSR $1,480 $1,200 $925 $750 $650 $550 $450 $395

Add $20 for .300 WSM cal.

* *A-Bolt Target Stainless II* – .223 Rem., .308 Win., .300 WSM cal., similar to A-Bolt Target, except has 28 in. stainless steel barrel. New 2009.

MSR $1,730 $1,425 $1,225 $1,050 $900 $775 $675 $575

Add $50 for .300 WSM cal.

RIFLES: BOLT ACTION, CENTERFIRE X-BOLT SERIES

The X-Bolt Series was introduced during 2008, and features a new three-lever Feather trigger system, which is adjustable from 3-5 lbs. It also has a 3-4 shot detachable rotary mag., 60-degree bolt lift, top safety with bolt unlock button feature, free floating barrel, X-lock scope mounting system (four screws per base, instead of two), and a soft recoil pad using Inflex technology. The various models listed all have these features.

X-BOLT HUNTER – various cals. in both super short, short, and long action, right or left (new 2011) hand action, satin finished walnut stock with checkering, low luster blue finish, 22-26 in. barrel (depending on caliber) w/o sights, 3 or 5 shot mag., approx. 6 1/2 - 7 lbs. New 2008.

MSR $1,000 $775 $625 $500 $425 $375 $325 $295

Subtract approx. $100 for 2008-2012 mfg. w/o raised cheekpiece on stock.
Add $40 for standard Mag. or WSM cals.
Add $20 for left-hand action (new 2011).

During 2013, this model became available through Full Line Browning dealers only. The only difference is that models made from 2008-2012 have stocks without a cheekpiece, while the Full Line dealer model has a raised cheekpiece.

X-BOLT MICRO MIDAS – .22-.250 Rem., .243 Win., .308 Win., or 7mm-08 Rem. cal., short or super short action, low luster bluing with satin finished stock, 20 in. barrel w/o sights, 4 shot mag., 12 1/2 in. LOP stock, approx. 6 lbs. New 2011.

MSR $840 $675 $550 $475 $425 $360 $310 $275

X-BOLT MICRO HUNTER – various cals., 20 or 22 in. blue barrel, right or left (new 2011) hand action, 3 or 4 shot mag., low luster blue finish, satin finished walnut stock, smaller dimensions, drilled and tapped, approx. 6 lbs. New 2009.

MSR $900 $715 $575 $465 $415 $360 $310 $275

Add $40 for Standard Mag. or WSM cals.
Add $20 for left-hand action (new 2011).

X-BOLT RMEF SPECIAL HUNTER – .325 WSM cal., 23 in. steel barrel, 3 shot mag., low luster blue finish, checkered satin finished walnut stock with raised cheekpiece, rosewood grip cap with RMEF logo inset, drilled and tapped, 6 lbs., 14 oz. New 2009.

MSR $1,100 $875 $700 $525 $475 $425 $350 $325

RIFLES: BOLT ACTION, RIMFIRE A-BOLT SERIES

MSR	100%	98%	95%	90%	80%	70%	60%

X-BOLT RMEF WHITE GOLD – .325 WSM cal., 23 in. stainless barrel, 3 shot mag., gold engraved matte finished receiver, drilled and tapped, checkered select gloss finish walnut stock with raised cheekpiece, rosewood grip cap, RMEF logo inset, 7 lbs., 3 oz. New 2009.

MSR $1,500 $1,075 $925 $785 $650 $575 $500 $450

X-BOLT MEDALLION – similar to X-Bolt Hunter, except has a gloss finished walnut stock with rosewood pistol grip and forend caps, right or left (new 2011) hand action, 3-5 shot mag. New 2008.

MSR $1,030 $860 $675 $550 $450 $375 $325 $275

Add $40 for standard Mag., WSM, or .375 H&H (new 2012) cals.
Add $30 for left-hand action (new 2011).

X-BOLT WHITE GOLD – various cals., 22, 23, 24, or 26 in. barrel, 3-5 shot mag., stainless steel free floating receiver and barrel, scroll engraving, gloss finished walnut stock with rosewood forend grip and pistol grip cap, drilled and tapped, 6 lbs., 8 oz. - 7 lbs. New 2010.

MSR $1,400 $1,195 $1,050 $935 $850 $725 $600 $525

Add $40 for Mag. cals.

X-BOLT COMPOSITE STALKER – similar cals. as X-Bolt Hunter, features matte black composite stock with palm swell and DuraTouch Armor coating, matte blued steel receiver and barrel, 22-26 in. barrel w/o sights, 3-5 shot mag., 6 lbs. 5 oz. - 6 lbs. 13 oz. New 2008.

MSR $840 $675 $550 $475 $415 $360 $310 $275

Add $40 for standard Mag. or WSM cals.

X-BOLT STAINLESS STALKER – similar to X-Bolt Composite, except has matte finished stainless steel receiver and barrel. New 2008.

MSR $1,120 $925 $750 $625 $525 $425 $375 $350

Add $40 for regular Mag. or WSM cals. or $40 for .375 H&H with open sights (new 2011).

X-BOLT VARMINT STALKER – .22-250 Rem., .223 Rem., .243 Win., or .308 Win. cal., 24 or 26 in. heavy blue barrel, low luster blue finish, 4 or 5 shot mag., matte black checkered composite stock with DuraTouch Armor coating and palm swell, approx. 8 lbs. New 2009.

MSR $1,120 $925 $750 $625 $525 $425 $375 $350

RIFLES: BOLT ACTION, RIMFIRE A-BOLT SERIES

A-BOLT GRADE I RIMFIRE – .22 LR or .22 WMR (new 1989) cal., 60 degree bolt throw, 22 in. barrel, checkered walnut stock and forearm or laminated stock (scarce - approx. 1,500 mfg., 390 had no sights), 5 or 15 (optional) shot mag., adj. trigger, available with or without open sights, 5 lbs. 9 oz. Mfg. 1986-96.

* *A-Bolt Grade I .22 LR cal.*

$575 $495 $425 $350 $295 $250 $210

Last MSR was $425.

Add $14 for open sights.

A 15 shot mag. was also available for this model at $45 retail.

* ***A-Bolt Grade I .22 WMR cal.***

MSR	100%	98%	95%	90%	80%	70%	60%
	$650	$550	$450	$375	$325	$295	$250

Last MSR was $493.

Add $21 for open sights.

A-BOLT GOLD MEDALLION RIMFIRE – .22 LR cal. only, similar to A-Bolt, except has high grade select walnut stock checkered 22 lines per inch, rosewood pistol and forend cap, high gloss finish, gold filled lettering and moderate engraving, solid recoil pad. Mfg. 1988-96.

$625 $550 $450 $385 $325 $295 $250

Last MSR was $567.

RIFLES: LEVER ACTION

BL-17 – .17 Mach 2 cal., otherwise similar to the BL-22, 5 lbs., 2 oz. New 2005.

* ***BL-17 Grade I*** – uncheckered stock with choice of blued or nickel (BL-17 Field) receiver, blued trigger. Mfg. 2005.

$420 $370 $315 $285 $230 $190 $145

Last MSR was $484.

Add $32 for nickel.

* ***BL-17 Grade II*** – features choice of engraved blued or nickel (Field) receiver, gold trigger, checkered stock and forearm. Mfg. 2005.

$465 $405 $350 $315 $255 $210 $165

Last MSR was $524.

Add $53 for nickel.

* ***BL-17 Grade II Field Octagon*** – similar to BL-22 Classic/Field octagon, 5 lbs., 6 oz., mfg. 2005 by Miroku.

$750 $675 $600 $550 $400 $325 $250

Last MSR was $744.

BL-22 GRADE I – .22 S, L, and LR cal., 20 in. barrel, short throw (33 degree) lever, folding leaf sight, 15 shot (LR) mag., blue finish, exposed hammer, Western style gloss finished unchecked stock and forearm, 5 lbs. Mfg. 1970-2003 by Miroku.

$450 $395 $325 $280 $230 $185 $145

Last MSR was $436.

* ***BL-22 Grade I (Classic/Field)*** – similar to BL-22 Grade I, except has choice of gloss or satin finished stock and forearm, 20 in. barrel, blue or nickel (new 2005) receiver. New 1999, mfg. by Miroku.

MSR $620 $485 $400 $350 $300 $240 $195 $150

Add $40 for satin nickel finished frame and satin finished stock (Field, new 2005).

The satin nickel model is available through Full-Line and Medallion dealers only.

MSR	100%	98%	95%	90%	80%	70%	60%

* **BL-22 Grade I Micro Midas** – .22 LR cal. only, features 19 3/8 in. barrel, 12 shot mag., and shortened 12 in. LOP unchecked stock, 4 3/4 lbs. New 2011.

  MSR $530　　$435　$365　$315　$280　$230　$185　$150

* **BL-22 Grade I NRA** – similar to BL-22 Grade I, except has NRA logo laser engraved in stock. Mfg. 2006-2007.

  　　　　$485　$400　$340　$305　$250　$205　$160

  Last MSR was $514.

BL-22 GRADE II – same general specifications as BL-22, except scroll engraved blue receiver and deluxe high gloss checkered walnut stock and forearm. Disc. 2003.

  　　　　$550　$475　$395　$325　$275　$225　$175

  Last MSR was $494.

* **BL-22 Grade II (Classic/Field)** – similar to BL-22 Grade II, except has choice of gloss or satin finished stock and forearm, engraved blue or nickel (new 2005) receiver. New 1999, mfg. by Miroku.

  MSR $700　　$565　$485　$400　$350　$275　$225　$175

  Add $50 for satin nickel receiver and satin finished stock and forearm (Field, new 2005).

  This model is available through Full-Line and Medallion dealers only.

* **BL-22 Grade II Classic/Field Octagon** – features 24 in. octagon barrel and silver nitride finished receiver with scroll engraving, adj. buckhorn rear sight, checkered satin finished stock and forearm, 5 1/4 lbs. New 2004, mfg. by Miroku.

  MSR $980　　$815　$700　$575　$500　$400　$350　$295

  This model is available through Full-Line and Medallion dealers only.

MODEL 53 DELUXE LIMITED EDITION – .32-20 WCF cal. (round nose or hollow point bullets only), patterned after the original Winchester Model 53 (redesigned Model 1892), 7 shot tube mag., high polished blue metal, open sights, 22 in. tapered barrel, high grade checkered walnut stock featuring full pistol grip cap and shotgun style metal buttplate, 6 1/2 lbs. Only 5,000 mfg. in 1990.

  　　　　$925　$795　$675　N/A　N/A　N/A　N/A

  Last MSR was $675.

MODEL 65 GRADE I LIMITED EDITION – .218 Bee cal., patterned after the Winchester Model 65, round tapered 24 in. barrel, open sights (hooded front), blue metal finish, 7 shot tube mag., unchecked pistol grip stock and semi-beavertail forearm, metal buttplate, 6 3/4 lbs. 3,500 total mfg. for Grade I in 1989 only, inventory depleted in 1990.

  　　　　$725　$625　$525　N/A　N/A　N/A　N/A

  Last MSR was $550.

MSR	100%	98%	95%	90%	80%	70%	60%

* *Model 65 High Grade* – greyed receiver (and lever) with scroll engraving and gold plated animals, gold plated trigger, deluxe checkered walnut stock and semi-beavertail forearm. 1,500 total mfg. in 1989, inventory depleted in 1990.

	$1,050	$925	$800	N/A	N/A	N/A	N/A

Last MSR was $850.

MODEL 71 LIMITED EDITION CARBINE – .348 Win. cal., reproduction of the Winchester Model 71 Carbine, 20 in. barrel, open sights, 4 shot mag., 8 lbs. New 1987 with inventory depleted in 1990.

* *Model 71 Limited Edition Carbine Grade I* – uncheckered satin finished walnut stock and forearm. 4,000 mfg. 1986-87 only.

	$875	$750	$650	N/A	N/A	N/A	N/A

Last MSR was $600.

* *Model 71 Limited Edition Carbine High Grade* – deluxe checkered walnut stock and forearm with high gloss finish, scroll engraved grey receiver with gold inlays and trigger. 3,000 mfg. 1986-1987 only.

	$1,325	$1,075	$925	N/A	N/A	N/A	N/A

Last MSR was $980.

MODEL 71 LIMITED EDITION RIFLE – .348 Win. cal., reproduction of the Winchester Model 71 Rifle, 24 in. barrel, open sights, 4 shot mag., 8 lbs. 2 oz. Mfg. 1986-87 only with inventory depleted in 1990.

* *Model 71 Grade I Rifle* – uncheckered satin finished walnut stock and forearm. 3,000 mfg. 1986-1987 only.

	$895	$775	$675	N/A	N/A	N/A	N/A

Last MSR was $600.

* *Model 71 High Grade Rifle* – deluxe checkered walnut stock and forearm with high gloss finish, scroll engraved grey receiver with gold inlays and trigger. 3,000 mfg. 1986-1987 only.

	$1,425	$1,175	$900	N/A	N/A	N/A	N/A

Last MSR was $980.

MODEL BLR SHORT ACTION – .22-250 Rem., .222 Rem. (disc. 1989), .223 Rem., .243 Win., .257 Roberts (disc. 1992), 7mm-08 Rem., .284 Win. (disc. 1994), .308 Win., or .358 Win. (disc. 1992) cal., steel receiver, rotary bolt locking lugs, 20 in. barrel with band, 3 (.284 Win. only) or 4 shot detachable mag., adj. rear sight, checkered straight grip stock, recoil pad, no sights optional 1988-89, approx. 7 lbs. Mfg. 1970-1981.

.243 Win. and .308 Win. cals. are the most popular in this model.

* *Model BLR USA* – .243 Win. or .308 Win. cal., this model was originally scheduled to be manufactured by TRW in Cleveland, OH for Browning. Originally assembled in 1966, these rifles are considered prototypes as they

| MSR | 100% | 98% | 95% | 90% | 80% | 70% | 60% |

were never sold through regular channels and at one time were scheduled to be destroyed. Approx. 50-250 of these rifles exist, some still NIB.

| | $995 | $870 | $745 | $675 | $545 | $450 | $350 |

This variation has a 2-line legend on the right side marked "MADE IN USA" and "PATENT PENDING". This model is dangerous to operate and should not be fired.

* *Model BLR Belgian* – .243 Win. or .308 Win. cal., mfg. was moved to FN in Belgium with original assembly beginning 1969 and concluding in 1973. This FN model included a number of small dimensioning and engraving changes.

| | $925 | $810 | $695 | $630 | $510 | $415 | $325 |

* *Model BLR Japan* – .243 Win. or .308 Win. cal., mfg. was moved to Miroku in Japan 1974-1980. Early guns during 1974 had stocks with impressed checkering. By 1975, cut checkering and gloss wood finish was used on stocks and forearms. Last ser. no. for Belgian production was 27,XXX. Japanese mfg. started with ser. no. 30,000.

| | $775 | $675 | $575 | $525 | $425 | $350 | $275 |

Last MSR was $550.

Add $40 without sights (scarce).

MODEL BLR '81 SHORT ACTION (MIROKU) – similar cals. and features as Model BLR short action, mfg. 1981-1995 by Miroku in Japan.

Standard cals.	$700	$625	$550	$450	$375	$300	$230
.257 Roberts	$900	$790	$675	$610	$495	$405	$315
.284 Win./.358 Win.	$900	$790	$675	$610	$495	$405	$315
.222 Rem.	$1,550	$1,355	$1,165	$1,055	$855	$700	$545

Last MSR was $550.

MODEL BLR '81 LONG ACTION – .270 Win., .30-06, or 7mm Rem Mag. cal., incorporates distinct design changes, 22 or 24 in. barrel, approx. 8 1/2 lbs. Mfg. 1991-95 by Miroku.

| | $750 | $655 | $565 | $510 | $415 | $340 | $265 |

Last MSR was $580.

NEW MODEL LIGHTNING BLR (SHORT ACTION) – .22-250 Rem., .223 Rem. (disc. 1998), .243 Win., 7mm-08 Rem., or .308 Win. cal. rotary bolt locking lugs, 20 in. barrel w/o barrel band, similar action as the BLR 81, but features aluminum alloy receiver, checkered pistol grip stock and forearm, rack and pinion geared slide, fold down hammer trigger travels with lever, 3-5 shot detachable mag., adj. rear sight approx. 6 1/2 lbs. Mfg. by Miroku late 1995 - 2002.

| | $625 | $545 | $470 | $425 | $345 | $280 | $220 |

Last MSR was $681.

RIFLES: LEVER ACTION

MSR	100%	98%	95%	90%	80%	70%	60%

* ***BLR Lightweight Stainless Short Action*** – various cals., similar to BLR Lightweight Short Action, except has 20 or 22 in. stainless steel barrel, pistol grip stock, 6 1/2 - 7 lbs. New 2010.

MSR $1,100 $895 $775 $635 $565 $450 $365 $285

Add $80 for WSM cals. Add $130 for takedown.

NEW MODEL LIGHTNING BLR (LONG ACTION) – .270 Win., .30-06, .300 Win. Mag. (new 1997), or 7mm Rem. Mag. cal., 22 or 24 (Mag. cals.) in. barrel, approx. 7 1/4 - 7 3/4 lbs. Mfg. by Miroku 1995-2002.

                               $650 $570 $490 $440 $360 $295 $230

Last MSR was $721.

* ***BLR Lightweight Stainless Long Action*** – various cals., similar to BLR Lightweight Short Action, except has 20 (disc.), 22, or 24 in. stainless steel barrel, pistol grip stock, 7 1/4 or 7 3/4 lbs. New 2010.

MSR $1,150 $925 $785 $660 $600 $475 $390 $305

Add $130 for takedown.

BLR LIGHTWEIGHT '81 (SHORT ACTION) – .22-.250 Rem., .223 Rem. (new 2010), .243 Win., .270 WSM (new 2004), 7mm-08 Rem., .325 WSM (pistol grip only, new 2005), .300 WSM (new 2004), 7mm WSM (new 2004), .308 Win., .358 Win., or .450 Marlin cal., 20 or 22 (WSM cals. only) in. barrel with barrel band, solid or takedown (new 2007) action, aluminum alloy receiver, choice of checkered Model 81 styled straight grip and forearm with gloss finish or checkered, gloss finished pistol grip with Schnabel forearm w/o barrel band (new 2005) stock, sling swivels (pistol grip only), rack and pinion geared slide with rotating breech head, fold down hammer, trigger travels with lever, 3-4 shot detachable mag., adj. rear sight, approx. 6 1/2 - 7 lbs. Mfg. by Miroku beginning 2003.

MSR $960 $775 $650 $540 $480 $380 $315 $245

Add $80 for WSM cals. (new 2004).
Add $60 for checkered pistol grip stock and Schnabel forearm (new 2005).
Add $80 for takedown action (new 2007).
Add $70 for one-piece scope mount (new 2007).

BLR LIGHTWEIGHT '81 (LONG ACTION) – .270 Win., .30-06, .300 Win. Mag., or 7mm Rem. Mag. cal., 22 or 24 in. barrel, 7 1/4 or 7 3/4 lbs. Mfg. by Miroku beginning 2003.

MSR $1,020 $845 $725 $600 $540 $440 $350 $270

Add $80 for takedown action (new 2007).
Add $60 for checkered pistol grip and Schnabel forend.

MODEL 1886 LIMITED EDITION GRADE I RIFLE – .45-70 Govt. cal. only, patterned after the Winchester Model 1886, blue receiver, 26 in. octagon barrel, 8 shot full mag., crescent buttplate, open sights. 7,000 mfg. 1986 only.

                               $1,250 $1,075 $950   N/A   N/A   N/A   N/A

Last MSR was $578.

MSR	100%	98%	95%	90%	80%	70%	60%

* *Model 1886 Limited Edition High Grade Rifle* – same general specifications as Model 1886, except has checkered high grade walnut stock and forearm, greyed steel receiver, with game scene engraving including elk and American Bison, gold accenting with "1 of 3,000" engraved on top of barrel. 3,000 mfg. 1986 only.

    $2,050 $1,795 $1,540 N/A N/A N/A N/A

    Last MSR was $935.

* *Model 1886 Montana Centennial Rifle* – similar to Model 1886 High Grade. 2,000 mfg. 1989 only to commemorate Montana Centennial.

    $1,975 $1,730 $1,480 N/A N/A N/A N/A

    Last MSR was $935.

MODEL 1886 LIMITED EDITION GRADE I CARBINE – .45-70 Govt. cal. only, saddle ring carbine, patterned after the Winchester Model 1886 Carbine, blue receiver, 22 in. round barrel, 7 shot full mag., crescent buttplate, open sights. 7,000 total mfg. 1992-93.

$1,095 $925 $800 N/A N/A N/A N/A

Last MSR was $750.

* *Model 1886 Limited Edition High Grade Carbine* – same general specifications as Model 1886, except has checkered high grade walnut stock and forearm, greyed steel receiver, with game scene engraving including bear and elk, gold accenting, 3,000 total mfg. 1992-93.

    $1,695 $1,485 $1,270 N/A N/A N/A N/A

    Last MSR was $1,175.

B-92 CARBINE – .357 Mag. or .44 Rem. Mag. cal., 20 in. barrel, patterned after the Winchester Model 92, 11 shot mag. (tubular), blue finish. Disc. 1986.

$600 $525 $450 $410 $330 $270 $210

Last MSR was $342.

Add 25% for .357 Mag. cal.

* *B-92 Centennial* – .44 Mag. cal., 6,000 mfg. in 1978.

    $685 $600 $515 N/A N/A N/A N/A

    Last MSR was $220.

* *B-92 BCA Commemorative* – mfg. to commemorate BCA's third anniversary.

    $750 $650 $550 N/A N/A N/A N/A

MODEL 1895 LIMITED EDITION GRADE I – .30/40 Krag or .30-06 cal. only, patterned after the Winchester Model 1895, blue receiver, 24 in. barrel, 4 shot mag. (box type), select walnut, rear buckhorn sight, 8 lbs. Mfg. 1984 only.

.30/40 Krag	$925	$800	$700	N/A	N/A	N/A	N/A
.30-06	$875	$750	$650	N/A	N/A	N/A	N/A

Production totaled 6,000 in the .30-06 cal. and 2,000 in .30/40 Krag for this model.

RIFLES: O/U 47

MSR	100%	98%	95%	90%	80%	70%	60%

* *Model 1895 Limited Edition High Grade* – same general specifications as Model 1895, except gold plated game scenes on satin finish receiver, gold trigger, and finely checkered select French walnut.

$1,625 $1,420 $1,220 N/A N/A N/A N/A

Production totaled 1,000 in the .30-06 cal. and 1,000 in .30/40 Krag for this model.

RIFLES: O/U

Currently, the Browning Custom Shop in Belgium is producing the CCS25 double rifle in the following grades: B2E ($15,059 MSR), B5 ($15,059), D5G ($32,435 MSR), M1 ($43,343 MSR), Bavarian ($17,280 MSR), CCS Herstal ($11,150 MSR), and the 375 H&H African Classic ($27,256 MSR).

Previous custom shop models included: CCS Africa ($15,266 last MSR, disc. 2005), Bavarian ($25,149 last MSR), CCS25 D5G ($43,665 last MSR), and the M1 ($57,498 last MSR).

EXPRESS RIFLE – .270 Win., .30-06 cal., or 9.3x74R cal., Superposed Superlight style action. 24 in. barrels, checkered straight grip stock and forearm, auto ejectors, Fleur-de-lis engraving, single trigger, folding leaf rear sight, 6 lbs. 14 oz., cased. Disc. 1986.

$6,000 $5,500 $4,775 $4,250 $3,500 $2,750 $2,250

Last MSR was $3,125.

GRADE I CONTINENTAL SET – includes .30-06 O/U rifle barrels with extra set of 20 ga. O/U shotgun barrels (26 1/2 in.), rifle barrels are 24 in., 20 ga. frame, SST, ejectors, blue receiver with scroll engraving, straight grip checkered stock and forearm, supplied with 2 barrel takedown case. Mfg. 1978-86.

$7,500 $6,500 $5,500 $4,850 $3,925 $3,225 $2,500

RIFLES: SEMI-AUTO, .22 LR

Miroku manufactured .22s can be determined by year of manufacture in the following manner: RV suffix - 1975, RT - 1976, RR - 1977, RP - 1978, RN - 1979, PM - 1980, PZ - 1981, PY - 1982, PX - 1983, PW - 1984, PV - 1985, PT -1986, PR - 1987, PP - 1988, PN - 1989, NM - 1990, NZ - 1991, NY - 1992, NX - 1993, NW - 1994, NV - 1995, NT - 1996, NR - 1997, NP - 1998, NN - 1999, MM - 2000, MZ - 2001, MY - 2002, MX - 2003, MW - 2004, MV - 2005, MU - 2006, MT - 2007, MS - 2008, MN - 2009, ZM - 2010, ZZ - 2011, ZY - 2012, ZX - 2013, ZW - 2014.

Currently, the Browning Custom Shop in Belgium is making the following .22 LR cal. semi-auto models: Grade II ($2,386 MSR), and the Grade III ($3,407 MSR).

On the following FN (Belgian mfg.) models, add approx. 10% if in NIB condition.

AUTO RIFLE GRADES I - VI – .22 LR or .22 Short (FN only, disc. - rare) cal., takedown design, 10 shot (16 for .22 Short) tube mag. in buttstock, 19 1/4 in. barrel for all .22 LR, .22 Shorts had various barrel lengths according to mfg. year: 19 1/4 in. for 1956, 22 3/8 in. for 1957, and 22 in. from 1958 until general production was disc. in 1983, checkered pistol grip stock, semi-beavertail forearm, stock has hole machined

MSR	100%	98%	95%	90%	80%	70%	60%

halfway to allow partial filling of tube mag., adj. folding rear or earlier wheel sight, grades differ in finish, amount of engraving, and quality of wood, 4 3/4-5 3/4 lbs. Early top loaders were mfg. from 1914 until approx. 1955. Modern tube loader mfg. 1956 to 1974 by FN Belgium Mfg. beginning 1976 by Miroku in Japan.

* ***Auto Rifle Grade I - FN (Belgian Mfg.)***

	$875	$750	$650	$550	$450	$400	$350

Add 50% for guns in .22 Short cal., if in 98% or better condition.
Add 25% for wheel sight guns if in 98% or better condition.

FN Postwar Grade Is have a lightly engraved blue steel receiver checkered walnut, blue trigger, and a variety of rear sights.

» ***Auto Rifle Grade I - FN Custom Shop***

	$995	$900	$750	$650	$525	$450	$375

Add 10% for .22 Short cal.

* ***Auto Rifle Grade I - Miroku (Japan Mfg.)*** – .22 LR cal., 19 3/8 in. barrel, polished blue receiver finish with scroll engraving, gloss finished checkered walnut stock and forearm, 10 shot mag., approx. 5 1/4 lbs.

MSR $700	$535	$465	$385	$340	$275	$225	$175

* ***Auto Rifle Grade II - FN (Belgian Mfg.)***

	$1,650	$1,375	$1,100	$975	$825	$675	$525

Add $100 for guns initialed by the engraver.
Add $200 for guns fully signed by the engraver.
Add $150 for original box.
Add 35% for Grade II with wheel sight.
Add 50% for guns in .22 Short cal., if in 95% or better condition.

FN Grade IIs have grey receiver, deluxe wood with finer checkering, gold plated trigger, and engraving depicting two squirrels and two prairie dogs. Unsigned, signed, or initialed by engraver.

» ***Auto Rifle Grade II - FN Custom Shop***

	$1,895	$1,500	$1,250	$1,050	$825	$675	$525

Add 10% for .22 Short cal.

* ***Auto Rifle Grade II - Miroku (Japan Mfg.)*** – disc. 1984.

	$795	$675	$575	$525	$425	$350	$275

Add $50 for original box.

* ***Auto Rifle Grade III - FN (Belgian Mfg.)***

	$3,300	$2,925	$2,500	$2,275	$1,950	$1,575	$1,225

Add 15% for guns signed by the engraver.
Add $200 for original box.
Add 50% for guns in .22 Short cal., if in 98% or better condition.

FN Grade IIIs have coin finish or grey chromed receiver, extra deluxe walnut with skipline checkering, gold plated trigger, and more elaborate game scene engraving usually featuring a dog flushing

MSR	100%	98%	95%	90%	80%	70%	60%

ducks or upland game. Signed or unsigned by engraver (Funken, J. Baerten, Vrancken, and Watrin will command premiums over values listed). A few were also special ordered with blue finish and special engraving - these command an extra premium.

» *Auto Rifle Grade III - FN Custom Shop*

| | $3,500 | $3,100 | $2,600 | $2,350 | $2,000 | $1,600 | $1,250 |

Add 15% for guns signed by the engraver.
Add 50% for "transition" guns signed by FN engravers with barrels and boxes marked "Made in Japan."

* *Auto Rifle Grade III - Miroku (Japan Mfg.)* – disc. 1983.

| | $1,550 | $1,375 | $1,275 | $995 | $800 | $675 | $525 |

* *Auto Rifle Grade VI - Miroku (Japan Mfg.)* – game scene engraved with gold plated animals (typically fox and squirrel on receiver sides), choice of blue or greyed receiver, deluxe walnut. New 1987.

| MSR $1,580 | $1,250 | $1,050 | $895 | $795 | $650 | $550 | $450 |

Add at least 50% for small run of .22 Short cal. Grade VI mfg. during 2003.

* *Auto Rifle Grade VI 125th Anniversary Miroku* – features silver nitride receiver with gold enhanced 125th Anniversary logo and delicate scroll engraving. 500 mfg. 2003-2004.

| | $1,275 | $975 | $795 | N/A | N/A | N/A | N/A |

Last MSR was $1,271.

BAR-22 – .22 LR cal., 20 1/4 in. barrel, 15 shot tube mag., folding leaf sight, high polish steel receiver, checkered pistol grip stock, 5 lbs. 13 oz. Mfg. 1977-85 by Miroku.

| | $695 | $625 | $550 | $450 | $350 | $300 | $250 |

Last MSR was $245.

BAR-22 GRADE II – engraved model of BAR-22 featuring game scenes on silver greyed steel receiver, select French walnut. Disc. 1985.

| | $1,050 | $925 | $775 | $725 | $575 | $450 | $350 |

Last MSR was $350.

BUCK MARK RIFLE – .22 LR cal., Buck Mark pistol blowback action, 18 in. tapered barrel with Hi-Viz fiber optic sights (Sporter Rifle), heavy barrel w/o sights (Target or Field Target Rifle), or carbon composite barrel (disc. 2006), includes integral scope rail, uncheckered walnut or grey laminate (new 2002, no sights) Monte Carlo stock that attaches to non-detachable, one-piece skeletonized and enclosed rear grip assembly, separate forearm, 10 shot mag., 3 lbs. 10 oz. (Classic Carbon -disc. 2006), 4 lbs. 6 oz. (Sporter) or approx. 5 1/2 lbs. (Target & Classic Target). New 2001.

| MSR $670 | $525 | $465 | $385 | $340 | $275 | $225 | $175 |

Add $20 for grey laminate stock (Classic/Field Target Rifle, new 2002).
Add $95 for carbon composite barrel (disc. 2006).

The Buck Mark Classic/Field Target with grey laminate stock &

RIFLES: SEMI-AUTO, BAR SERIES

MSR	100%	98%	95%	90%	80%	70%	60%

Classic/Field Carbon Rifles are available through Full-Line and Medallion dealers only.

RIFLES: SEMI-AUTO, BAR SERIES

Currently, the Browning Custom Shop in Belgium is making the following BAR custom shop rifles: Grade 4 VB ($9,086 MSR), Grade 4 PH ($9,086 MSR). Until 2006, the Custom Shop produced the Grade D ($6,543 last MSR).

BROWNING PATENT 1900 – please refer to model listing under F.N.

BAR SEMI-AUTO – .243 Win., .270 Win., .280 Rem. (new 1990), .308 Win., or .30-06 cal. available in standard model, Mag. cals. include 7mm Rem., .300 Win., and .338 Win. Mag. (reintroduced 1990), gas operated, blued steel receiver, 22 or 24 (Mag. only) in. barrel, rotary bolt with seven lugs, folding leaf sight, walnut stock, grades differ in engraving, finish, and quality of wood, in 1993, to celebrate the 25th Anniversary of the BAR, Browning introduced the BAR MK II Safari (see model listing), approx. 7 lbs. 6 oz. New 1967 (includes BAR MK II).

Add 20% for FN mfg. and assembled BARs (marked "Made in Belgium").
Add 10% for .338 Win. Mag. cal. (FN mfg. only).

Note: Original .338s were limited production, mostly seen in the deluxe Grade II only. During the last year of FN .338 production, several were delivered in a Grade I by FN. Although being rarer than the Grade II, it is not as desirable. The following prices are for Portuguese assembled guns, manufactured by FN, and so stamped on the barrel.

* **BAR Grade I** – standard grade without engraving, blue finish. Ordering this model without sights became an option in 1988. Disc. 1992.

$725	$635	$545	$495	$400	$325	$250

Last MSR was $633.

Add 15% for .280 Rem. cal. if in 98%+ condition.
Subtract $16 if without sights

FN mfg. and assembled Grade Is can be denoted by light scroll engraving on the receiver.

* **BAR Grade I Magnum** – standard grade without engraving, with recoil pad, 8 lbs. 6 oz. Disc. 1992.

$765	$675	$575	$525	$425	$350	$275

Last MSR was $680

Subtract $16 without sights.

Ordering this gun without sights became an option in 1988.

* **BAR Grade II** – blue receiver, engraved with big game heads. Mfg 1967-74.

$1,175	$1,025	$875	$800	$650	$525	$415

This model was previously designated Deluxe.

RIFLES: SEMI-AUTO, BAR SERIES

MSR	100%	98%	95%	90%	80%	70%	60%

* ***BAR Grade II Magnum*** – magnum version of Grade II. Mfg. 1967-74.

  $1,295 $1,100 $925 $875 $700 $550 $435

* ***BAR Grade III*** – features antelope and deer game scenes etched on greyed steel receiver, select checkered stock and forearm. Disc. 1984.

  $1,750 $1,500 $1,275 $1,100 $950 $825 $725

* ***BAR Grade III Magnum*** – magnum version of Grade III, features elk and moose game scenes. Disc. 1984.

  $1,850 $1,600 $1,375 $1,200 $1,050 $925 $825

* ***BAR Grade IV*** – engraved satin finish greyed receiver depicts big game animal scenes and trigger guard, carved borders on checkering. Disc. 1989.

  $2,800 $2,500 $2,200 $1,825 $1,525 $1,275 $1,050

  Last MSR was $1,670.

* ***BAR Grade IV Magnum*** – magnum version of Grade IV. Disc. 1984.

  $2,950 $2,650 $2,350 $2,000 $1,650 $1,375 $1,150

  Last MSR was $1,720.

* ***BAR Grade V*** – more elaborate engraving than Grade IV, with gold inlays. Mfg. 1971-74.

  $6,500 $5,700 $4,900 $4,500 $3,515 $2,875 $2,250

* ***BAR Grade V Magnum*** – magnum version of Grade V.

  $6,850 $5,995 $5,150 $4,650 $3,775 $3,075 $2,400

BAR NORTH AMERICAN DEER RIFLE ISSUE – .30-06 cal. only, BAR style action with silver grey finish and engraved action, 600 total production, walnut cased with accessories. Disc. 1983 but were sold through 1989.

  $4,500 $3,950 $3,400 $3,100 N/A N/A N/A

  Last MSR was $3,550.

BAR MK II SAFARI – .22-250 Rem. (mfg. as prototype only during 1997), .25-06 Rem. (new 1997), .243 Win., .270 Win., .30-06, .308 Win., .270 Wby. Mag. (mfg. 1996-2000), 7mm Rem. Mag., .300 Win. Mag., or .338 Win. Mag. cal., improved BAR action featuring redesigned bolt release, new gas operating system, and reduced recoil, removable trigger assembly, 22, 23 (WSM cals. only, disc.), or 24 (Mag. cals. only) in. barrel with (adj. for windage and elevation) or without sights, BOSS became optional 1994, and is available with ported BOSS, (approx. 30% less recoil), or unported BOSS-CR (Conventional Recoil) muzzle brake, blue finish with scroll engraved receiver, checkered walnut stock and forearm, gold trigger, detachable 3 (.300 WSM cal. only), 4 (Mag. cals. only) or 5 shot box mag., approx. 7 lbs. 6 oz. except for Mag. cals. (8 lbs. 6 oz.). Mfg. by FN in Belgium. New 1993.

MSR $1,230 $995 $850 $725 $625 $525 $450 $375

Add $120 for Mag. cals. Add $19 for open sights (not available in .270 Wby. Mag., disc.).

The new BAR MK II Safari does not have interchangeable magazine capability with the older pre-1993 BARs.

MSR	100%	98%	95%	90%	80%	70%	60%

* ***BAR Classic Mark II Safari*** – .270 Win. (disc. 2001), .270 WSM (new 2003), .30-06 (disc. 2001), 7mm Rem. Mag., (disc. 2001), 7mm WSM (new 2003), .300 Win. Mag. (disc. 2001), or .300 WSM (new 2002) cal., similar to BAR Mark II Safari, except has satin finished checkered stock and forearm, 7 lbs. 6 oz. or 8 lbs. 6 oz. Mfg. 1999-2003.

    $785 **$685** **$595** **$525** **$425** **$350** **$275**

Last MSR was $908.

Subtract approx. 10% for non-Mag. cals.
Add $17 for open sights (disc. 2000).

This model was available through Full-line and Medallion dealers only.

* ***BAR Mark II Safari with BOSS*** – .243 Win. (disc. 1999), .308 Win. (disc. 1999), .270 Win., .270 WSM (new 2003), .30-06, 7mm Rem. Mag., 7mm WSM (new 2003), .300 Win. Mag., .300 WSM (new 2003), .338 Win. Mag. cal., similar to BAR MK II Safari, with BOSS (ballistic optimizing shooting system), no sights, approx. 7 1/2 or 8 1/2 lbs. New 1994.

MSR $1,390 **$1,150** **$995** **$825** **$725** **$625** **$525** **$425**

Add $110 for Mag. and WSM cals.

* ***BAR Mark II Lightweight*** – .243 Win., .270 Win., .30-06, .308 Win., 7mm Rem. Mag. (new 1999), .300 Win. Mag. (new 1999), or .338 Win. Mag. (new 1999) cal., features alloy receiver and 20 or 24 (Mag. cals only) in. barrel, matte wood and barrel finish, open sights, 7 lbs. 2 oz. or 7 lbs. 12 oz. Mfg. 1997-2003.

    $715 **$625** **$525** **$475** **$395** **$325** **$250**

Last MSR was $850.

Add $77 for Mag. cals. (new 1999).

* ***BAR MK II Lightweight with BOSS*** – 7mm Rem. Mag., .300 Win. Mag. or .338 Win. Mag. (disc. 1999) cal., similar to BAR Mark II Lightweight except has 24 in. barrel with BOSS, 8 lbs. 6 oz. Mfg. 1999-2000.

    $800 **$700** **$600** **$550** **$450** **$365** **$275**

Last MSR was $939.

* ***BAR MK II Lightweight Stalker*** – .243 Win., .270 Win., .270 WSM (new 2003), .30-06, .308 Win., 7mm Rem. Mag. (disc. 2004), 7mm WSM (new 2003), .300 Win. Mag., .300 WSM (new 2002), or .338 Win. Mag. cal., similar to BAR Mark II Safari, except has aluminum alloy receiver and checkered black synthetic stock and forearm, matte metal finish, 20, 22, 23 (new 2002, WSM cals. only), or 24 (Mag. cals. only) in. barrel with open sights, 7 lbs. 2 oz. - 7 lbs. 12 oz. New 2001.

MSR $1,230 **$995** **$850** **$725** **$625** **$525** **$450** **$375**

Add $110 for Mag. or WSM cals.

» ***BAR MK II Lightweight Stalker with BOSS*** – .270 WSM (new 2003), 7mm Rem. Mag., 7mm WSM (new 2003), .300 Win. Mag., .300 WSM

MSR	100%	98%	95%	90%	80%	70%	60%

(new 2002), or .338 Win. Mag. cal., similar to BAR Mark II Stalker, except has 23 (new 2002, WSM cals. only) or 24 in. barrel with BOSS, approx. 7 3/4 lbs. Mfg. 2001-2003.

	$835	$725	$625	$575	$450	$375	$295

Last MSR was $981.

* **BAR MK II High Grade** – .270 Win., .30-06, .300 Win. Mag., or 7mm Rem. Mag. cal., satin finished receiver with either whitetail/mule deer or moose/elk etched game scenes and gold border, checkered high grade gloss finished walnut stock and forearm, no sights, 7 lbs. 6 oz. or 8 lbs. 6 oz. Mfg. 2001-2003.

	$1,475	$1,295	$1,100	$1,000	$815	$675	$515

Last MSR was $1,856.

Add $58 for Mag. cals.

* **BAR MK II Grade III** – features Grade III engraving pattern. Mfg. by the FN custom shop 1996-99.

	$3,400	$2,975	$2,550	$2,300	$1,875	$1,525	$1,195

Last MSR was $3,754.

* **BAR MK II Grade IV** – features Grade IV engraving pattern. Mfg. by the FN custom shop beginning 1996.

	$3,500	$3,075	$2,625	$2,375	$1,925	$1,575	$1,225

Last MSR was $3,859.

BAR SHORTTRAC – .243 Win., .270 WSM, .300 WSM, .308 Win., 7mm-08 Rem. (new 2010), 7mm WSM, or .325 WSM (new 2009) cal., features new styling with black (disc. 2008) or satin nickel finished (new 2009) aluminum alloy gas operated short action receiver with light etching and gold Browning logo at rear, composite trigger guard and mag. floorplate, 22 or 23 in. hammer forged barrel w/o sights, mfg. in Belgium, drilled and tapped, checkered satin (disc. 2008) or oil (new 2009) finished walnut stock supplied with 6 adj. shims and squared off forearm, 3 or 4 shot detachable mag., 6 lbs. 10 oz (regular cals.) or 7 1/4 lbs. (WSM cals.). New 2004.

MSR $1,230	$995	$850	$725	$625	$525	$450	$375

Add $110 for WSM cals.
Add $40 for left-hand model with left-side ejection port.

* **BAR Shorttrac Stalker** – similar to BAR Shorttrac, except has matte black metal finish and black composite stock and forearm. New 2006.

MSR $1,260	$1,050	$875	$750	$650	$525	$425	$325

Add $90 for WSM cals.

* **BAR Shorttrac Camo** – similar to BAR Shorttrac, except has 100% Mossy Oak New Break Up (disc. 2009) or Break Up Infinity (new 2010) camo coverage. New 2007.

MSR $1,360	$1,175	$995	$850	$750	$650	$495	$375

Add $120 for WSM cals.

MSR	100%	98%	95%	90%	80%	70%	60%

BAR LONGTRAC – .270 Win., .30-06, .300 Win. Mag., or 7mm Rem. Mag. cal., similar to BAR Shorttrac, except has long action, 3 or 4 shot mag., 7 or 7 1/2 lbs. New 2004.

MSR $1,230	$995	$850	$725	$625	$525	$450	$375

Add $90 for Mag. cals.
Add $40 for left-hand model with left-side ejection port.

* **BAR Longtrac Stalker** – similar to BAR Longtrac, except has matte black metal finish and black composite stock and forearm. New 2006.

MSR $1,260	$1,050	$875	$750	$650	$525	$425	$325

Add $90 for Mag. cals.

* **BAR Longtrac Camo** – similar to BAR Longtrac, except has 100% Mossy Oak New Break Up (disc. 2009) or Break Up Infinity (new 2010) camo coverage. New 2007.

MSR $1,360	$1,175	$995	$850	$750	$650	$495	$375

Add $100 for Mag. cals.

BAR ZENITH – various cals., features a manual cocking system on the upper tang and wood inserts in the receiver, 20 in. barrel with Battue/fixed rear sight and fiber optic front sight. European distribution only. New 2012.

This model is not available for U.S. importation, and is sold in Europe exclusively.

RIFLES: SEMI-AUTO, FAL & CAL SERIES

FN manufactured FALs and CALs imported by BAC can be found under the Fabrique Nationale heading.

Above Average	Average	Below Average

RIFLES: SINGLE SHOT

MODEL 1878 STANDARD – various cals., J.M. Browning's first patent, falling block action, fewer than 600 made (highest known ser. no. is 542) by Browning Brothers in Ogden, Utah between 1878-1883, octagon barrel marked "Browning Bros. Ogden, Utah USA", plain wood stock and forearm with and without pistol grips, crescent steel buttplate, with or without ramrod, several receiver configurations, a very few were made in the deluxe model, seldom found in better than average used condition, with or w/o serial number. Approx. only 100 have survived - Browning Arms Co. and the Winchester Museum have no factory records on this model.

$50,000 - $40,000	$35,000 - $30,000	$25,000 - $20,000

Add 50% for Deluxe Rifle (checkered stock and forearm), 10% for Early Rifle with Sharps Borchardt type lever, 40% for Early Rifle stamped "Ogden, U.T.", 20% for any caliber other than .40-70 SS or .45-70 Govt., 25% for Late Model with ramrod under barrel held by two thimbles (known as "Montana Model").
Subtract 20% if the original sights have been removed or replaced incorrectly.

MSR	100%	98%	95%	90%	80%	70%	60%

Calibers in this model are listed from rarest to most commonly encountered: .50-70 Govt., .45 Sharps, .44 Rem., .40-90 Sharps, .44-77 Sharps, .45-70 Govt., and .40-70 Sharps Straight.

This model is rare since approx. only 550 were mfg. (approx. ser. range 1-550). This patent was sold to Winchester, which became their Model 1885 single shot. To date, less than 100 original Model 1878s have been encountered indicating a high mortality rate (most remaining specimens are in poor original condition). An inherent weakness of the original design was the way the stock attached to the action - Winchester later corrected this design flaw. A few remaining examples are not serial numbered. Barter guns are rifles which have Browning stamped actions but with another gunsmith's barrel.

MODEL B-78 – .22-250 Rem., 6mm Rem., .243 Win. (only 671 mfg.), .25-06 Rem., 7mm Mag., .30-06, or .45-70 Govt. (octagon barrel only) cal., 24 or 26 in. round or octagon barrel, lever activated falling block, no sights except .45- 70 Govt., checkered walnut stock, approx. 24,000 mfg. 1973-1982.

$1,495 $1,275 $1,125 $1,000 $825 $675 $525

Add 30% for .243 Win. cal.

Production statistics on the various calibers are as follows: .22-250 - 2,431 mfg. in round barrel, 3,482 mfg. in octagon, .243 Win. - 280 mfg. in round barrel, 391 mfg. in octagon, 6mm Rem - 1,280 mfg. in round barrel, 1,911 mfg. in octagon, .25-06 - 1,475 mfg. in round barrel, 3,293 mfg. in octagon, .30-06 - 1,588 mfg. in round barrel, 2,330 mfg. in octagon, .45-70 - 0 mfg. in round barrel, 3,839 mfg. in octagon, 7mm Rem. Mag. - 635 mfg. in round barrel, 961 mfg. in octagon.

The Model B-78 was superceded by the Model 1885 in 1985.

* *Model B-78 Sporter* – various cals., utilizes a Model 1885 barrelled action with B-78 wood (pistol grip and cheekpiece).

$1,495 $1,275 $1,125 $1,000 $825 $675 $525

MODEL 1885 HIGH WALL – .22-250 Rem., .223 Rem. (disc. 1994), .270 Win., .30-06, 7mm Rem. Mag., .45-70 Govt., or .454 Casull (new 1998) cal., falling block action, sear safety, 28 in. octagonal barrel, adj. gold trigger, no sights, checkered straight grip English walnut stock without cheekpiece and Schnabel forearm, exposed hammer, approx. 8 3/4 lbs. Mfg. 1985-2001.

$1,450 $1,270 $1,090 $985 $800 $655 $510

Last MSR was $1,027.

This model was equipped with open sights in .45-70 Govt. and .454 Casull cals.

MSR	100%	98%	95%	90%	80%	70%	60%

MODEL 1885 LOW WALL – .22 Hornet, .223 Rem. (disc. 2000), .243 Win. (disc. 2000), or .260 Rem. (new 1999) cal., action patterned after the Winchester Low Wall receiver, features thinner 24 in. barrel, adj. trigger, 6 1/4 lbs. Mfg. 1995-2001.

$1,225 $1,070 $920 $835 $675 $550 $430

Last MSR was $997.

Add $100 for .260 Rem. cal.

MODEL 1885 HIGH WALL TRADITIONAL HUNTER – .30-30 Win., .38-55 WCF or .45-70 Govt. cal., High-Wall action, 30 in. octagon barrel with ejector, blue receiver, rear tang aperture sight, crescent buttplate, checkered stock and forearm, approx. 9 lbs. Mfg. 1997-2000.

$1,325 $1,160 $995 $900 $730 $595 $465

Last MSR was $1,220.

* *Model 1885 High Wall Traditional Hunter 125th Anniversary* – .45-70 Govt. cal., features delicate scroll receiver engraving and gold enhanced 125th anniversary logo with gold border. 500 mfg. 2003-2004 only.

$1,675 $1,465 $1,255 N/A N/A N/A N/A

Last MSR was $1,516.

MODEL 1885 LOW WALL TRADITIONAL HUNTER – .357 Mag., .44 Mag., or .45 LC cal., 24 in. half-round, half-octagon barrel, case colored receiver and buttplate, gold bead front, semi-buckhorn rear, and rear tang aperture sights, 6 1/2 lbs. Mfg. 1998-2001.

$1,375 $1,205 $1,030 $935 $755 $620 $480

Last MSR was $1,289.

MODEL 1885 BPCR (BLACK POWDER CARTRIDGE RIFLE) – .40-65 Win. (black powder only) or .45-70 Govt. (black powder or smokeless) cal., case colored high wall action, 30 in. half-round, half-octagon barrel, checkered pistol grip stock with shotgun butt, w/o ejector system and shell deflector, vernier tang rear sight and globe front sight with spirit level, approx. 11 lbs. Mfg. 1996-2001.

$1,900 $1,665 $1,425 $1,290 $1,045 $855 $665

Last MSR was $1,766.

* *Model 1885 BPCR Creedmoor* – .45-90 cal., blue receiver, 34 in. half-round, half-octagon barrel with globe front and aperture rear tang sights, 11 3/4 lbs. Mfg. 1998-1999.

$1,900 $1,665 $1,425 $1,290 $1,045 $855 $665

Last MSR was $1,764.

RIFLES: SLIDE ACTION

BPR – .243 Win., .270 Win., .30-06, .308 Win., .300 Win. Mag., or 7mm Rem. Mag. cal., 7 lug rotary bolt, blue alloy receiver, 22 or 24 (Mag. cals. only) in. barrel with open sights, features downward camming slide action assembly, checkered walnut stock and forend, cross-bolt safety, 3

SHOTGUNS: BOLT ACTION, A-BOLT SERIES

MSR	100%	98%	95%	90%	80%	70%	60%

or 4 shot mag., approx. 7 lbs. 3 oz. Mfg. 1997-2001.

	$750	$650	$525	$475	$375	$315	$250

Last MSR was $725.

Add $55 for Mag. cals.

BPR-22 – .22 LR or .22 WMR cal., short-stroke action, 20 1/4 in. barrel, 11 shot tube mag., mfg. 1977-1982.

	$550	$495	$425	$375	$315	$275	$225

Add 30% for .22 WMR cal.

* *BPR-22 Grade II* – similar to BPR-22, only engraved action, select walnut.

	$850	$750	$650	$550	$450	$400	$315

Add 30% for .22 WMR cal.

TROMBONE MODEL – .22 LR cal. only, slide action with tube mag., fixed sights, takedown, 24 in. barrel, hammerless, with either FN or U.S. (rare) barrel address, approx. 150,000 Grade I's were mfg.

Add $150 for original box.

* *Trombone Model w/FN Barrel Address* – most common variation.

	$1,375	$1,200	$1,025	$925	$750	$625	$475

* *Trombone Model w/BAC Barrel Markings* – approx. 3,200 Grade Is were imported by BAC during the late 1960s.

	$1,895	$1,650	$1,425	$1,295	$1,050	$850	$675

Add $250 for original box.

* *Trombone Model Grade I* – limited mfg. for the BCA circa 1985, 30 mfg., with only 10 sold individually, engraved by Custom Shop at FN for wholesaler.

	$1,650	$1,425	$1,175	N/A	N/A	N/A	N/A

* *Trombone Grades I & II 2 Gun Set* – limited mfg. for the BCA circa 1985, 10 sets mfg., available in 2 gun set.

	$3,925	$3,425	$2,950	N/A	N/A	N/A	N/A

* *Trombone Grades I, II, & III 3 Gun Set* – 10 sets mfg. for BCA circa 1985.

	$7,500	$6,575	$5,625	N/A	N/A	N/A	N/A

* *Trombone Custom Shop Models* – limited mfg. from the FN Custom Shop.

Values for 100% rifles are as follows: Grade I - $1,350, Grade II - $2,350, Grade III - $3,750, Grade III C or Grade III w/gold inlays (sometimes referred to as Grade IV) - $4,500, Grade V (wood and water or Squirrel gun) - $3,000.

SHOTGUNS: BOLT ACTION, A-BOLT SERIES

A-BOLT SHOTGUN MODEL (DISC.) – 12 ga. only, 3 in. chamber, 2 shot mag., same bolt system as A-Bolt II Rifle, 22 or 23 in. barrel (rifled or Invector with rifled tube), available in Stalker Model with graphite fiberglass composite stock or Hunter Model with select satin finished walnut stock, dull matte finished barrel and receiver, top tang safety, choice of no sights (new 1996) or adj. rear sight, drilled and tapped receiver, approx. 7 lbs. Mfg. by Miroku 1995-98.

* ***A-Bolt Stalker Model Shotgun***

	100%	98%	95%	90%	80%	70%	60%
	$895	$825	$700	$625	$595	$475	$375

Last MSR was $720.

Add $45 for open sights.
Add $150 for rifled barrel.

* ***A-Bolt Hunter Model Shotgun***

	100%	98%	95%	90%	80%	70%	60%
	$895	$825	$700	$625	$595	$475	$375

Last MSR was $805.

Add $40 for open sights.
Add $150 for rifled barrel.

A-BOLT SHOTGUN HUNTER SERIES (CURRENT) – 12 ga. only, 3 in. chamber, 22 in. rifled barrel with adj. rear and Truglo fiber optic front sights, matte blued finish, 60 degree bolt lift, 2 shot detachable mag., choice of satin finish, checkered walnut stock (Hunter Model), black composite stock with Dura-Touch armor coating (Stalker Model), or Camo Model with Mossy Oak Break-Up Infinity camo finish with armor coating, vent. recoil pad, sling swivels, approx. 7 lbs. New 2011.

MSR $1,150 $975 $875 $750 $675 $650 $525 $400

Add $130 for Hunter Model with wood stock.
Add $150 for Camo Model with Mossy Oak Break-Up Infinity finish.

SHOTGUNS: O/U, CYNERGY SERIES

During 2010, Vector Pro chokes became standard on 12 and 20 ga. models.

CYNERGY SERIES – 12, 20 (new 2005), 28 (new 2005) ga., or .410 bore (new 2007), silver nitride finished receiver, features new MonoLock hinge system allowing low receiver profile, mechanical striker based SST, reverse striker ignition system (triple trigger system included on Sporting models), 26 or 28 in. backbored and ported vent. barrels with VR, Vector Pro lengthened forcing cones became standard on all 12 and 20 ga. models beginning 2010, Invector-Plus chokes, choice of wood or composite (12 ga. only) stock and forearm, solid, vent., or Inflex recoil pad, impact ejectors. New 2004.

* ***Cynergy Field (Current)*** – 12, 20, 28 ga. or .410 bore, similar to discontinued Cynergy Field, except has Vector Pro lengthened forcing cones on 12 and 20 ga., engraving features pheasants and ducks on 12 ga., or quail and grouse on small gauge, gloss oil finished Grade II/III walnut stock, approx. 6 - 7 3/4 lbs. New 2010.

MSR $2,800 $2,420 $2,000 $1,800 $1,450 $1,150 $925 $775

Add $50 for 20, 28 ga. or .410 bore.

* ***Cynergy Field (Disc.)*** – 12 (disc. 2006), 20, or 28 ga., 2 3/4 (28 ga. only) or 3 in. chambers, 26 or 28 in. non-ported barrels with 5/16 in. slanted VR, flush choke tubes, silver nitride finished receiver with cla

SHOTGUNS: O/U, CYNERGY SERIES

MSR	100%	98%	95%	90%	80%	70%	60%

pigeon motif, checkered Grade I walnut or non-glare black composite (disc. 2006) stock and forearm, stock has adj. comb with built in Inflex recoil pad system allowing LOP adjustment, approx. 6 1/4 - 7 1/2 lbs. Mfg. 2004-2007.

$1,575 $1,200 $950 $875 $775 $700 $625

Last MSR was $2,062.

Subtract approx. 10% for composite stock and forearm.

* ***Cynergy Classic Field*** – 12, 20 (new 2007), 28 ga. (new 2007), or .410 bore (new 2007), 3 in. chambers, features traditional satin finished walnut stock with standard vent. recoil pad and Schnabel forearm, etched mallard and pheasant on receiver sides, approx. 6 1/4 - 7 3/4 lbs. New 2006.

MSR $2,530 $2,350 $1,900 $1,500 $1,200 $950 $750 $700

Add $60 for 20, 28 ga. or .410 bore.

* ***Cynergy Classic Field Grade III*** – 12 or 20 ga., 3 in. chambers, similar to Classic Field, except has gloss finished upgraded wood (Grade III/Grade IV) and fully engraved receiver, approx. 6-8 lbs. New 2007.

MSR $4,000 $3,475 $2,925 $2,600 $2,200 $1,875 $1,575 $1,200

Add $50 for 20 ga.

* ***Cynergy Classic Field Grade VI*** – 12 or 20 ga., similar to Classic Field Grade III, except has upgraded wood (Grade V/VI), fully engraved receiver with multiple gold inlays. New 2007.

MSR $6,100 $5,260 $4,475 $4,000 $3,400 $2,890 $2,300 $1,800

Add $30 for 20 ga.

* ***Cynergy Euro Field*** – 12, 20, 28 ga. or .410 bore, 26 or 28 in. barrel, jewelled mono-bloc, full coverage high relief engraving (pheasants and ducks on 12 ga., quail and grouse on 20 ga.) on receiver, forearm iron and top lever, gloss oil finished Grade II/III walnut stock and forearm, choke tubes, 5 lbs., 15 oz. - 7 lbs., 11 oz. Mfg. 2009.

$2,300 $1,850 $1,475 $1,195 $950 $750 $700

Last MSR was $2,509.

Add $20 for 20, 28 ga. or .410 bore.

This model's nomenclature was changed to the Cynergy Field during 2010.

* ***Cynergy Feather*** – 12, 20 (new 2008), 28 (new 2008) ga. or .410 bore (new 2008), 3 in. chambers, choice of checkered black composite stock with adj. comb or checkered satin-finished walnut stock and Schnabel forearm, Inflex recoil pad, 26 or 28 in. barrels with flush Invector-Plus choke tubes, jewelled mono-bloc (new 2009), approx. 5 1/2 - 6 3/4 lbs. New 2007.

MSR $2,900 $2,525 $2,025 $1,650 $1,325 $1,100 $950 $800

Add $30 for 20, 28 ga. or .410 bore.
Subtract $100 for black adj. composite stock and forearm (12 ga. only).

SHOTGUNS: O/U, CYNERGY SERIES

MSR	100%	98%	95%	90%	80%	70%	60%

* *Cynergy Sporting* – 12 (disc. 2006), 20, or 28 ga., 2 3/4 in. chambers, 28, 30, or 32 in. ported barrels with tapered VR (non-tapered 5/16 in. rib on 28 ga.), Hi-Viz fiber optic front sight, silver nitride receiver with clay pigeon motif, oil finished checkered walnut (with or w/o adj. comb) or black composite (12 ga. only, disc. 2006) stock and forearm, stock has adj. comb with built in Inflex recoil pad system allowing LOP adjustment (disc. 2006), extended choke tubes, approx. 6 1/2 - 8 lbs. Mfg. 2004-2007.

$1,875 $1,640 $1,405 $1,275 $1,030 $845 $655

Last MSR was $3,080.

Add 25% for adj. comb (mfg. 2006 only).
Subtract approx. 20% for composite stock and forearm.

* *Cynergy Classic Sporting* – 12, 20 (new 2007), 28 ga. (new 2007) or .410 bore (new 2007), 2 3/4 or 3 in. chambers, 28, 30, or 32 in. ported barrels with extended choke tubes, features traditional oil finished walnut stock with solid recoil pad and Schnabel forearm, etched Browning logo on receiver sides, approx. 6 1/4 - 8 lbs. New 2006.

MSR $3,600 $3,100 $2,625 $2,375 $1,900 $1,600 $1,400 $1,100

Add $30 for 20, 28 ga. or .410 bore.
Add $400 for adj. comb (new 2007, not available in 28 ga. or .410 bore).

* *Cynergy Sporting (Euro Sporting)* – 12 or 20 (new 2008) ga., 2 3/4 in. chambers, 28, 30, or 32 in. VR barrels with porting and extended choke tubes, features traditional checkered oil finished walnut stock and Schnabel forearm, or black composite (adj. comb only) stock with Inflex recoil pad, jewelled mono-bloc (new 2009), high relief scroll engraving on receiver forearm and top lever (new 2009), approx. 6 1/4 - 8 lbs. New 2007.

MSR $4,000 $3,525 $2,900 $2,400 $1,925 $1,650 $1,350 $1,175

Add $500 for adj. comb (12 ga. only) with oil finished walnut stock and Schnabel forearm.
Add $30 for 20 ga.
Subtract $120 for adj. comb black composite stock and forearm (not available in 20 ga.).
Subtract 10% if w/o scroll engraving.

This model's nomenclature changed from Euro Sporting to Sporting during 2010.

* *Cynergy Classic Trap* – 12 ga. only, 2 3/4 in. chambers, 30 or 32 in. VR barrels with porting, extended Invector-Plus chokes and Hi-Viz fiber optic front sight, checkered walnut stock with or w/o adj. comb and competition forearm, vent. recoil pad, approx. 8 3/4 lbs. New 2007.

MSR $3,880 $3,340 $2,840 $2,550 $2,100 $1,785 $1,500 $1,300

Add $400 for adj. comb.

* *Cynergy Classic Trap Unsingle Combo* – 12 ga. only, includes choice of 32 or 34 in. ported single barrel and choice of 30 or 32 in. O/U ported

SHOTGUNS: O/U, CITORI HUNTING SERIES

MSR	100%	98%	95%	90%	80%	70%	60%

barrels with adj. top rib, gloss finished Grade III/VI walnut stock with adj. comb and semi-beavertail forearm with finger grooves, includes aluminum (disc.) or green canvas case, approx. 8 3/4 lbs. New 2008.

MSR $6,000 $5,180 $4,335 $3,685 $3,130 $2,665 $2,265 $1,800

SHOTGUNS: O/U, CITORI HUNTING SERIES

All Citori shotguns which incorporate the Invector choke tube system may be used with steel shot. Invector Plus choke tubes are designed for backbored barrels. DO NOT USE Standard Invector choke tubes in barrels marked for the Invector Plus choking system. During 2010, Vector Pro chokes became standard on 12 and 20 ga. models.

Hand engraving was replaced by machine engraving in late 1982 on all higher grade models.

Subtract $100 for 26 in. barrels on used guns.

CITORI HUNTING MODELS - 12, 16 (mfg. 1986-89), 20, 28 ga. (disc. 1994) or .410 bore (disc. 1994), 26, 28, or 30 in. barrels, various chokes, boxlock, auto ejectors, SST, vent. rib, features checkered semi-pistol grip stock with grooved semi-beavertail forearm, grades differ in amount of engraving, finish, and wood. Invector chokes became standard in 1988, Invector Plus chokes became standard 1995 on 12 or 20 ga., 6 lbs. 9 oz. - 8 lbs. 5 oz. Mfg. 1973-2001 by Miroku.

* *Citori Hunting Grade I 12 or 20 ga.* – blue finish with light scroll engraving beginning 1978.

  » *Citori Hunting Grade I Earlier Mfg. without Invector Choking*

       $950 $800 $700 $600 $575 $500 $450

Add 15% for 16 ga. if in 90%+ original condition.
Add approx. 40% for extra 20 ga. barrels originally ordered with gun.

  » *Citori Grade I Hunter Model w/Invector Choking* – recent mfg. with Invector Choking, 12 or 20 ga., 3 in. chambers, 20 ga. available with Standard Invector or Invector Plus (new 1994) choking system, Invector Plus choking standard on recently mfg. 12 and 20 ga., 6 lbs. 9 oz. - 8 lbs. 5 oz. Disc. 2001.

       $1,150 $950 $825 $700 $650 $575 $525

  Last MSR was $1,486.

Add $100 for Invector Plus choke tubes.

* *Citori Hunting Grade I Smaller Gauges*

  » *Citori Hunting Grade I 28 ga. or .410 bore* – without Invector choking. Disc. 1994.

       $1,000 $850 $700 $600 $550 $500 $450

  Last MSR was $1,097.

* *Citori Hunting Grade II* - 12, 20, 28 ga., or .410 bore. Mfg. 1978-1983.

       $1,200 $1,000 $800 $650 $600 $550 $500

* *Citori Hunting Grade III* - 12, 16 (mfg. 1986-89), 20, 28 ga. (disc. 1994), or .410 bore (disc. 1994), greyed steel receiver with engraved

SHOTGUNS: O/U, CITORI HUNTING SERIES

MSR	100%	98%	95%	90%	80%	70%	60%

game scenes featuring grouse (20 ga.) and ducks (12 ga.), Invector chokes standard, Invector Plus became standard in 12 ga. in 1994. Mfg. 1985-95.

$1,900 $1,600 $1,300 $1,000 $800 $700 $600

Last MSR was $1,875.

Add 15% for 16 ga. if in 90%+ original condition.
Add 15%-25% for 28 ga. or .410 bore (both disc. 1989).
Subtract $200 for standard Invector chokes.

* *Citori Hunting Grade V* – 12, 20, 28 ga., or .410 bore, extensive deep relief engraving with game scenes on satin grey receiver. Disc. 1984.

$2,750 $2,200 $1,850 $1,525 $1,300 $1,150 $995

Add 20% for 28 ga.

* *Citori Hunting Grade VI* – 12, 16 (mfg. 1986-89), 20, 28 ga. (disc. 1992), or .410 bore (disc. 1989), hand engraved (1983-1984 only) or machine engraving on blue or greyed receiver with extensive engraving including multiple gold inlays, Standard Invector (12 ga. disc. 1993) or Invector Plus chokes. Mfg. 1983-1995.

$2,750 $2,200 $1,900 $1,600 $1,350 $1,225 $1,100

Last MSR was $2,715.

Add 35% for factory hand engraving mfg. 1983-1984 only.
Add 15% for 16 ga. if in 90%+ original condition.
Add 15%-25% for 28 ga.
Subtract $200 for standard Invector chokes.

* *Citori Hunting 3 1/2 in. Magnum Model* – 12 ga., 3 1/2 in. chambers 28 or 30 in. VR barrels with back-bored Invector plus choke tubes, with recoil pad, approx. 8 lbs. 9 oz. Mfg. 1989-2000.

$1,250 $950 $825 $695 $600 $550 $495

Last MSR was $1,563.

* *Citori Sporting Hunter* – 12 or 20 ga., 3 or 3 1/2 (12 ga. only) in. chambers, 26, 28, or 30 (12 ga. only) in. barrels with Invector Plus choking, configured for both hunting and sporting clays shooting, Superposed style forearm, contoured recoil pad, front and middle bead sights, gloss or satin (3 1/2 in. only) wood finish, 6 lbs. 9 oz. - 8 lbs. oz. Mfg. 1998-2001.

$1,250 $950 $825 $695 $600 $550 $495

Last MSR was $1,607.

* *Citori Satin Hunter* – 12 ga. only, 3 or 3 1/2 (disc. 2000) in. chambers, 26, 28, or 30 (3 1/2 in. Mag. only, disc. 1998) in. VR backbored barrel with Invector Plus choking, features satin wood finish, approx. 8 1/ lbs. Mfg. 1998-2001.

$1,150 $895 $700 $600 $500 $450 $375

Last MSR was $1,53.

MSR	100%	98%	95%	90%	80%	70%	60%

* ***Citori Upland Special*** – 12, 16 (mfg. 1989 only), or 20 ga. (2 3/4 in. chambers), shortened checkered straight grip walnut stock (14 in. LOP) and Schnabel forearm, 24 in. barrels, blue finish, Invector (12 ga. disc. 1993) or Invector Plus choking, 6-6 3/4 lbs. Mfg. 1984-2000.

	$1,195	$975	$725	$625	$500	$450	$375

Last MSR was $1,514.

Add 15% for 16 ga. if in 90%+ original condition.
Subtract $200 for Invector choking.

* ***Citori White Upland Special*** – 12 or 20 ga., 2 3/4 in. chambers, similar to Upland Special, except features silver nitride finished receiver, 6 1/8 or 6 1/2 lbs. Mfg. 2000-2001.

	$1,250	$1,000	$875	$750	$650	$600	$550

Last MSR was $1,583.

CITORI SATIN HUNTER MICRO MIDAS – 12 or 20 ga., 3 in. chambers, 24 or 26 in. VR barrels with Vector Pro lengthened forcing cones, includes 3 Invector Plus choke tubes, blued receiver, SST, checkered satin finished walnut stock and forearm, 13 in. LOP, vent. recoil pad on 12 ga., approx. 6 - 6 3/4 lbs. New 2011.

MSR $1,600	$1,395	$1,175	$1,055	$900	$750	$650	$500

CITORI SUPERLIGHT MODELS – 12, 16, 20, 28 ga., or .410 bore, 2 3/4 in. chambers except for .410 bore, English stock, oil finish, Invector chokes became standard in 1988, Invector Plus became standard 1995 for 12 or 20 ga., approx. 5 lbs., 11 oz. - 6 3/4 lbs. New 1983.

* ***Citori Superlight Grade I 12, 16, or 20 ga.***

  » *Citori Superlight Grade I Earlier Mfg. without Invector Choking*

	$995	$850	$750	$650	$600	$550	$500

  » *Citori Superlight Grade I w/Invector Choking* – recent mfg. with Invector Choking 12 or 20 ga., 20 ga. available with Standard Invector or Invector Plus (new 1994, became standard 1995) choking system, Invector Plus choking standard on recently mfg. 12 ga. Disc. 2002.

	$1,250	$1,025	$850	$750	$675	$600	$525

Last MSR was $1,590.

Subtract $200 for Standard Invector choking in 12 or 20 ga.

* ***Citori Superlight Grade I 28 ga. or .410 bore*** – without Invector choking until 1993, Invector choking became an option in 1994 and standard in 1995. Disc. 2002.

	$1,300	$1,100	$875	$775	$700	$625	$550

Last MSR was $1,666.

Subtract $200 if without Invector choke tubes.

* ***Citori Superlight Feather*** – 12 or 20 (new 2002) ga., 2 3/4 in. chambers, greyed alloy receiver, 26 in. Invector choked VR barrels, gloss finished

SHOTGUNS: O/U, CITORI HUNTING SERIES

MSR	100%	98%	95%	90%	80%	70%	60%

straight grip English stock and scaled down Schnabel forearm, 5 3/4 or 6 1/4 lbs. New 1999.

MSR $2,390 $2,050 $1,650 $1,400 $1,175 $1,000 $850 $725

* *Citori Superlight Grade III* – same gauges as Grade I, Standard Invector on 12 or 20 (disc.) ga. or Invector Plus (standard in 12 ga. beginning 1994) chokes. Mfg. 1986-2002.

   $1,900 $1,600 $1,300 $1,000 $800 $700 $600

   Last MSR was $2,300.

Add $270 for 28 ga. or .410 bore (disc. 1997).
Subtract $300 if without Invector choke tubes or $200 for standard Invector choke tubes.

* *Citori Superlight Grade V* – sideplate available. Disc. 1984.

   $2,950 $2,300 $1,900 $1,500 $1,250 $1,075 $900

* *Citori Superlight Grade VI* – older mfg. has Invector chokes standard (option on 28 ga. or .410 bore beginning 1994) or Invector Plus (standard and available in 12 or 20 ga. only) chokes, choice of blue or grey (new 1996) receiver finish. Mfg. 1983-2002.

   $2,750 $2,350 $2,000 $1,700 $1,450 $1,325 $1,200

   Last MSR was $3,510.

Subtract 10% for 28 ga. or .410 bore without choke tubes.
Subtract $200 for standard Invector choke tubes.
Add $270 for 28 ga. or .410 bore with Standard Invector choking.

* *Citori Superlight Grade VI Sideplate* – 20 ga. only. Disc.

   $3,350 $2,750 $2,250 $1,950 $1,825 $1,650 $1,475

CITORI SPORTER MODELS – similar to Citori Superlight, except with 3 in. chambers, 26 in. barrels, various chokes, straight grip stock, Schnabel forearm. Disc. 1983.

   $1,100 $900 $825 $700 $600 $550 $500

Add 10% for 28 ga. or .410 bore.

* *Citori Sporter Grade II* – 12, 20, 28 ga., or .410 bore.

   $1,350 $1,100 $1,000 $965 $880 $770 $715

Add 10% for 28 ga.

* *Citori Sporter Grade V* – 12, 20, 28 ga., or .410 bore.

   $2,750 $2,200 $1,800 $1,600 $1,450 $1,300 $1,150

Add 10% for 28 ga.

CITORI LIGHTNING MODELS – 12, 16 (disc. 1989), 20, 28 ga., .410 bore, 2 3/4 (28 ga. only), or 3 in. (standard on 12 ga., 20 ga., and .410 bore) chamber, 26, 28, or 30 (disc.) in. barrels, Invector chokes standard on newer mfg. smaller ga.'s, Invector Plus became standard 1995 for 12 or 20 ga., boxlock, auto ejectors, SST, vent. rib, features checkered round knob pistol grip stock and slimmer forearm, grades differ in amount of engraving, finish, and quality of wood, approx. 6.5 lbs. Introduced 1988.

SHOTGUNS: O/U, CITORI HUNTING SERIES

MSR	100%	98%	95%	90%	80%	70%	60%

* **Citori Lightning Grade I** 12, 16 or 20 ga.

» **Citori Lightning Grade I Earlier Mfg. w/o Invector Choking** – without Invector Choking.

                       $995 **$850** **$750** **$650** **$600** **$550** **$500**

Add 15% for 16 ga.

» **Citori Lightning Grade I w/Invector Choking** – 12 or 20 ga., current mfg. with Invector Choking, 12 or 20 ga., Invector (disc. 1994) or Invector Plus choking (became standard on 12 ga. in 1994, 20 ga. in 1995), gloss finished walnut stock and forearm, buttplate replaced vent recoil pad in 2010, 6 1/2 - 8 lbs.

MSR $1,990   **$1,725** **$1,450** **$1,200** **$1,020** **$875** **$750** **$625**

Subtract 10% for Standard Invector choking.

This model was supplied with scroll engraving with rosette design until 2004. Beginning 2004, standard engraving is high relief, intricate, and sculpted.

* **Citori Lightning Grade I Smaller Gauges** – 28 ga. or .410 bore, without Invector choking until 1993, Invector choking became an option in 1994, standard in 1995.

MSR $2,070   **$1,785** **$1,520** **$1,290** **$1,095** **$900** **$750** **$625**

Subtract $200 if without Standard Invector choking.

* **Citori Lightning Grade III** – 12, 16 (disc. 1989), or 20 ga., greyed steel receiver with engraved game scenes (mallards/pheasants on 12 ga., quail/grouse on 20 ga.), older mfg. may or may not have Invector choking, Invector Plus choking is now standard on 12 or 20 ga. Mfg. 1988-2004.

                       $1,865 **$1,450** **$1,250** **$1,000** **$800** **$700** **$600**

Last MSR was $2,464.

Subtract 10% if without Invector choking.
Add 15% for 16 ga. (disc. 1989).

» **Citori Lightning Grade III 28 ga. or .410 bore** – features quail and grouse scene engraving. Disc. 2004.

                       $1,950 **$1,675** **$1,500** **$1,375** **$1,250** **$1,175** **$995**

Last MSR was $2,754.

* **Citori Lightning Grade IV** – 12 or 20 ga., high relief engraving on grey receiver (pheasants on left, mallards on right on 12 ga., quail and grouse on 20 ga.) trigger guard and tang screws, high gloss finished walnut stock and forearm. Mfg. 2005-2012.

                       $3,030 **$2,380** **$1,950** **$1,575** **$1,250** **$1,030** **$800**

Last MSR was $3,500.

» **Citori Lightning Grade IV 28 ga. or .410 bore** – features quail and grouse inlays. Disc. 2012.

                       $3,095 **$2,475** **$2,100** **$1,900** **$1,700** **$1,500** **$1,100**

Last MSR was $3,590.

SHOTGUNS: O/U, CITORI HUNTING SERIES

MSR	100%	98%	95%	90%	80%	70%	60%

* *Citori Lightning Grade VI* – 12, 16 (disc. 1989), or 20 ga., blue or greyed receiver with extensive deep relief engraving with 7 gold inlays, including mallards/pheasants on receiver sides. Disc. 2004.

　　　　$2,825　$2,400　$2,000　$1,650　$1,450　$1,225　$1,050

　　　　　　　　　　　　　　　Last MSR was $3,797.

Add 15% for 16 ga. (disc. 1989).

» *Citori Lightning Grade VI 28 ga. or .410 bore* – disc. 2004.

　　　　$3,075　$2,550　$2,100　$1,750　$1,550　$1,325　$1,100

　　　　　　　　　　　　　　　Last MSR was $4,090.

* *Citori Lightning Grade VII* – 12 or 20 ga., deep relief engraving on grey or blue receiver, trigger guard, top tang, takedown lever and bracket, 24Kt. gold bird inlays (two flushing ringnecks and pointer on right side with three mallards on left side on 12 ga., quail and grouse on 20 ga.), high gloss finished walnut stock and forearm. Mfg. 2005-2012.

　　　　$4,800　$3,840　$3,275　$2,625　$2,225　$1,895　$1,600

　　　　　　　　　　　　　　　Last MSR was $5,560.

» *Citori Lightning Grade VII 28 ga. or .410 bore* – features quail and grouse inlays. Disc. 2012.

　　　　$4,875　$3,900　$3,300　$2,800　$2,400　$1,925　$1,650

　　　　　　　　　　　　　　　Last MSR was $5,660.

CITORI LIGHTNING FEATHER – 12 or 20 (new 2000) ga., 3 in. chambers, greyed alloy receiver with dovetailed steel breechface and steel hinge pin, 26 or 28 in. Invector Plus choked VR barrels, select checkered round knob walnut stock and forearm with gloss finish, vent. recoil pad, approx. 6 1/4 - 7 lbs. Mfg. 1999-2007.

　　　　$1,400　$1,200　$1,000　$850　$550　$475　$450

　　　　　　　　　　　　　　　Last MSR was $1,944.

* *Citori Lightning Feather Combo* – includes set of 27 in. 20 ga. (3 in. chambers) and 28 ga. barrels with Invector Plus (20 ga.) and standard Invector (28 ga.) chokes, includes luggage case, approx. 6 1/4 lbs. New 2000.

MSR $3,580　　$3,150　$2,525　$2,100　$1,800　$1,500　$1,350　$1,125

CITORI FEATHER LIGHTNING – 12 or 20 ga., 3 in. chambers, greyed alloy receiver with dovetailed steel breechface and steel hinge pin, 26 or 28 in. Invector Plus choked VR barrels, select checkered round knob walnut stock and forearm with gloss finish, solid recoil plate, approx. 6 - 6 1/2 lbs. New 2012.

MSR $2,180　　$1,875　$1,500　$1,225　$1,000　$850　$725　$625

CITORI GRAN LIGHTNING (GL) MODEL – 12, 20, 28 ga. (new 1994) or .410 bore (new 1994) only, 2 3/4 (28 ga. only) or 3 in. chambers, similar to Lightning Model, except has Grade III walnut stock and forearm with satin/oil finish, includes recoil pad, 26 or 28 in. barrels, Invector chokes standard on newer mfg. smaller ga.'s, Invector Plu

SHOTGUNS: O/U, CITORI HUNTING SERIES

MSR	100%	98%	95%	90%	80%	70%	60%

became standard 1995 for 12 or 20 ga., 6 1/4 - 8 lbs. Mfg. 1990-2005.

                                            $1,850 $1,575 $1,350 $1,150 $975 $850 $725

Last MSR was $2,429.

Add $128 for 28 ga. or .410 bore.

Subtract $200 for standard Invector chokes on 12 or 20 ga.

Beginning 2004, high relief intricate sculpted engraving replaced rosette, scroll type engraving.

CITORI WHITE LIGHTNING – 12, 20, 28 (new 2000) ga., or .410 bore (new 2000), 3 in. chambers, silver nitride receiver with engraving, satin wood finish with round pistol grip stock and vent. recoil pad, 26 or 28 in. VR barrels with Invector Plus choking, 6 lbs. 7 oz - 8 lbs. 2 oz. New 1998.

MSR $2,070 $1,785 $1,475 $1,250 $1,075 $925 $795 $695

Add $70 for .28 ga. or .410 bore (new 2000).

Beginning 2004, high relief intricate sculpted engraving replaced rosette, scroll type engraving.

CITORI MICRO LIGHTNING – 20 ga. only, 2 3/4 in. chambers, 24 in. VR barrels, Invector (disc. 1993) or Invector Plus (new 1994) choking, 13 3/4 in. LOP (1/2 in. shorter), 6 lbs. 3 oz. Mfg. 1991-2001.

* *Citori Micro Lightning Grade I*

                         $1,250 $1,000 $850 $750 $650 $575 $525

Last MSR was $1,591.

Subtract 10% for standard Invector choking.

* *Citori Micro Lightning Grade III* – Invector (disc. 1993) or Invector Plus choking. Mfg. 1993-94.

                         $1,600 $1,300 $1,175 $950 $825 $700 $550

Last MSR was $1,850.

Subtract $200 for Standard Invector choking.

* *Citori Micro Lightning Grade VI* – Mfg. 1993-94.

                         $2,025 $1,725 $1,500 $1,250 $1,025 $900 $825

Last MSR was $2,680.

Subtract $200 for standard Invector choking.

CITORI CLASSIC LIGHTNING GRADE I – 12 or 20 ga., 3 in. chambers, 26 or 28 in. vent. rib barrels, Invector Plus chokes, silver nitride receiver with Grade I Superposed engraving, Grade II/III oil finished slender lightning style walnut stock and forearm with vent. recoil pad, 6 lbs. 10 oz. - 8 lbs., 2 oz. Mfg. 2005-2007.

                       $1,600 $1,300 $1,100 $850 $725 $650 $500

Last MSR was $1,968.

CITORI CLASSIC LIGHTNING FEATHER GRADE I – 12 or 20 ga., 3 in. chambers, 26 or 28 in. vent. rib barrels, Invector Plus chokes, lightweight alloy receiver with high relief sculpted engraving, Grade II/

MSR	100%	98%	95%	90%	80%	70%	60%

III satin finished lightning style stock and Schnabel forearm, vent. recoil pad, 6 lbs. 3 oz. - 7 lbs. Mfg. 2005-2006.

	$1,650	$1,350	$1,100	$850	$725	$650	$550

Last MSR was $1,991.

CITORI SUPER LIGHTNING GRADE I – 12 or 20 ga., 3 in. chambers, 26 or 28 in. vent. rib barrels, Invector Plus chokes, deep blue receiver with gold border accents, Grade II/III gloss finished lightning style stock with buttplate and Schnabel forearm, 6 lbs. 7 oz. - 8 lbs. 2 oz. Mfg. 2005-2007.

	$1,500	$1,200	$1,000	$825	$700	$600	$500

Last MSR was $1,941.

CITORI 525 FIELD – 12 (disc. 2007), 20, 28 (new 2003) ga. or .410 bore (new 2003), 3 in. chambers (except 28 ga.), engraved silver nitride receiver, 26 or 28 in. unported barrels featuring VR with forward angled posts, oil finished checkered walnut stock with pronounced pistol grip and European comb, flush fit Invector Plus choke tubes, vent. recoil pad, Schnabel forearm, 6 lbs. 6 oz. - 8 lbs. Mfg. 2002-2008.

	$1,650	$1,395	$1,175	$1,000	$750	$650	$550

Last MSR was $2,144.

Add $31 for 28 ga. or .410 bore. Subtract $50 for 12 ga.

CITORI 525 FIELD GRADE III – 12 ga. only, 3 in. chambers, similar to 525 Field, except has Grade III/VI wood and more engraving, includes case, approx. 8 lbs. Mfg. 2007.

	$1,950	$1,650	$1,400	$1,200	$800	$700	$600

Last MSR was $2,532.

CITORI 525 FEATHER – 12, 20 (new 2008), 28 (new 2008) ga. or .410 bore (new 2008), 3 in. chambers, silver nitride alloy receiver featuring high relief engraving, traditional oil finished checkered stock and Schnabel forearm, approx. 6 1/4 lbs. Limited mfg. 2007-2008.

	$1,750	$1,400	$1,200	$1,000	$800	$675	$550

Last MSR was $2,278.

Add $17 for 28 ga. or .410 bore.

CITORI ESPRIT – 12 ga. only, 3 in. chambers, 28 in. barrels with VR and 3 choke tubes, features removable and interchangeable sideplates, satin finished receiver, choice of scroll or pointer engraving scenes, gold enhancements were optional, 8 1/4 lbs. Mfg. 2002-2003.

	$1,950	$1,350	$1,025	$875	$725	$625	$550

Last MSR was $2,50.

CITORI PRIVILEGE – 12 or 20 (new 2001) ga., 3 in. chambers, boxlock with extensively hand engraved sideplates, silver finished receiver, 26 or 28 in. barrels with 5/16 in. VR and Invector Plus choking, approx. lbs. Mfg. 2000-2003.

	$4,235	$3,600	$3,050	$2,600	$2,475	$2,025	$1,750

Last MSR was $5,53.

SHOTGUNS: O/U, CITORI SKEET

MSR	100%	98%	95%	90%	80%	70%	60%

CITORI 625 FIELD – 12 (disc. 2011), 20 (new 2009), 28 (new 2009) ga. or .410 (new 2009) bore, 3 in. chambers, 26 or 28 in. VR barrels with Vector Pro choking system with extended forcing cones, gloss finished Grade II/III special cut checkered walnut stock and Schnabel forearm, vent recoil pad, silver nitride finished receiver with etched engraving, approx. 6 1/2 - 7 3/4 lbs. New 2008.

MSR $2,630 $2,275 $1,825 $1,525 $1,300 $1,100 $950 $795

Add $30 for 28 ga. or .410 bore.

CITORI 625 FEATHER – 12 (disc. 2011), 20, 28 ga., or .410 bore, 2 3/4 (20 or 28 ga.) or 3 in. chambers, 26 or 28 in. lightweight VR barrels with three Invector Plus choke tubes (12 or 20 ga.) or Standard Invector (28 ga. or .410 bore), lightweight alloy receiver with steel breech face and hinge pin, high relief etched engraving, SST, ejectors, gloss finished Grade II/III pistol grip walnut stock with Schnabel forearm, approx. 5 lbs. 9 oz - 7 lbs. New 2009.

MSR $2,800 $2,425 $1,975 $1,575 $1,350 $1,100 $1,000 $800

Add $60 for 28 ga. or .410 bore.

CITORI 725 FIELD – 12 ga. only, 3 in. chambers, features lower profile silver nitride boxlock action receiver with engraving, 26 or 28 in. VR barrels with three Invector-DS choke tubes, Fire Lite mechanical gold single trigger, checkered gloss finished walnut stock and forearm with solid pad, approx. 7 1/4 lbs. New 2012.

MSR $2,470 $2,175 $1,750 $1,475 $1,250 $1,050 $925 $825

CITORI 725 FEATHER – 12 ga. only, 3 in. chambers, similar to 725 Field, except has lightweight alloy frame, approx. 6 1/2 lbs. New 2013.

MSR $2,470 $2,175 $1,750 $1,475 $1,250 $1,050 $925 $825

CITORI 725 GRADE III – 12 ga. only, 26 or 28 in. VR barrels with three invector-DS choke tubes, features engraved pheasants on left side of frame, mallards on the right side, and a dog on the bottom, Grade III/IV checkered walnut with high gloss finish, Inflex II recoil pad, Fire Lite mechanical SST trigger, includes ABS case, approx. 7 3/8 lbs. Only 300 to be mfg. during 2013.

MSR $3,730 $3,250 $2,725 $1,425 $1,950 $1,650 $1,450 $1,125

CITORI 725 GRADE V – 12 ga. only, 26 or 28 in. VR barrels with three invector-DS choke tubes, features gold enhanced pheasants on left and mallards on the right side, Grade V/VI checkered walnut with high gloss finish, Inflex II recoil pad, Fire Lite mechanical SST trigger, includes canvas/Crazy Horse leather case, approx. 7 3/8 lbs. Only 200 to be mfg. during 2013.

MSR $5,600 $4,950 $4,450 $3,700 $3,200 $2,700 $2,300 $1,950

SHOTGUNS: O/U, CITORI SKEET

During 2010, Vector Pro chokes became standard on 12 and 20 ga. models.

Hand engraving was replaced by machine engraving in late 1982 on all higher grade models.

SHOTGUNS: O/U, CITORI SKEET

MSR	100%	98%	95%	90%	80%	70%	60%

Subtract 10%-15% for all Skeet models with 26 in. barrels.

CITORI SKEET/SPECIAL SKEET MODELS – 12, 20, 28 ga., or .410 bore, same action as Citori Field, only with high post target rib (standard 1985), 26 and 28 in. skeet barrels, recoil pad, Invector chokes became standard in 1990 in 12 and 20 ga., Invector Plus chokes with ported barrels were an option during 1992 and became standard on the 12 ga. in 1994, new Special Skeet models were introduced during 1995 with decreased weight (1/4 lb. lighter) and better swing/balance characteristics.

* *Citori Skeet Grade I*

» *Citori Skeet Grade I 12 or 20 Ga.* – Invector Plus choking, high-post target rib, and ported barrels became standard in 1994, 7 1/4 - 8 lbs. Disc. 2000.

	$1,295	$1,095	$995	$800	$625	$575	$500

Last MSR was $1,742.

Add $100 for factory adj. comb (mfg. 1995-98).
Subtract 10% if without Invector Plus chokes.
Subtract 30% for fixed chokes.
Add approx. 40% for extra 20 ga. skeet barrels originally ordered with gun.
Add $50 for 20 ga.

Earlier mfg. skeet guns had a low profile, wide VR.

» *Citori Skeet Grade I Smaller Gauges* – 28 ga. or .410 bore, 6 lbs. 15 oz. Disc. 1999.

	$1,400	$1,000	$850	$650	$550	$500	$450

Last MSR was $1,627.

Subtract 20% if without Invector chokes.

* *Citori Skeet Grade II* – 12, 20, 28 ga., or .410 bore, high rib. Disc. 1983.

	$1,600	$1,235	$925	$740	$690	$650	$600

* *Citori Skeet Grade III* – 12 or 20 ga., Invector chokes originally in 12 and 20 ga. and invector plus choking, high-post target rib, and ported barrels became standard in 1994. Mfg. 1986-1999.

	$1,700	$1,300	$1,000	$800	$700	$650	$600

Last MSR was $2,310.

Add $100 for factory adj. comb (mfg. 1995-98).
Subtract 10% if w/o Invector Plus choke system.

» *Citori Skeet Grade III Smaller Gauges* – 28 ga. or .410 bore, invector chokes became an option in 1994. Mfg. 1986-1999.

	$1,800	$1,500	$1,300	$1,000	$700	$650	$600

Last MSR was $2,316.

Subtract 20% if without standard Invector choking (new 1994).

* *Citori Skeet Grade V* – 12, 20, 28 ga., or .410 bore, high rib. Disc. 1984.

	$2,500	$2,100	$1,800	$1,500	$1,250	$1,050	$850

Add 20% for 20 ga. or 30% for 28 ga. or .410 bore.

MSR	100%	98%	95%	90%	80%	70%	60%

* ***Citori Skeet Grade VI*** – 12 or 16 ga., choice of blue or grey finished receiver with multiple gold inlays, deluxe walnut, invector plus choking high post target rib and ported barrels became standard in 1994. Disc. 1995.

	$2,400	$2,100	$1,800	$1,300	$1,100	$900	$800

Last MSR was $2,555.

Add approx. 35% for hand engraving (mfg. 1983-1984 only).
Subtract 10% if w/o Invector Plus choke system.

» ***Citori Skeet Grade VI Smaller Gauges*** – 28 ga. or .410 bore, barrels are choked SK/SK.

	$2,750	$2,250	$1,900	$1,400	$1,200	$1,000	$850

Last MSR was $2,518.

Add approx. 35% for hand engraving (mfg. 1983-1984 only).

* ***Citori Skeet Golden Clays (GC)*** – 12 or 20 ga., 26 or 28 in. ported VR barrels with Invector (disc. 1995) or Invector Plus choking, high post target rib and ported barrels (12 ga. only), Skeet features, satin grey receiver with Grade VI level of engraving and gold inlays depicting a transitional hunting to clay pigeon scene. Mfg. 1993-1999.

	$2,725	$2,400	$2,250	$2,000	$1,650	$1,300	$1,000

Last MSR was $3,434.

Add $100 for factory adj. comb (mfg. 1995-98).
Subtract approx. 20% if without Invector Plus choking.

» ***Citori Skeet Golden Clays Smaller Gauges*** – 28 ga. or .410 bore, standard Invector or fixed SK/SK choking.

	$3,000	$2,650	$2,400	$2,250	$1,800	$1,500	$1,250

Last MSR was $3,356.

Subtract approx. 20% with fixed choking.

CITORI XS SKEET – 12 or 20 (new 2001) ga., 2 3/4 in. chambers, ported 28 or 30 in. vent. barrels with raised 5/16 in. VR and Invector Plus choking, silver nitride receiver with gold accents, checkered walnut stock available with or without adj. comb, features similar to the Ultra XS Sporting Model, Hi-Viz fiber optic front sight, includes Triple Trigger System, approx. 7 - 8 1/4 lbs. New 2000.

MSR $3,180	$2,750	$2,350	$2,000	$1,700	$1,450	$1,200	$1,000

Add $420 for adj. comb.

This model's nomenclature was changed from Ultra XS Skeet to Citori XS Skeet in 2002.

CITORI 3-GAUGE SKEET SETS – supplied with one 20 ga. frame and one forearm, and 3 barrels consisting of 20, 28 ga. and .410 bore, cased. Mfg. 1987-1996.

* ***Citori 3-Gauge Skeet Set Grade I*** – with high post target rib, standard Invector choking became standard 1994.

	$2,650	$2,200	$1,900	$1,450	$1,275	$1,050	$975

Last MSR was $3,100.

MSR	100%	98%	95%	90%	80%	70%	60%

* *Citori 3-Gauge Skeet Set Grade III* – with high post target rib, available with standard Invector choking (new 1994) or fixed SK/SK chokes.

$3,400　$2,600　$2,100　$1,550　$1,395　$1,250　$1,125

Last MSR was $3,900.

Subtract 20% for fixed SK/SK chokes.

* *Citori 3-Gauge Skeet Set Grade VI* – with high post target rib, fixed SK/SK chokes only. Disc. 1994.

$3,600　$2,800　$2,300　$1,775　$1,600　$1,400　$1,275

Last MSR was $3,990.

* *Citori 3-Gauge Skeet Set Golden Clays* – features Golden Clays accents and engraving, standard Invector choking. Mfg. 1994-95 only.

$4,250　$3,075　$2,600　$2,100　$1,900　$1,750　$1,600

Last MSR was $5,100.

CITORI 4-GAUGE SKEET SETS – supplied with one 12 ga. frame and forearm, and 4 barrels consisting of 12, 20, 28 ga., and .410 bore, cased. Imported 1985 only.

* *Citori 4-Gauge Skeet Set Grade I* – with high post target rib, choice of standard Invector (new 1994) or fixed SK/SK choking.

$3,500　$2,850　$2,400　$1,975　$1,800　$1,775　$1,600

Last MSR was $4,450.

Subtract 10% for fixed SK/SK choking.

* *Citori 4-Gauge Skeet Set Grade III* – with high post target rib, choice of standard Invector (new 1994) or fixed SK/SK choking.

$4,250　$3,250　$2,700　$2,250　$1,950　$1,800　$1,700

Last MSR was $5,450.

Subtract 20% for fixed SK/SK choking.

* *Citori 4-Gauge Skeet Set Grade VI* – with high post target rib, fixed SK/SK choking only. Disc. 1994.

$4,600　$3,350　$2,775　$2,300　$2,100　$2,000　$1,900

Last MSR was $5,225.

* *Citori 4-Gauge Skeet Set Golden Clays* – features Golden Clays accents and engraving, standard Invector choking. Mfg. 1994 only.

$5,650　$4,100　$3,300　$2,600　$2,350　$2,100　$1,975

Last MSR was $6,750.

SHOTGUNS: O/U, CITORI SPORTING CLAYS

All sporting clays models mfg. after 1994 have the Triple Trigger System which includes 3 interchangeable trigger shoes. During 2010, Vector Pro chokes became standard on 12 and 20 ga. models.

Subtract 10% for 28 in. barrels on used guns.

CITORI 325 GRADE II – 12 or 20 ga., 28, 30, or 32 (12 ga. only) in. 10mm VR barrels with Invector Plus choking, ported barrels, European

| MSR | 100% | 98% | 95% | 90% | 80% | 70% | 60% |

styling featuring checkered walnut stock and Schnabel forearm, greyed nitrous finished receiver, top tang safety, SST, ejectors, 6 lbs. 12 oz. - 7 lbs. 15 oz. Mfg. 1993-94.

| | $1,195 | $995 | $850 | $715 | $575 | $495 | $450 |

Last MSR was $1,625.

CITORI 325 GOLDEN CLAYS – 12 or 20 ga., 28, 30, or 32 in. ported (12 ga. only) or unported (20 ga. only) VR barrels, Invector Plus choking, Model 325 Grade II features, satin grey receiver with engraving and gold inlays depicting a transitional hunting to clay pigeon scene. Mfg. 1994 only.

| | $2,450 | $2,050 | $1,450 | $1,150 | $975 | $875 | $825 |

Last MSR was $3,030.

CITORI 425 SPORTING CLAYS GRADE I – 12 or 20 ga., 28, 30, or 32 (disc. 2000 - 12 ga. only, adj. comb) in. 10mm VR barrels with Invector Plus choking, 12 ga. has ported barrels, with or without adj. comb (disc. 2000), European styling featuring checkered walnut stock and Schnabel forearm, mono-bloc action with greyed nitrous finished receiver, top tang safety, SST, ejectors, solid pad, approx. 6 3/4 - 8 lbs. Mfg. 1995-2001.

| | $1,625 | $1,200 | $1,000 | $825 | $725 | $625 | $525 |

Last MSR was $2,006.

Add $231 for adj. comb.

CITORI 425 GOLDEN CLAYS – 12 or 20 ga., 28, 30, or 32 (disc. 1999) in. ported (12 ga. only) or unported (20 ga. only) VR barrels, with (disc. 1998) or without adj. comb, Invector Plus choking, Model 425 Grade I features, satin grey receiver with engraving and gold inlays depicting a transitional hunting to clay pigeon scene, 6 lbs., 13 oz. - 7 lbs., 14 oz. Mfg. 1995-2001.

| | $2,725 | $2,400 | $2,250 | $2,000 | $1,650 | $1,300 | $1,000 |

Last MSR was $3,977.

Add $100 for factory adj. comb (disc. 1998).

CITORI 425 WSSF – 12 ga. only, special dimensions for Women's Shooting Sports Foundation, features painted turquoise finish with WSSF logo on stock or natural walnut finish (new 1997), 7 1/4 lbs. Mfg. 1995-99.

| | $1,750 | $1,300 | $1,100 | $925 | $800 | $675 | $550 |

Last MSR was $1,855.

CITORI 525 SPORTING – 12, 20, 28 (new 2003) ga., or .410 bore (new 2003), 2 3/4 or 3 (.410 bore) in. chambers, 28, 30, or 32 (new 2003) in. vent. barrels with 8-11 mm (12 ga. only) or 10 mm (20 ga. only) width canted VR and porting (12 or 20 ga. only), silver nitride receiver finish with high relief engraving, Hi-Viz Pro-Comp sights, redesigned stock, includes full set of Midas Grade Invector Plus choke tubes (non-flush), oil finished European style checkered Grade III/IV walnut stock with palm

| MSR | 100% | 98% | 95% | 90% | 80% | 70% | 60% |

swell and forearm, approx. 7-8 1/2 lbs. Mfg. 2002-2008.

$2,425 $2,050 $1,750 $1,400 $1,000 $800 $695

Last MSR was $3,035.

Add $11 for 28 ga. or .410 bore.

Add $298 for adj. comb stock (mfg. 2004-2007, 12 or 20 ga.).

* *Citori 525 Sporting Grade I* – 12 ga. only, 3 in. chambers, 28, 30, or 32 in. ported barrels, silver nitride receiver with light 525 style field engraving, oil finished Grade I American walnut stock and Schnabel forearm, right hand palm swell, tapered floating rib, triple trigger system, three flush Invector-Plus choke tubes, Hi-Viz Pro-Comp sight, approx. 8 lbs. Mfg. 2005-2007.

$1,950 $1,675 $1,425 $1,200 $800 $675 $575

Last MSR was $2,461.

CITORI 525 GOLDEN CLAYS – 12, 20, 28 (new 2003) ga. or .410 bore (new 2003), similar features to the Model 525 Sporting, except has oil finished Grade V/VI walnut stock with solid pad and Schnabel forearm, engraving pattern that depicts the transition of a game bird into a clay bird in 24Kt. gold, includes 5 Midas Grade Invector Plus choke tubes (non-flush), 7-8 1/2 lbs. Mfg. 2002-2007.

$3,775 $3,000 $2,300 $1,850 $1,500 $1,250 $995

Last MSR was $4,722

Add $215 for 28 ga. or .410 bore.

CITORI 625 SPORTING – 12 (disc.), 20 (new 2009), 28 (new 2009) ga., or .410 bore (new 2009), 2 3/4 or 3 (.410 bore only) in. chambers, 28, 30, or 32 in. ported VR barrels with Vector Pro choking system with extended forcing cones, checkered gloss finished Grade III/IV walnut stock with or w/o adj. comb and Schnabel forearm, Triple Trigger System, Hi-Viz fiber optic front sight, silver nitride finished receiver with gold accents, approx. 7-8 lbs. New 2008.

MSR $3,550 $3,275 $2,425 $2,100 $1,750 $1,450 $1,200 $1,000

Add $50 for adj. comb. (12 ga. only), disc.

Add $30 for 28 ga. or .410 bore.

CITORI 725 SPORTING – 12 ga. only, 3 in. chambers, features lower profile silver nitride boxlock action receiver, 28, 30, 32 in. vent ported barrels with VR and five Invector-DS choke tubes, adj. comb became an option during 2013, gold triple trigger system, oil finished Grade III/IV checkered forearm and walnut stock with Inflex II recoil pad, approx. 1/2 lbs. New 2012.

MSR $3,140 $2,775 $2,300 $1,950 $1,650 $1,375 $1,175 $1,000

Add $390 for adj. comb. (new 2013).

CITORI 802 EXTENDED SWING (ES) SPORTING – 12 ga. only, 2 3/ in. chambers, features 28 in. ventilated ported VR barrels (low post 6.2mm wide) which accept either Invector Plus stainless steel 2 or in. extension tubes (extends barrels to 30 or 32 in.), adj. pull trigger

MSR	100%	98%	95%	90%	80%	70%	60%

slimmer checkered and Schnabel forearm, 7 lbs. 5 oz. Mfg. 1996-2001.

	$1,395	$1,100	$975	$800	$700	$600	$550

Last MSR was $2,063.

CITORI GTI GRADE I – 12 ga. only, 28 or 30 in. barrel with 13mm vent. rib and barrels, red lettering on receiver during 1989 only - changed to gold lettering and borders with Browning logo in 1990, checkered stock and semi-beavertail forearm, ported barrels were introduced 1990 and became standard 1992, Invector chokes standard, back-bored Invector Plus chokes became standard in 1990, approx. 8 lbs. Mfg. 1989-1994.

	$1,100	$950	$850	$700	$625	$550	$475

Last MSR was $1,450.

Subtract $100 for standard chokes. Add $35 for Signature Painted Model.

The Signature Painted Model includes special paint treatment on stock and forearm featuring Browning logos and trademark - new 1993.

CITORI GTI GOLDEN CLAYS – 12 ga. only, 28, 30, or 32 in. ported VR barrels, Invector Plus choking, GTI features, satin grey receiver with Grade VI level of engraving and gold inlays depicting a transitional hunting to clay pigeon scene. Mfg. 1993-94.

	$2,350	$1,950	$1,600	$1,300	$1,050	$925	$825

Last MSR was $2,930.

CITORI GRADE I SPECIAL SPORTING – 12 ga. only, 2 3/4 in. chambers, target dimensions, high-post tapered rib, 28, 30, or 32 in. barrels, full pistol grip with palm swell, adj. comb became optional in 1994, approx. 8 lbs. 3 oz. Mfg. 1989-99.

	$1,195	$925	$775	$635	$525	$495	$450

Last MSR was $1,636.

Add $100 for factory adj. comb.
Add $35 for Signature Painted Model (disc. 1994).
Add $800 for 2 barrel set (28 and 30 in. barrels), disc. 1990.

The Signature Painted Model includes special paint treatment on stock and forearm featuring Browning logos and trademark - mfg. 1993-94.

Ported barrels were new in 1990 and became standard in 1992.

In 1990, the Grade I designation was added to this model. Changes include back-bored barrels with Invector plus choke tubes.

CITORI SPECIAL SPORTING GOLDEN CLAYS (GC) – 12 ga. only, 28, 30, or 32 in. ported barrels with high-post VR, Invector Plus choking, Special Sporting features, satin grey receiver with Grade VI level of engraving and gold inlays depicting a transitional hunting to clay pigeon scene. Mfg. 1993-98.

	$2,250	$1,900	$1,600	$1,250	$995	$875	$825

Last MSR was $3,203.

Add $100 for factory adj. comb.

SHOTGUNS: O/U, CITORI SPORTING CLAYS

MSR	100%	98%	95%	90%	80%	70%	60%

CITORI GRADE I SPECIAL SPORTING PIGEON GRADE – 12 ga. only, Invector Plus choking and ported barrels, higher grade of Special Sporting model featuring higher grade walnut and gold line receiver accents. Mfg. 1993-94.

	$1,395	$1,150	$950	$800	$700	$625	$550

Last MSR was $1,630.

CITORI ULTRA SPORTER – 12 ga. only, 28, 30, or 32 in. barrels with vent rib separating barrels, low tapered 13-10mm VR, blue or grey (new 1996) receiver with gold accents, satin finished checkered pistol grip stock and forearm, Invector Plus choking, 7 lbs. 10 oz. - 8 lbs. 4 oz. Mfg. 1995-99.

	$1,400	$1,050	$875	$750	$575	$495	$450

Last MSR was $1,800.

Add $210 for adj. comb (disc. 1998).

This model was designated GTI until 1995.

* *Citori Ultra Sporter Golden Clays (GC)* – 12 ga. only, features better wood and satin finished engraved receiver with gold inlays clay target scene. Mfg. 1995-99.

	$2,250	$1,900	$1,700	$1,500	$1,275	$1,075	$925

Last MSR was $3,396.

Add $210 for adj. comb (disc. 1997).

CITORI FEATHER XS SPORTING – 12, 20, 28 ga., or .410 bore, 2 3/4 in. chambers (3 in. standard on .410 bore), 28 or 30 in. vent. barrels with tapered VR (12 ga. only) and Invector Plus choking on 12 and 20 ga. (standard Invector on 28 ga. and .410 bore, 28 in. barrels), alloy receiver with dovetailed steel breechface and hinge pin, satin finished checkered walnut pistol grip stock with Schnabel forearm, Hi-Viz comp. sighting system (includes 8 interchangeable colored light pipes), Nitex receiver finish, includes Triple Trigger System (3 interchangeable trigger shoes), 6 lbs. (28 ga. or .410 bore) - approx. 7 lbs. (12 ga., 30 in barrels). Mfg. 2000-2002.

	$1,700	$1,375	$1,150	$995	$875	$775	$675

Last MSR was $2,311.

CITORI XS GOLDEN CLAYS – 12 or 20 ga. only, similar to 525 Golden Clays, except has traditional checkering pattern and 1/2 - 3/8 in. width VR, includes 3 choke tubes. Mfg. 2002-2003.

	$3,150	$2,600	$2,050	$1,650	$1,400	$1,150	$925

Last MSR was $3,914.

CITORI XS SPORTING (ULTRA) – 12, 20, 28 ga. (disc. 2003) or .410 bore (disc. 2003), greyed steel receiver with silver nitride finish, 24Kt gold accents and light engraving, 28, 30, or 32 (new 2003) in. barrels with or w/o (30 in. barrels only) barrel porting, 12 ga. features flush Invector Plus choking and right-hand palm swell, Hi-Viz Pro-Comp sight

SHOTGUNS: O/U, CITORI SPORTING CLAYS

MSR	100%	98%	95%	90%	80%	70%	60%

Triple Trigger System, select checkered walnut stock with satin finish and Schnabel forearm, 6 lbs. 5 oz. - 8 lbs. Mfg. 1999-2007.

$1,900 $1,600 $1,300 $995 $875 $750 $650

Last MSR was $2,597.

Add 10% for 28 ga. or .410 bore.

CITORI GRAND PRIX SPORTER – 12 ga. only, 2 3/4 in. chambers, steel receiver with silver nitride finish and gold enhanced engraving, 28, 30, or 32 in. VR ported barrels with extended Invector-Plus Midas Grade choke tubes and Hi-Viz fiber optic front sight, oil finished checkered pistol grip walnut stock and Schnabel forearm, select ejector system allows for either ejection or manual extraction, cased, approx. 8 1/4 lbs. Mfg. 2007-2009.

$2,800 $2,350 $1,800 $1,525 $1,250 $1,050 $925

Last MSR was $3,439.

CITORI LIGHTNING SPORTING (GRADE I) – 12 ga. only, features 3 in. chambers, rounded pistol grip, Lightning style forearm, choice of high or low post VR, standard or adj. (new 1995) comb stock, "Lightning Sporting Clays Edition" inscribed and gold-filled on receiver, triple trigger system, 28 in. ported or 30 in. ported or unported (disc.) barrels, approx. 8 1/2 lbs. Mfg. 1989-2004.

$1,300 $1,045 $885 $765 $650 $550 $495

Last MSR was $1,794.

Add $100 for adj. comb (disc. 1998).
Subtract $100 for low rib.

The Signature Painted Model includes special paint treatment on stock and forearm featuring Browning logos and trademark - mfg. 1993-94. Ported barrels were new in 1990 and became standard in 1992. Between 1990-2000, the Grade I designation was added to this model. Changes include back-bored barrels with Invector plus choke tubes.

* *Citori Lightning Sporting Golden Clays (GC)* – 12 ga. only, 28, 30, or 32 (disc.) in. ported barrels with choice of low or high-post VR, standard or adj. (new 1995) comb stock, Invector Plus choking, Lightning Sporting features, satin grey receiver with Grade VI level of engraving and gold inlays depicting a transitional hunting to clay birds scene, approx. 8 1/2 lbs. Mfg. 1993-98.

$2,600 $2,200 $1,750 $1,400 $1,175 $1,000 $875

Last MSR was $3,092.

Add $100 for factory adj. comb.
Subtract $100 for low post rib.

CITORI GRADE I LIGHTNING SPORTING PIGEON GRADE – 12 ga. only, higher grade model featuring higher grade walnut and gold line receiver accents. Mfg. 1993-94.

MSR	100%	98%	95%	90%	80%	70%	60%
	$1,500	$1,200	$950	$700	$575	$495	$450

Last MSR was $1,566.

Subtract $100 for low post rib.

CITORI SPORTING HUNTER – please refer to description and pricing under Shotguns: O/U Citori Hunting Series category.

SHOTGUNS: O/U, CITORI TARGET

During 2010, Vector Pro chokes became standard on 12 and 20 ga. models.

CITORI XS SPECIAL – 12 ga. only, 2 3/4 in. chambers, 30 or 32 in. vent barrels, silver nitride receiver with XS Special engraving, satin finished stock with adj. comb and semi-beavertail forearm, low/regular or high-post (new 2007) floating 8-11mm tapered rib, includes Triple Trigger System and 5 Midas Grade Invector Plus chokes (non-flush), approx. 8 3/4 lbs. New 2004.

MSR $3,600	$3,100	$2,475	$2,100	$1,825	$1,525	$1,325	$1,150

CITORI GTS GRADE I – 12 ga. only, 3 in. chambers, 28 or 30 in. 10mm VR barrels with flush Invector-Plus choke tubes, steel silver nitride finished receiver with game bird transforming into clay target engraving oil finished checkered Grade II/III walnut pistol grip stock and Schnabel forearm, Hi-Viz front sight, includes case, approx. 8 1/4 lbs. Mfg. 2007-2009.

	$2,150	$1,750	$1,400	$1,150	$950	$800	$700

Last MSR was $2,349.

CITORI GTS HIGH GRADE – 12 ga. only, similar to Grade I, except has gold game bird/clay target engraving. Mfg. 2007-2009.

	$3,475	$2,800	$2,350	$1,925	$1,600	$1,300	$1,175

Last MSR was $4,309.

CITORI ULTRA XS PRESTIGE – 12 ga., similar to Citori GTS High Grade, except has gloss oil finished adj. stock and gold accented Ultra XS special engraving, ported barrels, Hi-Viz fiber optic sight, includes case, approx. 8 lbs. Mfg. 2008-2009.

	$4,000	$2,850	$2,000	$1,600	$1,350	$1,125	$1,000

Last MSR was $4,75...

SHOTGUNS: O/U, CITORI TRAP

During 2010, Vector Pro chokes became standard on 12 and 20 ga. models.

Hand engraving was replaced by machine engraving in late 1982 on all higher grade models.

CITORI TRAP MODELS – 12 ga., similar to Standard Citori, 30 or 32 in. barrels, trap chokes, Monte Carlo stock, recoil pad. Invector chokes became standard in 1988, Invector Plus chokes with ported barrels became an option in 1992, and were made standard in 1993, new Special Trap models were introduced during 1995 with decreased weight (1/4 lb. lighter) and better swing/balance characteristics. Mfg. 1974-current.

* ***Citori Trap Grade I*** – w/o choke tube, mfg. 1974-1978, with choke tube 1979-1994.

	100%	98%	95%	90%	80%	70%	60%
w/o choke tube	$900	$800	$750	$650	$525	$495	$450
w/ choke tube	$1,150	$1,025	$900	$800	$750	$650	$525

* ***Citori Grade I Special Trap*** – approx. 8 1/2 lbs. Mfg. 1995-99.

  $1,395 $975 $795 $650 $525 $495 $450

  Last MSR was $1,658.

Add $100 for factory adj. comb.
Subtract 20% without Invector chokes or high rib.

* ***Citori Trap Combination Set*** – Grade I only, 32 in. O/U and 34 in. single barrel, or extra set of barrels in same ga., cased. Disc.

  $1,295 $1,100 $975 $900 $825 $775 $725

Add approx. 40% for extra 20 ga. barrels originally ordered with gun.

* ***Citori Grade I Plus Trap*** – features adj. rib and stock, back-bored barrels, Invector Plus choke system. Mfg. 1990-94.

  $1,900 $1,525 $1,225 $995 $700 $600 $500

  Last MSR was $2,005.

Add 5% for ported barrels.

In 1991 this model included a travel vault gun case at no extra charge. Subtract $50 for older mfg. without travel case.

* ***Citori Grade I Plus Trap Combo*** – includes ported barrels with Invector Plus choking and extra standard single ported barrel, luggage case. Mfg. 1992-94.

  $2,775 $2,475 $2,100 $1,900 $1,700 $1,500 $1,250

  Last MSR was $3,435.

* ***Citori Plus Trap Golden Clays*** – 12 ga. only, 30 or 32 in. ported VR barrels, Invector Plus choking, Trap features, satin grey receiver with Grade VI level of engraving and gold inlays depicting a transitional hunting to clay birds scene. Mfg. 1993-94.

  $3,000 $2,600 $2,000 $1,600 $1,400 $1,200 $995

  Last MSR was $3,435.

* ***Citori Plus Trap Golden Clays Combo*** – includes O/U ported barrels with Invector Plus choking and extra standard single ported barrel, luggage case. Mfg. 1993-94.

  $4,425 $3,300 $2,775 $2,250 $1,925 $1,800 $1,700

  Last MSR was $5,200.

* ***Citori XT Trap*** – 12 ga. only, features greyed receiver with 24Kt. gold accents and light engraving, Triple Trigger System (includes 3 interchangeable triggers for 1/8 in. adj. on LOP), 30 or 32 in. vent.

SHOTGUNS: O/U, CITORI TRAP

MSR	100%	98%	95%	90%	80%	70%	60%

backbored barrels with high-post VR, checkered high gloss Monte Carlo walnut stock and forearm, right hand palm swell, Hi-Viz front sight, waffle-style recoil pad, approx. 8 1/2 lbs. New 1999.

MSR $2,950 $2,550 $2,100 $1,575 $1,275 $1,000 $800 $650

Add $440 for adj. comb.

* ***Citori XT Trap Gold*** – 12 ga. only, 2 3/4 in. chambers, features intricate "Golden Clays" engraving with game bird/clay bird, Grade V/VI American walnut stock and semi-beavertail forearm, vented 30 or 32 in. ported barrels with high post VR and Invector Plus choke system with five flush Midas Grade chokes, adj. comb, adj. GraCo recoil reduction system, Triple Trigger System, Hi-Viz Pro-Comp, and mid-bead sights, approx. 9 lbs. New 2005.

    MSR $5,700 $4,950 $3,850 $3,050 $2,375 $1,875 $1,475 $1,175

* ***Citori Trap Pigeon Grade*** – 12 ga. only, features extra deluxe walnut, Invector Plus ported barrels, and receiver gold accents. Mfg. 1993-94.

    $1,715 $1,250 $950 $800 $700 $600 $500

    Last MSR was $2,225.

* ***Citori Trap Signature Painted*** – 12 ga. only, features painted red/black stock with Browning logos on stock and forearm, Invector Plus ported barrels. Mfg. 1993-94.

    $1,595 $1,200 $940 $800 $700 $600 $500

    Last MSR was $2,06

* ***Citori Trap Grade II*** – high post rib. Mfg. 1978-1983.

    $1,200 $900 $800 $700 $650 $600 $500

* ***Citori Trap Grade III*** – 12 ga. only, high post rib, Invector Plus choking and ported barrels became standard in 1994. Mfg. 1986-99.

    $1,500 $1,200 $900 $800 $725 $650 $550

    Last MSR was $2,31

Add $100 for factory adj. comb.
Subtract 10% if without Invector Plus chokes or ported barrels.

* ***Citori Trap Grade V*** – high post rib. Mfg. 1978-1984.

    $1,750 $1,400 $1,100 $880 $795 $710 $620

* ***Citori Trap Grade VI*** – 12 ga. only, Invector chokes became standard in 1985, Invector Plus chokes became standard in 1994. Disc. 1994.

    $1,995 $1,600 $1,300 $1,100 $960 $875 $825

    Last MSR was $2,59

Add approx. 20% for hand engraving (mfg. 1983-1984 only).
Subtract $150 if without Invector Plus chokes or ported barrels.
Subtract $250 for fixed chokes.

* ***Citori Trap Golden Clays (GC)*** – 12 ga. only, 30 or 32 in. ported barrels, Invector Plus choking, Trap features, Monte Carlo or regular stock, satin grey receiver with Grade VI level of engraving and gold inlay

depicting a transitional hunting to clay pigeon scene. Mfg. 1993-99.

MSR	100%	98%	95%	90%	80%	70%	60%
	$2,750	$2,400	$2,100	$1,750	$1,500	$1,250	$1,025

Last MSR was $3,434.

Add $220 for adj. comb (new 1995).

CITORI XS PRO-COMP – 12 ga. only, 2 3/4 in. chambers, 28 or 30 in. vent. and ported VR barrels with spreader chokes, adj. comb, beavertail forearm, GraCoil recoil reduction system, right-hand palm swell, Triple Trigger System, features removable tungsten alloy forearm weight which approximates the same weight as barrel tubes, also has removable front barrel weight to adj. the swing through, approx. 9 lbs. Mfg. 2002-2004.

	$2,750	$2,300	$1,900	$1,425	$1,100	$975	$850

Last MSR was $4,027.

SHOTGUNS: O/U, SUPERPOSED GENERAL INFO & CHOKE CODES

SUPERPOSED MODEL – 12, 20 (introduced circa 1948-49), 28 ga. (introduced 1959) or .410 bore (introduced 1958), 26 1/2, 28, 30, or 32 in. barrels, various chokes, boxlock, auto ejectors, various trigger combinations (single & double), checkered pistol grip stock, mfg. 1931-40 and 1948-76 by FN, grades differ in amount of engraving, inlays, general quality of workmanship and wood.

NOTE: The use of steel shot is NOT recommended in any Superposed Series manufactured in Belgium (B-25 variations).

BROWNING CHOKES AND THEIR CODES (MARKED NEXT TO EJECTORS)

* designates full choke (F).

*- designates improved modified choke (IM).

** designates modified choke (M).

**- designates improved cylinder choke (IC).

**$ designates skeet (SK).

*** designates cylinder bore (CYL).

SKEET MODELS were available in every ga. and grade.

TRAP MODELS were available in every grade in 12 ga. only.

BROADWAY TRAP MODELS (mfg. 1961-75) featured a 5/8 in. wide vent. rib and were also available in every grade.

Please refer to the new expanded Browning Superposed serialization section in this text for determining year of manufacture.

SUPERPOSED: 1931-1940 MFG. (PRE-WWII)

Early pre-war guns had long slender forearms with a metal plate at the front called a horseshoe plate. Approx. circa 1936, the forearm was changed to the one used post war - smaller with a transverse bolt to hold the forearm on. The earlier forearm had a long bolt that ran from front to back through the metal plate. The earlier transverse bolts were recessed into the sides of the forearms. Later the head and fastener on the other side of the forearm were flush with the wood.

Pre-war cases were manufactured in black or brown, with a textured surface called elephant hide, in leather or tex leather. Insides were lined with grey or blue cloth, and the Browning brass label was on the inside top of the case, not the outside. Depending on original condition, these cases sell in the $200-$400 range - single barrel cases are more common than multi-barrel ones. Extra barrels (same ga. only) could be ordered with the original gun, and were supplied in a Browning hard case.

Very few pre-war Pigeon, Diana, and Midas Grades were signed by the engraver.

Add approx. 35%-50% per extra set of barrels (same ga. only), depending on condition.

Subtract 10%-25% for recoil pad (depending on originality, deterioration, and condition).

SUPERPOSED STANDARD GRADE/GRADE I/LIGHTNING

12 ga. only, boxlock action, blue w/border receiver engraving until 1938, when a simple small center rosette engraving pattern was introduced, 4 trigger options until 1938, when the barrel selector was moved to the top tang, trigger options included: double normal, selective single with the selector on the bottom next to the trigger, twin single, and non-selective single, Standard model nomenclature was changed to Grade I during 1938, in addition to changing the trigger to SST with the barrel selector on the top tang, raised hollow or ventilated rib, Lightning Model introduced during 1936 in Standard grade with striped barrels - ribs were extra cost. Original buttplates featured intertwined twin circles and were made of horn.

	MSR	100%	98%	95%	90%	80%	70%	60%
12 ga.		N/A	$2,900	$2,200	$1,800	$1,400	$1,200	$1,000

Original buttplates with unaltered (uncut) stock are very important to collectors for this period of Superposed manufacture.

First year production Superposed will command a premium (approx ser. no. range 1-2,000). The twin single trigger is also very desirable for collectors.

Recoil pads were an extra option during this time, and even though they might be factory installed, they are not desirable to collectors and as a result, prices could be reduced substantially based on pad deterioration. Pad makers included: Jostam, Hawkins, Noshoc, D&W and Black Diamond - these pads were $5 options pre-WWII.

SUPERPOSED PIGEON GRADE

grey receiver with 2 pigeons on either side, these earlier guns had larger engraved pigeons than later production (1960 and later). Mfg. 1931-1940.

	MSR	100%	98%	95%	90%	80%	70%	60%
12 ga.		N/A	$5,950	$4,850	$3,950	$2,950	$2,200	$1,900

The Pigeon Grade style of engraving is the only pre-war style that was continued after WWII.

MSR	100%	98%	95%	90%	80%	70%	60%

SUPERPOSED DIANA GRADE – grey receiver with lighter style, delicate European style engraving, boars and stags were pictured in the 1931 catalog, but dogs and birds could also be special ordered at no additional cost until 1936, after which it became extra cost, dogs and birds engraving are more common than boars and stag. Mfg. 1931-1940.

12 ga.	N/A	$8,500	$6,750	$5,250	$4,150	$3,500	$2,750

The Diana Grade was changed dramatically in post-WWII production.

SUPERPOSED MIDAS GRADE – featured gold inlaid pigeons with outstretched wings on blue frame sides and bottom plus trigger guard. This Germanic syle engraving also exhibited multiple gold escutcheons and gold lining, ejector trip rods, ejector hammers and firing pins are also 18Kt. gold plated, finest checkered walnut.

12 ga.	N/A	$10,500	$8,500	$6,750	$5,000	$4,000	$3,000

The Midas Grade was changed dramatically in post-WWII production.

SUPERPOSED: 1948-1960 MFG. (POST-WWII)

Model nomenclature was changed from pre-war designations to Grades I-VI. During this period, extra barrels could only be ordered in the same gauge as the original gun. Hardshell cases from this era are referred to as Tolex cases - they have blue velvet lining, and a brass Browning label on the outside top.

Engraved guns signed by Browning's top engravers (Funken, Vrancken, Watrin, Doyen, Müller, and Magis) will command a premium over unsigned guns. Felix Funken retired in 1960, and died in 1966.

On most Superposed with added recoil pads, the stock has usually been cut to keep the LOP the same. The correct LOP on a Superposed is 14 1/4 inches, with or w/o a recoil pad.

The twin circle buttplate was always horn, and was used on very early post war guns until 1949-1950.

Barrel addresses appeared as follows: circa 1947-1958 "St. Louis, M.O." (earliest BAC markings) or "St. Louis, Missouri", 1959-1968 "St. Louis, Missouri and Montreal P.Q.", and 1969-1975 "Morgan, Utah and Montreal, P.Q.". Make sure barrel address date matches year of mfg. (see listings in the back of this text).

The original factory configuration of almost all Superposed shotguns can be verified by grade, gauge/bore, and barrel length. To obtain information on a specific Belgian Superposed serial number, please contact the Browning historian directly (refer to Contact Information for more information).

Add approx. 35%-50% per extra set of barrels (same ga. only), depending on condition.

Add $300-$500 for correct Tolex hardshell case with paperwork.

Subtract 25% for non-original recoil pads on Grade I models, depending on condition.

Subtract 25% for non-original recoil pads on the higher grades, depending on condition.

Special order Superposed with non-standard factory engraving, checkered buttstocks, 3 piece forearms, and other special orders will command premiums over standard configurations.

MSR	100%	98%	95%	90%	80%	70%	60%

SUPERPOSED GRADE I STANDARD WEIGHT – 12 or 20 ga. (3 in. chambers were introduced in the 12 ga. during 1955, and in 20 ga. during 1957), otherwise similar to pre-war mfg., blue finish and triggers until 1955, gold trigger(s) became standard in 1955, raised (standard until 1959) or vent. rib only beginning in 1959, round knob long tang (RKLT) stock configuration, this earlier period of mfg. also featured smaller, narrower forearms and thinner pistol grip stock with horn buttplate (can be determined by the rounded "g" in Browning, not square), early post-war production had similar pre-WWII minimal engraving until circa 1952-53, more standard engraving continued through 1955, when Grade I models featured considerably more engraving, post-war 12 ga. serialization began at approx. 17,100, and with 200 on 20 ga. Mfg. 1948-1960.

12 ga.	N/A	$1,700	$1,475	$1,300	$1,000	$895	$675
20 ga.	N/A	$2,800	$2,500	$2,000	$1,500	$1,200	$1,000

Grade I models had 3 levels of standard engraving coverage.

* *Superposed Grade I Lightning Hunting Model* – 12 or 20 ga., 6 oz. lighter than Standard Weight. Introduced in all Grades beginning 1956.

12 ga.	N/A	$1,700	$1,475	$1,300	$1,000	$895	$675
20 ga.	N/A	$2,800	$2,500	$2,000	$1,500	$1,250	$1,100

* *Superposed Grade I Magnum* – 12 ga. only, 3 in. chambers, 28, 30, or 32 (rare) in. barrels with raised or vent. rib, recoil pad standard introduced in all Grades in 1955.

N/A	$1,850	$1,625	$1,450	$1,150	$950	$750

This model with 30 or 32 (rare) in. barrels is now popular again, as Sporting Clays shooters like this desirable configuration.

* *Superposed Grade I Trap Standard Weight Model* – 12 ga. only, various configurations. Introduced 1952.

N/A	$1,825	$1,595	$1,450	$1,150	$950	$725

Pre-war trap guns and those manufactured post-war until approx. 1955 were virtually indistinguishable from field guns as they had field style forearms, round knob (semi-pistol grip) and long tangs. The only way to tell the difference is they had a longer LOP (14 1/2 in.) and a shorter drop at the heel - 1 3/4 in. vs. 2 1/2 in. for field stocks. These early trap guns did not come with recoil pads. Between 1956-1960, trap guns had the forearm changed to semi-beavertail. These late guns with semi-beavertail forearms are very desirable today due to their rarity and overall desirability.

SUPERPOSED GRADE II – 12 or 20 ga., featured pre-war Pigeon Grade engraving with large pigeons, some early post-war mfg. were signed by Funken.

12 ga.	N/A	$4,200	$3,675	$3,325	$2,650	$2,175	$1,675
20 ga.	N/A	$7,300	$6,395	$5,750	$4,600	$3,795	$2,925

MSR	100%	98%	95%	90%	80%	70%	60%

SUPERPOSED GRADE III – 12 or 20 ga., European style engraving, commonly referred to as "fighting cocks," pheasants on right side, fighting cocks on left, most were signed by the engraver.

12 ga.	N/A	$4,800	$4,200	$3,795	$3,025	$2,500	$1,925
20 ga.	N/A	$9,000	$7,875	$7,100	$5,675	$4,675	$3,600

SUPERPOSED GRADE IV – 12 or 20 ga., features deeper European style engraving with dogs and foxes, most were signed by the engraver.

12 ga.	N/A	$8,000	$7,000	$6,325	$5,050	$4,150	$3,200
20 ga.	N/A	$12,500	$10,950	$9,875	$7,875	$6,500	$5,000

SUPERPOSED GRADE V – 12 or 20 ga., features deeper engraving than pre-war Diana Grade, pheasants and ducks on receiver, most were signed by the engraver - Doyen was prevalent on this model.

12 ga.	N/A	$7,000	$6,125	$5,525	$4,400	$3,650	$2,800
20 ga.	N/A	$12,000	$10,500	$9,475	$7,500	$6,250	$4,800

SUPERPOSED GRADE VI – 12 or 20 ga., engraving pattern similar to later production Midas Grade, almost all of these were signed by Müeller. Introduced in July, 1957, changed in 1960, limited production, and rarest of the 6 grades.

12 ga.	N/A	$10,000	$8,750	$7,900	$6,300	$5,200	$4,000
20 ga.	N/A	$20,000	$17,500	$15,800	$12,600	$10,400	$8,000

SUPERPOSED: 1960-1976 MFG.

In early 1960, a major change was made in the manner in which the various grades of Superposed were designated. The Roman numerals used in the 1950s were dropped, and Browning once again returned to names. The Pigeon, Diana, and Midas names used for pre-war designations were brought back and replaced the Grade II, Grade V, and Grade VI respectively. Grades III & IV were dropped and replaced by the Pointer. The Grade I remained unchanged.

The Broadway Trap Model was introduced in 1961. Browning's lifetime Superposed warranty began in 1963. During 1965, the Hydro Coil stock (1 year only) and barrel Super Tubes were introduced. During 1966, a major change was implemented to save money when Browning switched from a long tang to short tang. During 1970-71, the stock configuration was once again changed to a full pistol grip (referred to as flat knob), and the long tang was brought back. Also at this time, mechanical triggers were implemented vs. the older inertial design, and silver solder vent. ribs vs. tin solder. As a result, this period of Superposed manufacture was mechanically better and more reliable. The Superlight Model was introduced in 12 ga. during 1967, 20 ga. during 1969, and became available in all Grades beginning in 1971. All gauge Skeet sets became available in all Grades during 1972.

During late 1966, Browning's salt wood problems began to emerge, and continued until 1970. The majority of salt wood Superposed models from this era are in the round knob short tang configuration (RKST), but some flat knob short tang (FKST) guns with salt problems have also been observed. Depending on the damage (it can vary a lot), values for salt damaged guns can be reduced by as much as 50% (heavy pitting and original salt wood). Those salt guns that have been restocked by Browning are accepted by the shooting fraternity, and can command as much as 90% of the value of non-salt original guns. To determine if a Superposed has salt damage, examine carefully any gun where the serial number is within the 1966-1971 production range (please refer to the Browning Superposed serialization section), and carefully inspect the wood around the buttplate, forearm, and where the wood joins the receiver metal for any telltale rusting or pitting.

Engraved guns signed by Browning's top engravers (Funken, Vrancken, Watrin, Magis, Müeller, and J. Baerten) will command a premium over unsigned guns. Also, more and more Superposed models are appearing with Angelo Bee's signature (while non-factory, Mr. Bee's work is universally recognized. He engraved in Belgium at FN from 1951-1974.) Louis Vrancken and Andre Watrin took over as heads of the engraving department in 1960.

The following values are for 1960-1976 Superposed production non-salt damaged guns. Most desirable period of mfg. is 1960-1966 (round knob, long tang, limited salt, rarely encountered with salt damage). Guns made during 1972-1976 (FKLT) are worth more than RKST. Lowest values are for 1966-1971 mfg. (round/flat knob, short tang - should be inspected carefully for potential salt wood problems). Many Browning collectors/dealers feel that round/flat knob, short tang Superposed are getting harder to sell every year.

Barrel addresses appeared as follows: circa 1947-1958 "St. Louis, M.O." (earliest BAC markings) or "St. Louis, Missouri", 1959-1968 "St. Louis, Missouri and Montreal P.Q.", 1969-1975 "Morgan, Utah and Montreal, P.Q." Make sure barrel address date matches year of mfg. (see listings in the back of this text).

The original factory configuration of almost all Superposed shotguns can be verified by grade, gauge/bore, and barrel length. To obtain information on a specific Belgian Superposed serial number, please contact the Browning historian directly (refer to Contact Information for more information).

SUPERPOSED WITH EXTRA BARREL(S) OR SUPER-TUBES – The Superposed could be special ordered from the factory in the following combinations: 12 or 20 ga. with one extra set of barrels in same ga., 12 ga. with one extra set in 20 ga., 12 or 20 ga. with two extra barrel sets of same ga., 20 ga. with one extra set in either 28 ga. or .410 bore, 20 ga. with both 28 ga. and .410 bore barrel sets, and 28 ga. with extra set of .410 bore barrels. Super-Tubes were adaptable on 12 ga. guns only; came from the factory cased with accessories, 16 1/2 in. long, factory installation.

Add 40%-50% of the gun's value for each Grade I extra barrel set(s). For higher grades, add approx. $1,000-$2,500 per barrel set, depending on grade.
Add $250 for Super-Tubes - available for 12 ga. only, introduced in 1965.
Add $400 for Super-Tube Set - 3 ga. set (20, 28 ga., and .410 bore).
Subtract $150-$500 for non-original recoil pads on Grade I models, depending on condition.
Subtract $250-$750 for non-original recoil pads on the higher grades, depending on condition.

SUPERPOSED VARIATIONS – On most Superposed with added recoil pads, the stock has usually been cut to keep the LOP the same. The correct LOP on a Superposed is 14 1/4 inches (14 1/2 in. on Trap & New Style Skeet), with or w/o a factory recoil pad, unless special ordered from the factory. Except for the Superlight Model, individual

MSR	100%	98%	95%	90%	80%	70%	60%

configurations have not been broken out on the Pigeon, Pointer, Diana, and Midas grades, but values will be similar to each other in most cases.

Subtract approx. 25%-40% for salt wood (depending on extent of damage).
Subtract 10% for new style Skeet configuration on models.
Subtract 15%-20% for Broadway Trap Model.
Special order Superposed with non-standard factory engraving, checkered buttstocks, 3 piece forearms, and other special orders will command premiums over standard configurations.

SUPERPOSED GRADE I STANDARD WEIGHT & LIGHTNING – 12, 20, 28 ga., or .410 bore (the 28 ga. & .410 bore were not cataloged until 1960), 28 ga. and .410 bore were built on a 20 ga. frame, the buttplate was changed from horn to plastic during 1961, 12 and 20 ga. Lightning Models were approx. 6 oz. lighter than Standard Weight.

12 ga.	$2,000	$1,600	$1,300	$975	$825	$750	$695
20 ga.	$3,500	$3,000	$2,800	$2,200	$1,550	$1,275	$1,100
28 ga.	$7,000	$6,500	$5,500	$4,250	$3,250	$2,650	$2,300
.410 bore	$5,500	$4,500	$3,500	$3,000	$2,200	$1,475	$1,225

Subtract 10%-15% for Grade I Standardweight (12 ga. only).
Add 20%-25% for round knob, long tang stock variations (pre-1966), unless Skeet choked.

* *Superposed Grade I Magnum* – 12 ga. only, 3 in. chambers, 28, 30, or 32 (rare) in. barrels with vent. rib, recoil pad standard.

12 ga.	$1,950	$1,600	$1,200	$1,000	$825	$775	$725

This model with 30 or 32 (very rare) in. barrels is now popular again, as Sporting Clays shooters like this desirable configuration.

* *Superposed Grade I Superlight* – 12 (mfg. 1967-1976), 20 (1969-1976), 28 (very rare, approx. 12-14 mfg.) ga. or .410 bore (mfg. 1970-76) features lightweight construction and straight grip stock. During 1971, the Superlight was offered in all Grades.

12 ga.	$3,375	$2,675	$2,175	$1,550	$1,075	$975	$875
20 ga.	$5,150	$4,425	$3,650	$2,850	$2,000	$1,650	$1,425
28 ga.	$17,500	$16,250	$13,750	$10,500	$8,125	$6,625	$5,750
.410 bore	$8,250	$6,750	$5,250	$4,500	$3,300	$2,200	$1,850

A Quail Unlimited limited edition was also available in the Superlight Series, add 10%-15% if in 98%+ original condition.
20 ga. with solid rib barrels are very rare and will command a premium over vent. rib variations.

* *Superposed Grade I Skeet/New Model Skeet* – 12, 20, 28 ga. or .410 bore, 26 1/2 or 28 in. VR barrels with fixed SK/SK chokes, New Model Skeet was introduced during 1968, and was available in both Standard and Lightning weights in 12 and 20 ga., this New Model featured a flat bottom pistol grip stock with factory vent. recoil pad and beavertail forearm, pre-'68 mfg. was basically a hunting model with skeet chokes. Mfg. circa 1950s-1976.

SUPERPOSED: 1960-1976 MFG.

MSR	100%	98%	95%	90%	80%	70%	60%
12 ga.	$1,675	$1,400	$1,100	$950	$825	$750	$700
20 ga.	$2,450	$2,100	$1,700	$1,250	$975	$850	$775
28 ga.	$4,950	$4,500	$3,500	$2,750	$2,250	$1,550	$1,275
.410 bore	$2,800	$2,400	$1,950	$1,450	$1,100	$925	$850

Add approx. 10%-15% for pre 1968 mfg. (w/o beavertail forearm and recoil pad.)
Subtract 20% for 26 in. (New Skeet style) barrels.

* *Superposed Grade I Four Gauge Skeet Set* – includes 12, 20, 28 ga. and .410 bore barrels, 26 1/2 or 28 in. VR barrels, 12 ga. frame, beavertail forearm, includes fitted luggage case. Mfg. 1972-1976.

$5,250 $4,950 $4,500 $4,150 $3,850 $3,350 $2,650

Subtract 20% for 26 in. (New Skeet style) barrels.

* *Superposed Grade I Trap Model (Lightning and Broadway)* – 12 ga. only, FKLT, Trap dimension stock with recoil pad, 14 3/8 in. LOP, semi-beavertail forearm, 30 or 32 (rare in Lightning model) in. barrels with either standard 5/16 in. VR (Lightning) or 5/8 in. Broadway VR, first cataloged in 1961, this new Lightning Model Trap was approx. 6 oz. lighter than previous mfg., front and middle ivory bead sights standard, Broadway is approx. 1 lbs. heavier than Lightning with same length barrels.

$1,950 $1,600 $1,200 $1,000 $825 $750 $700

SUPERPOSED PIGEON GRADE – 12, 20, 28 ga. or .410 bore, features a silver grey receiver with 2 smaller flying pigeons surrounded by fine scroll engraving on each side of the frame, receiver bottom and tangs also exhibit fine scroll work. Disc. 1974.

12 ga.	$5,500	$3,850	$2,900	$2,000	$1,700	$1,570	$1,485
20 ga.	$9,000	$7,500	$6,000	$4,000	$2,750	$2,100	$1,850
28 ga.	$12,500	$9,000	$7,800	$6,000	$4,500	$3,500	$2,500
.410 bore	$9,000	$7,500	$6,000	$4,500	$3,300	$2,800	$2,200

Add 20%-25% for round knob, long tang stock variations (pre-1966), unless Skeet choked.
Subtract 20% for newer Skeet style model with beavertail forearm and recoil pad.

Between 1948-1960, this model was designated the Grade II.

* *Superposed Pigeon Grade Superlight* – 12 (mfg. 1967-1976), 20 (1969-1976), 28 (very rare, approx. 6 mfg.) ga. or .410 bore (mfg. 1970-76) features lightweight construction and straight grip stock. During 1971, the Superlight was offered in all Grades.

12 ga.	$8,500	$6,850	$5,500	$4,150	$3,100	$2,200	$1,800
20 ga.	$11,500	$10,000	$8,750	$7,500	$6,250	$5,000	$4,000
28 ga.	$15,000	$12,500	$9,250	$7,750	$6,150	$5,00	$3,750
.410 bore	$12,000	$10,500	$9,250	$8,000	$6,750	$5,500	$4,500

SUPERPOSED POINTER GRADE – features engraved silver grey receiver with a pointer on one side, and a setter on the other, select checkered walnut, early production was engraved by Funken, while the

MSR	100%	98%	95%	90%	80%	70%	60%

final design was executed by Vrancken. Mfg. 1959-disc. 1966, except for special orders.

12 ga.		$8,750	$6,850	$5,500	$4,150	$3,100	$2,200	$1,800
20 ga.		$15,000	$12,500	$9,250	$7,600	$6,000	$5,000	$3,750
28 ga. (rare)		$21,500	$18,000	$15,500	$12,500	$8,000	$5,000	$3,800
.410 bore (rare)		$17,500	$14,000	$12,250	$9,250	$6,000	$4,600	$3,500

Add 40% for round knob, long tang stock variations (pre-1966), unless Skeet choked (add 40% if 28 ga.).

Subtract 20% for newer Skeet style model with beavertail forearm and recoil pad.

* *Superposed Pointer Grade Superlight* – this model was available by special order only, and was never cataloged by BAC (approx. 10 mfg. in 28 ga.).

12 ga.	$12,250	$9,600	$7,700	$5,800	$4,350	$3,075	$2,525
20 ga.	$21,000	$17,500	$12,950	$10,500	$8,400	$7,000	$5,250
28 ga. (very rare)	$30,000	$25,750	$19,750	$15,000	$11,000	$8,500	$7,000
.410 bore (very rare)	$25,000	$21,000	$15,500	$12,000	$9,000	$7,750	$6,000

SUPERPOSED DIANA GRADE – deeper engraving with duck and pheasant game scenes - similar to 1948-60 mfg. Grade V. Disc. 1976.

12 ga.	$7,750	$6,500	$4,300	$2,750	$2,450	$2,200	$1,975
20 ga.	$13,000	$10,000	$8,500	$5,950	$4,850	$3,650	$3,150
28 ga.	$22,500	$18,000	$15,000	$10,000	$7,350	$5,750	$4,750
.410 bore	$14,500	$12,000	$9,000	$6,550	$5,000	$4,200	$3,650

Add 20% for round knob, long tang stock variations (pre-1966, add 40% if 28 ga.).

Subtract 20% for newer Skeet style model with beavertail forearm and recoil pad.

Between 1948-1960, this model was designated the Grade V.

* *Superposed Diana Grade Superlight* – 12 (mfg. 1967-76), 20 (1969-76), 28 (very rare, approx. 7-9 mfg.) ga. or .410 bore (mfg. 1970-76) features lightweight construction and straight grip stock. During 1971, the Superlight was offered in all Grades.

12 ga.	$11,650	$9,750	$6,450	$3,850	$3,425	$3,075	$2,775
20 ga.	$18,000	$15,000	$11,500	$8,000	$6,500	$4,950	$4,000
28 ga. (very rare)	$35,000	$30,000	$25,000	$21,000	$17,500	$14,000	$10,000
.410 bore (very rare)	$27,500	$23,000	$17,000	$13,500	$10,000	$8,500	$7,250

SUPERPOSED MIDAS GRADE – features new design by Vrancken with deep relief scroll engraving with gold inlaid ducks and pheasants on frame sides and a quail on the bottom, ejector trip rods, ejector hammers, and firing pins are also 18Kt. gold plated, best quality walnut with fine checkering. Disc. 1976.

12 ga.	$12,500	$10,500	$8,750	$6,250	$5,000	$4,000	$3,500
20 ga.	$19,500	$16,500	$14,000	$11,750	$8,750	$7,250	$5,000
28 ga.	$27,500	$23,000	$20,000	$16,500	$12,500	$9,000	$7,350
.410 bore	$19,500	$16,500	$14,000	$11,750	$8,750	$7,250	$5,000

MSR	100%	98%	95%	90%	80%	70%	60%

Add 20% for round knob, long tang stock variations (pre-1966), unless Skeet choked (add 40% if 28 ga.).

Subtract 20% for newer Skeet style model with beavertail forearm and recoil pad.

Between 1948-1960, this model was designated the Grade VI.

* *Superposed Midas Grade Superlight* – 12 (mfg. 1967-76), 20 (1969-76), 28 (very rare, approx. 9 mfg.) ga. or .410 bore (mfg. 1970-76) features lightweight construction and straight grip stock. During 1971, the Superlight was offered in all Grades.

12 ga.	$15,625	$13,125	$11,000	$7,800	$6,250	$5,000	$4,375
20 ga.	$24,375	$20,500	$17,500	$14,500	$11,000	$9,000	$6,250
28 ga. (very rare)	$39,500	$33,500	$26,000	$21,000	$17,500	$14,750	$11,500
.410 bore (very rare)	$27,250	$23,000	$19,500	$16,450	$12,250	$10,150	$7,000

SUPERPOSED BICENTENNIAL SUPERLIGHT – specially engraved limited edition Model, 51 mfg. - one for each state and Washington, D.C. Left side has U.S. Flag, bald eagle and state emblem inlaid in gold. Right side has gold inlaid hunter and turkey. Blue receiver, fancy checkered English stock, Schnabel forend, velvet lined wood case. Made 1976 by FN.

$12,000	$10,000	$8,000	N/A	N/A	N/A	N/A

SUPERPOSED EXPOSITION/EXHIBITION MODEL – this specially manufactured Superposed saw limited production from pre-WWII through 1976. There are true exhibition models and a "C" series. Most "C" series did not have carved stocks, and were a special BAC sale of FN guns which did not sell well in Europe. True exhibition guns had gold lettering on the barrels in most cases, and many also had carved stocks. These guns were made for a very special reason, purpose, or person. Prices usually start in the 5 digit level - the C Series is typically priced between $20,000-$50,000, with the Exhibition guns comparably priced as long as they are not Trap or Skeet guns. Field choked RKLT and Superlite small bore guns bring the most, with small bore, all option side plated Exhibitions at the top of the heap, whether C Series or not.

SUPERPOSED PRESENTATION MODELS (P1-P4) – custom made versions of the Lightning Field, Super Light, Trap, and Skeet guns specifications the same as Standard models, with differences in finish engraving and inlay(s), and grade of wood and checkering. These guns were introduced by FN in 1977 and were disc. after 1984. Gauge premiums below refer to Models P1-P3.

Add 50% for 20 ga.
Add 75% for 28 ga.
Add 40% for .410 bore.
Add $1,500 for each P1 extra barrel set(s). For higher grades, add approx. $1,500-$2,500 per barrel set, depending on grade.
Subtract 25% for P Series Trap Models.
Subtract 25% for P Series Broadway Trap Models.
Subtract 20% for P Series Skeet 12 and 20 ga. guns.

SUPERPOSED: 1960-1976 MFG.

MSR	100%	98%	95%	90%	80%	70%	60%

Since P Series Superposed were disc. in 1985, collector interest has increased substantially. Interestingly, the P series models are rarer than most of the pre-1976 high grade Superposed models.

* ***Superposed Presentation 1*** – silver grey or blue receiver, oak leaf and fine scroll engraved, choice of 6 different animal scenes.

	$3,300	$2,500	$2,100	$1,850	$1,500	$1,250	$1,000

* ***Superposed Presentation 1 w/gold inlays*** – similar to Presentation 1, only with gold inlays.

	$4,750	$3,500	$3,000	$2,100	$1,825	$1,700	$1,500

* ***Superposed Presentation 2*** – silver grey or blue receiver, high relief engraving, choice of 3 different sets of game scenes.

	$4,800	$4,000	$2,750	$2,050	$1,825	$1,700	$1,500

* ***Superposed Presentation 2 w/gold inlays*** – similar to Presentation 2, only with gold inlays.

	$7,000	$6,000	$4,200	$2,150	$1,925	$1,750	$1,550

* ***Superposed Presentation 3*** – silver grey or blue receiver, more elaborate high relief engraving with choice of partridges, mallards, or geese depicted on frame sides in 18Kt. gold.

	$9,000	$7,500	$5,500	$3,750	$3,200	$2,875	$2,300

* ***Superposed Presentation 4*** – features engraved side plates in either silver grey or blue finish, hand engraved game scenes include waterfowl on right frame side, 5 pheasants on left frame side, 2 quail on receiver bottom, and a retriever's head on trigger guard. Extra figure walnut stock and forearm.

	$8,000	$6,900	$5,250	$4,000	$3,350	$2,950	$2,375

Add 30% for 20 ga., 70% for 28 ga., or 50% for .410 bore.

* ***Superposed Presentation 4 w/gold inlays*** – similar to Presentation 4, only with game scenes inlaid in 18Kt. gold.

	$12,000	$10,500	$8,700	$6,000	$4,250	$3,650	$2,950

Add 50% for 20 ga., 75% for 28 ga., or 50% for .410 bore.

SUPERPOSED PRESENTATION SERIES SUPERLITE (PI - PIV) – available in various configurations including multi-barrel sets.

* ***Superposed Presentation I Superlite w/Gold*** – G, H, I, J, K, or L style engraving.

	100%	98%	95%	90%	80%	70%	60%
12 ga. (25 mfg.)	$6,750	$6,000	$5,200	$3,600	$3,000	$2,250	$1,800
20 ga. (80 mfg.)	$9,500	$8,000	$7,000	$5,500	$4,000	$3,200	$2,500
28 ga. (38 mfg.)	$13,000	$11,000	$9,800	$7,700	$6,200	$4,000	$3,400
.410 bore (47 mfg.)	$9,500	$8,500	$6,800	$5,500	$4,000	$3,200	$2,600

Add $1,500 per extra barrel.
Add 40% for an all option gun (checkered buttstock, oil finish, three piece forend, rare).
Add 15% for J. Baerten signed gun (rare).
Subtract 35% for Trap or Skeet Models.
Subtract 30% for A, B, C, D, E, or F models w/o gold.

MSR	100%	98%	95%	90%	80%	70%	60%

* *Superposed Presentation II Superlite* – P, Q, or R style engraving.

12 ga. (23 mfg.)	$9,500	$9,000	$8,000	$7,000	$6,000	$4,500	$2,200
20 ga. (93 mfg.)	$14,000	$12,500	$9,500	$7,500	$6,000	$5,000	$3,000
28 ga. (57 mfg.)	$16,000	$14,500	$11,000	$9,000	$7,500	$6,000	$4,000
.410 bore (44 mfg.)	$14,000	$12,500	$9,500	$7,500	$6,000	$5,000	$3,000

Add $2,000 per extra barrel.
Add 40% for an all option gun (checkered buttstock, oil finish, three piece forend, rare, 50% if 28 ga.).
Add 15% for J. Baerten signed gun (rare).
Subtract 40% for Trap or Skeet Models.
Subtract 30% for M, N, or O models w/o gold.

* *Superposed Presentation III Superlite* – S, T, or U style engraving.

12 ga. (16 mfg.)	$13,000	$12,000	$10,000	$8,500	$7,000	$5,000	$3,500
20 ga. (85 mfg.)	$18,500	$17,000	$14,000	$10,000	$7,500	$5,500	$4,500
28 ga. (36 mfg.)	$22,500	$20,500	$17,000	$14,000	$10,000	$8,000	$6,500
.410 bore (37 mfg.)	$18,000	$16,500	$13,500	$9,500	$7,000	$5,000	$4,000

Add $2,000 per extra barrel.
Add 30% for an all option gun (checkered buttstock, oil finish, three piece forend, 40% if 28 ga.).
Add 25% for an all option FKLT gun (very rare).
Add 15% for J. Baerten signed gun (rare).
Subtract 40% for Trap or Skeet Models.

* *Superposed Presentation IV Superlite w/Gold* – W style engraving.

12 ga. (14 mfg.)	$21,000	$20,000	$17,500	$14,000	$11,000	$8,500	$6,000
20 ga. (44 mfg.)	$25,000	$23,000	$19,500	$15,000	$10,000	$8,000	$6,500
28 ga. (20 mfg.)	$32,000	$30,000	$24,000	$18,000	$15,000	$12,000	$10,000
.410 bore (35 mfg.)	$25,000	$23,000	$19,500	$15,000	$10,000	$8,000	$6,500

Add $3,000 per extra barrel.
Add 40% for an all option gun (checkered buttstock, oil finish, three piece forend 50% if 28 ga.).
Add 40% for an all option FKLT gun (very rare).
Add 15% for J. Baerten signed gun (rare).
Subtract 35% for Trap or Skeet Models.
Subtract 35% for plain models w/o gold.

LIEGE (FN B-26) – 12 ga., 26 1/2, 28 or 30 in. barrels, various chokes boxlock, auto ejectors, non-selective single trigger, vent. rib, checkered pistol grip stock. Approx. 10,000 mfg. 1973-1975 by FN.

$1,325	$1,050	$850	$685	$610	$570	$540

This model is also known as the B-26.

GRAND LIEGE – similar to Liege, except has deluxe checkered walnut stock and forearm, and engraved receiver. Disc.

$1,650	$1,225	$1,000	$850	$750	$700	$650

MSR	100%	98%	95%	90%	80%	70%	60%

B-26 – with BAC markings. Mfg. 1973-75.

$1,250 $1,000 $825 $685 $610 $570 $540

B-27 – F.N. manufactured modified B-26, imported into the U.S. in 1984, same action as Liege (B 26), blue or satin finished receiver with light engraving, no BAC markings and never cataloged.

* *B-27 Standard Game* – 28 in. barrels, 9/32 in. vent. rib, pistol grip stock, Schnabel forearm, SST, blue receiver, choking M/F only.

$1,325 $1,050 $850 $685 $610 $570 $540

Also available in Skeet model with gold "Browning" logo on blue receiver. Prices are the same.

* *B-27 Deluxe Game (Grade II)* – similar to Standard Grade, except has 30 in. barrels, better wood and English scroll engraved satin finished receiver, choking M/F only.

$1,425 $1,100 $1,000 $850 $750 $650 $550

* *B-27 Grand Deluxe Game* – 28 in. IC/IM & M/F choked barrels, game scene engraved, signed by the engraver, 90% receiver coverage.

$1,575 $1,200 $1,075 $900 $775 $660 $595

This model was also available in a Trap configuration - values are about the same as above.

* *B-27 Deluxe Skeet* – similar to Deluxe Game (Grade II), except is designed for skeet shooting.

$1,325 $1,050 $850 $685 $610 $570 $540

International Skeet was also available at same price; hand fit pistol grip with stippling and International Type recoil pad.

* *B-27 Deluxe Trap* – similar to Deluxe Game (Grade II), except is configured for trap shooting.

$1,325 $1,050 $850 $685 $610 $570 $540

* *B-27 City of Liege Commemorative* – limited edition of 250 units manufactured to commemorate the 1,000th anniversary of the city of Liege, cased. Only 29 imported into the U.S.

$1,750 $1,500 $1,225   N/A   N/A   N/A   N/A

ST-100 – 12 ga., Belgian mfg., O/U trap configuration with separated barrels and adj. point of impact, manufactured 1979-81 for European sale mostly, floating VR, ST, deluxe checkered walnut stock and forearm, non-BAC model.

$3,500 $2,750 $2,000 $1,850 $1,200 $975 $825

SUPERPOSED WATERFOWL SERIES – 12 ga., 500 made of each issue, 7 gold inlays with extensive engraving on French Grey receiver, lightning action, 28 in. barrels, checkered buttstock, full-length walnut case, factory inventories were depleted on Mallard, Pintail, and Black Duck Issues in 1989.

Add 20% for 3 gun set with same serial number.

MSR	100%	98%	95%	90%	80%	70%	60%

* *Superposed Waterfowl 1981 Mallard Issue*

	$9,500	$7,500	$6,000	N/A	N/A	N/A	N/A

Last MSR was $7,000.

This issue was sold out in 1988.

* *Superposed Waterfowl 1982 Pintail Issue*

	$9,500	$7,500	$6,000	N/A	N/A	N/A	N/A

Last MSR was $7,000.

* *Superposed Waterfowl 1983 Black Duck Issue*

	$9,500	$7,500	$6,000	N/A	N/A	N/A	N/A

Last MSR was $8,800

SUPERPOSED SHOTGUN: 1983-86 MFG. – 12 or 20 ga. In 1983, Browning announced renewed production of the famous Belgian "Superposed" O/U in Grade I only. Available in Lightning or Superlight models, 3 in. chambers in Lightning 20 ga., 26 1/2 or 28 in. barrels. Belgian manufactured from 1983-86.

* *Superposed Shotgun Grade I (1983-86 mfg.)* – limited mfg., not compatible with steel shot, featured select walnut stock/forearm and extra engraving.

	100%	98%	95%	90%	80%	70%	60%
Lightning	$2,800	$2,150	$1,550	$950	$800	$675	$550
Superlight	$3,750	$3,300	$2,750	$1,850	$1,400	$1,000	$850

Last MSR was $1,995

Add 25% for 20 ga.

SUPERPOSED CLASSIC SERIES – 20 ga. only, 26 in. barrels, less than 2,500 manufactured in Classic model and under 350 manufactured in Gold Classic. Both editions feature multiple engraved scenes and a special silver grey finish. Select American walnut featuring oil finish. Available 1986 only.

	$4,000	$3,350	$2,750	N/A	N/A	N/A	N/A

Last MSR was $2,000

* *Superposed Gold Classic* – 8 gold inlays, select walnut forearm and stock are both checkered and carved, many were shipped back to Belgium due to poor sales domestically. Available 1986 only.

	$7,250	$6,000	$4,150	N/A	N/A	N/A	N/A

Last MSR was $6,00

SHOTGUNS: O/U, SUPERPOSED HIGH GRADES: 1985-PRESENT

Browning, in 1985, resumed production of the Superposed in Pigeon, Pointer, Diana and Midas grades. They were available in 12 and 20 ga. only, in either a Lightning or Superlight configuration. These higher grades were custom ordered from the factory with delivery ranging from 8 to more than 12 months. Custom options could be special ordered on each grade with corresponding prices being higher than shown below. B-25 engraving patterns on these various grades will nearly duplicate those styles manufactured before 1976. Skeet models were not available.

SUPERPOSED: CUSTOM SHOP CURRENT PRICING & MODELS

MSR	100%	98%	95%	90%	80%	70%	60%

Be wary of non-factory upgraded Superposed higher grade models. These upgraded guns have very nice workmanship, but are valued at approx. 50% less than a factory guns in similar grade/gauge, and barrel length. Non-factory engraving has been done by: R. Capece, Dubois, Diet, and Bee. It is strongly advised to get a factory letter from Glen Jensen in the Browning Historical Dept. to guarantee the original configuration of a Superposed.

Superposed: Custom Shop Current Pricing & Models

In 2000, Browning changed the nomenclature of their B-25 shotgun Series. Prices reflect current custom shop MSRs. These new boxlock grades include: Special Woodcock $16,558, Special Duck $16,968, Special Pigeon $18,091, Trap Evolution 2 $19,215, Traditionnel $16,968, Sporting 207 Gold 25 $17,273, Diana UK $21,913, and Grades B11 - $17,887 (disc. 2003, reintroduced 2006), B12 - $18,091 (disc. 2003, reintroduced 2006), B2G - $18,296 (disc. 2003, reintroduced 2004), C11 - $21,668, C12 - $22,896, C1G - $19,421, C2G - $22,896, C3 - $25,553, D11 - $30,970, D12 - $29,845, D2L $37,309, D4G $35,773, D5G - $35,773, Special Automn - $36,797, Cheverny - $41,907.

Additionally, the Browning Custom Shop also offers the following shotguns in various grades with engraved sideplates: Grade II - $23,234 (disc. 2003), C2S - $31,992, Grade E1 - $40,931 Grade F1 - $40,931, Grade I1 - $40,931, Grade M1 - $43,343, Grade M2 - $43,343, Special Perdrix - $54,058, Windsor Or - $54,058, Chenonceau - $56,376, Cheverny - $56,376, D5G Sideplate - $56,376, and the Special Automn $56,376. These new grades are special order only through the Browning Custom Shop.

Grade I Traditional, Pigeon Grade, Pointer Grade, Diana Grade, and Midas Grade Superposed are listed separately under the B-25 model listing.

Add 20% for 20 ga. on previously owned models.
Add approx. $1,250 for a previously owned extra set of barrels.
Add $6,479 - $11,954 per extra set of barrels on currently manufactured Superposed models, depending on the grade.

B-25 – 12 or 20 ga. only, original Superposed Model manufactured entirely from parts fabricated in Herstal, Belgium. Also available in Superlight configuration. This older nomenclature series was discontinued domestically in 1999, but the Custom Shop is still producing these grades.

* *B-25 Grade I Traditional*

MSR	100%	98%	95%	90%	80%	70%	60%
	$10,500	$8,750	$6,500	N/A	N/A	N/A	N/A

Last MSR was $19,433.

* *B-25 Pigeon Grade*

MSR	100%	98%	95%	90%	80%	70%	60%
MSR $17,280	$12,500	$9,500	$7,250	N/A	N/A	N/A	N/A

* *B-25 Pointer C Grade*

MSR	100%	98%	95%	90%	80%	70%	60%
MSR $18,920	$14,500	$10,750	$8,500	N/A	N/A	N/A	N/A

* *B-25 Diana C Grade*

MSR	100%	98%	95%	90%	80%	70%	60%
MSR $19,886	$15,750	$11,750	$9,500	N/A	N/A	N/A	N/A

* *B-25 Midas D Grade*

MSR	100%	98%	95%	90%	80%	70%	60%
MSR $25,678	$17,750	$12,500	$10,000	N/A	N/A	N/A	N/A

SUPERPOSED: CUSTOM SHOP CURRENT PRICING & MODELS

MSR	100%	98%	95%	90%	80%	70%	60%

B-25 125th ANNIVERSARY – 12 ga. only, 2 3/4 in. chamber, 28 in. VR barrels with fixed M/F chokes and 8mm rib, Lightning style stock and forearm with oil finish and black buttplate, case colored receiver with gold border and gold enhanced 125th Anniversary logo. 10 mfg. 2003 only.

$13,750 $5,250 $3,750 N/A N/A N/A N/A

Last MSR was $15,219

B-125 – 12 or 20 ga. only, retains all the features of the original Superposed except parts were subcontracted worldwide to decrease production costs and were assembled "in the white" at Herstal's Custom Gun Shop in Belgium, choice of three different engraving styles and two receiver finishes. Mfg. 1988-2003.

* **B-125 Hunting Model** – available in either Hunting Lightning or Superlight configuration.

» **B-125 Hunting Model w/"A" Style Engraving** – blue frame with border engraving featuring Browning logo engraved on each side.

$3,400 $2,750 $2,150 $1,700 $1,450 $1,275 $1,050

Last MSR was $3,925

» **B-125 Hunting Model w/"B" Style Engraving** – coin finished frame with smaller game scene engravings.

$3,700 $3,100 $2,250 $1,800 $1,500 $1,300 $1,100

Last MSR was $4,360

» **B-125 Hunting Model w/"C" Style Engraving** – coin finished frame with elaborate scroll work and game scene engraving.

$4,100 $3,475 $2,450 $1,900 $1,600 $1,400 $1,200

Last MSR was $4,90

* **B-125 Sporting Clays Model** – 12 ga. only, designed for sporting clays competition and included Invector-Plus choke tube system.

» **B-125 Sporting Clays Model w/"A" Style Engraving** – blue frame with border engraving featuring Browning logo engraved on each side.

$3,400 $2,750 $2,150 $1,700 $1,450 $1,275 $1,050

Last MSR was $3,92

» **B-125 Sporting Clays Model w/"B" Style Engraving** – coin finished frame with smaller game scene engravings.

$3,700 $3,100 $2,250 $1,800 $1,500 $1,300 $1,100

Last MSR was $4,36

» **B-125 Sporting Clays Model w/"C" Style Engraving** – coin finished frame with elaborate scroll work and game scene engraving.

$4,100 $3,475 $2,450 $1,900 $1,600 $1,400 $1,200

Last MSR was $4,9

MSR	100%	98%	95%	90%	80%	70%	60%

* **B-125 Trap Model** – standard F-1 style engraving.

	$4,950	$3,550	$2,325	$1,750	$1,450	$1,275	$1,050

Last MSR was $5,452.

SHOTGUNS: SxS

The Browning Custom Shop in Herstal, Belgium offered several SxS sidelock models manufactured by Lebeau-Courally until circa 2006. Models include the LC1 (blued receiver, $17,516 last MSR), and LC2 (coin finished receiver, $22,799 last MSR).

B-SS – 12 or 20 ga., 26, 28, or 30 in. barrels, various chokes, engraved boxlock action, auto ejectors, checkered pistol grip walnut stock, beavertail forearm, SST. Mfg. 1971-1988 by Miroku.

12 ga.	$1,175	$1,000	$850	$725	$650	$550	$450
20 ga.	$2,250	$2,000	$1,775	$1,525	$1,300	$1,100	$950

Last MSR was $775.

Early guns had a single non-selective trigger (silver plated) - subtract 10%.

* **B-SS Grade II** – satin greyed steel receiver featuring an engraved pheasant, duck, quail, and dogs. Disc. 1983.

	$3,250	$2,850	$2,250	$1,775	$1,350	$1,100	$925

B-SS SPORTER – 12 or 20 ga., straight grip stock, longer lower tang, slimmed down beavertail forearm, oil finish, 26 or 28 in. barrels. Disc. 1988.

	$2,000	$1,750	$1,500	$1,225	$950	$800	$650

Last MSR was $775.

Add 50% for 20 ga., if in 95%+ condition.

* **B-SS Sporter Grade II** – satin greyed steel receiver featuring an engraved pheasant, duck, quail and dogs. Disc. 1983.

	$3,150	$2,700	$2,225	$1,800	$1,350	$1,100	$925

Add 50% for 20 ga., if in 95%+ condition.

* **B-SS "Bottle" Sporter Set** – 12 and 20 ga., wild turkey and wood duck inlays on 12 ga., wood ducks only on 20 ga., straight grip sporter stock, shoulders are sculpted and engraved, Exhibition grade walnut, engraving was done in Belgium by custom shop, cased in Browning Airways case. Less than 100 mfg. circa 1976.

Set	$9,500	$8,750	$7,500	$6,250	$5,000	$4,500	$4,000
12 ga.	$2,995	$2,750	$2,400	$2,100	$1,850	$1,600	$1,400
20 ga.	$3,750	$3,300	$2,950	$2,650	$2,300	$2,000	$1,800

This model got its nickname from a Mr. Bottles Sporting Goods store in Wichita, KS, who special ordered 100 sets of these guns circa 1976.

B-SS SIDELOCK – 12 or 20 ga., engraved sidelock action in satin grey finish, ST, 26 or 28 in. barrels, English select walnut stock, splinter forend. Mfg. 1983-88 by Miroku in Japan.

12 ga.	$3,750	$3,300	$2,725	$2,275	$1,875	$1,500	$1,250
20 ga.	$4,995	$4,300	$3,650	$2,900	$2,300	$1,875	$1,500

Last MSR was $2,000.

SHOTGUNS: SEMI-AUTO, A-5 1903-1998, 2012-CURRENT MFG.

BROWNING CHOKES AND THEIR CODES (ON REAR LEFT-SIDE OF BARREL)

* designates full choke (F).

*- designates improved modified choke (IM).

** designates modified choke (M).

**- designates improved cylinder choke (IC).

**$ designates skeet (SK).

*** designates cylinder bore (CYL).

INV. designates barrel is threaded for Browning Invector choke tube system.

INV. PLUS designates back-bored barrels.

Miroku manufactured A-5s can be determined by year of manufacture in the following manner: RV suffix - 1975, RT - 1976, RR - 1977, RP - 1978, RN - 1979, PM - 1980, PZ - 1981, PY - 1982, PX - 1983, PW - 1984, PV - 1985, PT - 1986, PR - 1987, PP - 1988, PN - 1989, NM - 1990, NZ - 1991, NY - 1992, NX - 1993, NW - 1994, NV - 1995, NT - 1996, NR - 1997, NP - 1998, ZY - 2012, ZX - 2013, ZW - 2014.

Browning resumed importation from F.N. in 1946. On November 26, 1997, Browning announced that the venerable Auto-5 would finally be discontinued. Final shipments were made in February, 1998. Over 3 million A-5s were manufactured by Fabrique Nationale in all configurations between 1903-1976. 1976-1998 manufacture was by Miroku in Japan. The A-5 was reintroduced in 2012 with a Kinematic Drive System, aluminum receiver, and a fixed barrel.

NOTE: Barrels are interchangeable between older Belgian A-5 models and recent Japanese A-5s manufactured by Miroku, if the gauge and chamber length are the same. A different barrel ring design and thicker barrel wall design might necessitate some minor sanding of the inner forearm on the older model, but otherwise, these barrels are fully interchangeable.

NOTE: The use of steel shot is recommended ONLY in those recent models manufactured in Japan - NOT in the older Belgian variations.

The "humpback" design on the Auto-5 (both Belgian and Japanese mfg.) features recoil operation with a scroll engraved steel receiver. During 1909, Browning introduced the magazine cutoff, and moved the safety from inside to the front of the triggerguard. 1946-1951 mfg. has a safety in front of triggerguard. 1951-1976 mfg. has crossbolt safety behind the trigger. Post-war 16 ga. imports by Browning are chambered for 2 3/4 in., and have either a horn (disc. 1964) or plastic (1962-1976) buttplate, high luster wood finish (disc. 1962) or glossy lacquer (1962-1976) finish. Walnut buttstock has either round knob pistol grip (disc. 1967) or flat knob (new 1967). In today's Auto-5 marketplace, all gauges of the A-5 have become extremely collectible. Obviously, the Belgian A-5s are the most desirable. However, the pre-1998 Miroku guns are gaining in collectible popularity. It also has become very apparent that the demand for the FN lightweight 20 ga. has supercedes the Sweet 16 due to availability. Both the lightweight 20 ga. and the Sweet 16 are the most desirable and have seen a dramatic increase in collectibility. Rarity of configurations such as choke designations, and barrel lengths are very important factors in determimming value. Older rare barrels such as the solid rib and the 16 and 20 ga. guns with shorter barrels and open chokes are more desirable than a 30 in. 12 ga. gun with full choke barrel.

MSR	100%	98%	95%	90%	80%	70%	60%

The publisher would like to thank Mr. Richard "Doc" Desira for his recent contributions to the Auto-5/A-5 section.

Add 15% for NIB condition on Belgian mfg. Auto-5 models only, depending on desirability. Beware of reproduced boxes and labels, especially on the more desirable configurations.

Add 15% for the round knob (rounded pistol grip knob on stock, pre-1967 mfg.) variation on FN models only, depending on desirability.

Add $250-$500 per additional barrel, depending on the gauge, barrel length, choke, condition, and rarity (smaller gauge open chokes are the most desirable).

Add 15% on FN models with blonde stock and forearm - mfg. mid-1960s.

AUTO-5 STANDARD - 1903-1940 MFG. – 12 ga. (introduced in Sept., 1903, Browning discontinued imports Dec., 1903), 16 ga. (introduced in 1909, but not in the U.S.), in 1923, Browning resumed importing both 12 and 16 ga. in four grades that differ in engraving, inlays, and grade of wood, both gauges were available with 26-32 in. barrel, recoil operated, 4 shot mag. with cutoff, various chokes, checkered pistol grip stock, horn buttplate, also available in a 3 shot version with shorter magazine tube to limit capacity to 3 rounds from 1932-1940. Importation temporarily ceased in 1940 with the German occupation of Belgium, ser. no. range 1-224,596 (12 ga.) and 1-126,175 (16 ga.). Mfg. in Herstal, Belgium 1903-1940.

Grade 1	$925	$825	$700	$575	$525	$475	$450
Solid matte rib	$1,175	$1,075	$975	$875	$775	$675	$625
With vent. rib	$1,075	$975	$875	$775	$665	$575	$525
Grade 2 (disc.1937)	$1,625	$1,375	$1,150	$1,025	$925	$850	$775
Solid matte rib	$2,150	$1,925	$1,625	$1,350	$1,125	$1,075	$725
With vent. rib	$2,050	$1,825	$1,525	$1,250	$1,025	$975	$875
Grade 3 (disc. 1940)	$3,050	$2,725	$2,425	$2,175	$1,825	$1,600	$1,325
Solid matte rib	$3,700	$3,250	$2,900	$2,625	$2,325	$2,025	$1,675
With vent. rib	$3,600	$3,150	$2,800	$2,525	$2,225	$1,925	$1,575
Grade 4 (disc. 1940)	$4,500	$4,050	$3,650	$3,300	$2,800	$2,300	$1,900
Solid matte rib	$5,250	$4,650	$4,450	$3,550	$3,150	$2,650	$2,450
Grade 4 w/vent. rib	$5,150	$4,550	$4,350	$3,450	$3,050	$2,550	$2,350

Add 100% for first year production (No. 1-10,000) with "Browning Automatic Arms Co." marking on barrel.

Subtract 25% for pre-WWII 16 ga. A-5s chambered for 2 9/16 in. shells.

Early models with safety mounted in front of trigger guard are not as desirable as there are potential safety problems inherent in the design.

Pre-WWII 16 ga. A-5s could be chambered for 2 9/16 in. shells. These shotguns are considerably less desirable than 16 ga. A-5s chambered for 2 3/4 in. modern shotshells. Since some guns have been modified to 2 3/4 in., careful inspection is advised before purchasing or shooting. The 2 9/16 chambered guns can be modified by the Browning Service Dept. to accept 2 3/4 in. shells if so desired.

SHOTGUNS: SEMI-AUTO, A-5 1903-1998, 2012-CURRENT MFG.

MSR	100%	98%	95%	90%	80%	70%	60%

"AMERICAN BROWNING" AUTO-5 – 12, 16, or 20 ga., Remington-produced variation of the Browning Auto-5, very similar to the Remington Model 11, except with Browning logo, mag. cut-off, and different engraving, over 38,000 mfg. in 12 ga. (ser. no. range B5000- B43129), over 14,000 in 16 ga. (ser. no. range A5000-A19450), and 11,000 in 20 ga. (ser. no. range C5000- C16152), stocks have Remington style round knob pistol grip. Mfg. 1940-1947.

	$695	$575	$500	$450	$400	$375	$350

Add 15% for 20 ga.

An easy way to identify this configuration is to look for the "A", "B", or "C" serial number prefix on the left side of receiver.

AUTO-5 STANDARDWEIGHT – 12 (disc. 1970) or 16 (disc. 1964) ga., 26-32 in. barrel, various chokes, checkered walnut stock and forearm, between 7 1/3-8 lbs. Browning resumed importation from F.N. in 1946.

Plain barrel	$1,150	$975	$800	$675	$600	$550	$500
Matted rib (solid)	$1,450	$1,275	$1,100	$1,000	$900	$800	$700
Vent rib	$1,350	$1,175	$1,000	$900	$800	$700	$600

Add 20% for 16 ga.
Subtract 20% for front safety.

Note: Watch for cracked forearms on all A-5 models (due to barrel recoil.)

Barrel addresses appeared as follows: circa 1930-1958 "St. Louis, M.O.", 1959-1968 "St. Louis, Missouri and Montreal P.Q.", 1969-1976 "Morgan, Utah and Montreal, P.Q.". Barrels are serial numbered to the gun until 1953. Make sure barrel address date matches year of mfg. (see listings in the back of this text).

AUTO-5 LIGHTWEIGHT (LIGHT 12 & LIGHT 20) – 12 (new 1947) or 20 (new 1958) ga., recoil operated, 26, 28, or 30 in. barrel, various chokes, gold plated trigger, checkered pistol grip round knob (disc. 1967) or flat knob (mfg. 1967-1976) stock, approx. 10 oz. lighter than Standard weight.

FN model	$1,300	$1,125	$925	$850	$750	$650	$550
FN-vent. rib	$1,525	$1,350	$1,125	$1,050	$950	$850	$750

Add 60% for 20 ga.
Add 15% for round knob NIB condition.
Add 15% for blonde stock and forearm (mfg. mid-1960s).
Subtract 30% for Cutts or Polychoke.

* ***Auto-5 Light 12 Miroku*** – 12 ga. only, 22, 26, 28, or 30 in. VR (became standard 1986) barrel with Invector choke system, approx. 8-8 1/2 lbs. Mfg. 1976-Feb. 1998.

	$1,050	$925	$775	$700	$625	$550	$500

Last MSR was $840.

Subtract 10% without Invector chokes.

MSR	100%	98%	95%	90%	80%	70%	60%

* ***Auto-5 Light 20 Miroku*** – 20 ga. only, 2 3/4 in. chamber, similar to original Belgian Light 20, VR, 22 (new 1995), 26, or 28 in. barrel, Invector chokes standard until 1993, Invector Plus choking became standard 1994, 6 lbs. 12 oz - 7 lbs. 2 oz. Mfg. 1987-1997.

$1,350 $1,225 $975 $900 $825 $750 $650

Last MSR was $840.

AUTO-5 MAGNUM – 12 (new 1958) or 20 (new 1967) ga., 3 in. chamber, 26, 28, 30, or 32 in. barrels, various chokes, VR or etched, 8 1/2 - 9 lbs. Mfg. 1958-1976 by FN, 1976-Feb. 1998 by Miroku.

FN model	$1,150	$975	$800	$675	$600	$550	$500
FN-vent. rib.	$1,350	$1,175	$1,000	$900	$800	$700	$600

Add 50% for 20 ga.

Add 15% for round knob, NIB condition.

Add 15% for blonde stock and forearm (mfg. mid-1960s).

Between 1976-1985 approx. 2,000 Belgian 12 ga. A-5 Mags. were imported into the U.S. These late models can be differentiated by serialization - also, slight premiums may be asked.

* ***Auto-5 Mag. Miroku*** – 12 or 20 ga., VR barrel with Invector choke system until 1993, Invector Plus choking became standard 1994, 8 1/2 - 9 lbs. Disc. 1997.

$1,025 $900 $750 $675 $595 $525 $475

Last MSR was $866.

Add 30% for 20 ga. Subtract 10% without Invector chokes.

AUTO-5 STALKER – 12 ga. only, 2 3/4 (Light-12) or 3 (Mag. Stalker) in. chamber, 22 (Light-12 only), 26, 28, 30, or 32 (Mag. only) in. VR barrel with Invector chokes, black matte finish graphite-fiberglass stock and forearm, matte finished metal, recoil pad, 8 lbs. 1 oz. - 8 lbs. 13 oz. Mfg. by Miroku 1992-1997.

$975 $825 $675 $625 $550 $525 $450

Last MSR was $840.

Add approx. $100 for Mag. Stalker.

AUTO-5 BUCK SPECIAL – 12, 16, or 20 ga., included Lightweight, Standardweight, and Magnum Models, 24 in. barrel, slug bore, adj. sight, optional sling studs and sling, between 1985-88, Buck Special barrels were available at additional cost. Introduced in 1962, mfg. by F.N. until 1976, and by Miroku from 1976-1984, and again in 1989.

* ***Auto-5 Buck Special FN Mfg. 12 Ga.***

$1,375 $1,200 $1,000 $925 $825 $725 $625

Add 75% for Sweet 16 model.

Add 60% for 20 ga. Add 50% for Standard Weight 16 ga.

This model was made in Light 12, Standard 12, 3 in. Mag. 12, Sweet 16, Standard 16, Lightweight 20 and Lightweight 20 Mag. (new 1967) configurations.

MSR	100%	98%	95%	90%	80%	70%	60%

* *Auto-5 Buck Special Miroku Model* – mfg. 1989-97.

        $1,050 $925 $775 $700 $625 $575 $525

Last MSR was $829.

AUTO-5 SKEET – 12, 16, or 20 ga., Lightweight models with 26 or 28 in. skeet bored, vent. rib barrel. Pre 1976 mfg. by F.N., 1976-1983 mfg. by Miroku.

* *Auto-5 Skeet FN Mfg.*

        $1,325 $1,150 $950 $875 $775 $675 $575

Add 20% for vent. rib.
Add 60% for 20 ga.

* *Auto-5 Skeet Miroku Model*

        $1,000 $895 $750 $675 $600 $550 $500

Add 30% for 20 ga.

AUTO-5 TRAP MODEL – 12 ga. only, similar to Standard, 30 in. full vent. rib barrel, 8 1/2 lbs., mfg. by FN until 1970.

        $1,300 $1,125 $925 $850 $750 $650 $550

AUTO-5 SWEET 16 – 16 ga., 2 9/16 in. chamber from 1937-1940, and 2 3/4 in. chamber from 1947-1975, similar configuration to Lightweight, 12 and 20 ga., gold plated trigger, 10 oz. lighter than Standardweight Model 16 ga., 1937-1940 mfg. Sweet Sixteens were available in pre-war Grades I, III, and IV. Mfg. 1937-1975 by F.N.

	100%	98%	95%	90%	80%	70%	60%
Plain Barrel	$1,700	$1,400	$1,200	$1,100	$1,000	$875	$800
Solid Matte Rib	$2,500	$2,100	$1,625	$1,425	$1,275	$1,175	$1,075
Vent. Rib	$2,400	$2,000	$1,525	$1,325	$1,175	$1,075	$975

Add 15% for round knob, NIB condition.
Add 15% for blonde stock and forearm (mfg. mid-1960s).
Subtract 20% for front safety.
Subtract 20% for 2 9/16 in. chamber.

* *Auto-5 Sweet 16 Miroku* – 16 ga. only, similar to original Belgian Sweet 16, VR, Invector choke standard. Mfg. 1987-92.

        $1,625 $1,325 $1,175 $1,075 $975 $825 $750

Last MSR was $720.

AUTO-5 TWO MILLIONTH COMMEMORATIVE – 12 ga., 2,500 mfg., 1971-74 mfg., special walnut, engraving, high-lustre bluing, cased with Browning book. Issue price was $550-$700, serial range 2,000,000-1 to 2,000,000-2,500.

        $2,950 $2,250 $1,750 N/A N/A N/A N/A

Subtract 25%-40% for guns damaged from salt wood problems, depending on salt wood damage.

AUTO-5 POLICE CONTRACT – 12 ga. only, 5 or 8 (factory extended) shot mag., black enamel finish on receiver and barrel, can be recognized by the European "POL" police markings below serial number, 24 in.

MSR	100%	98%	95%	90%	80%	70%	60%

barrel. Imported in limited quantities during 1999.

5 shot mag.	N/A	$700	$650	$625	$575	$525	$500
8 shot mag.	N/A	$1,300	$1,095	$995	$895	$850	$750

A-5 CLASSIC SERIES - 12 ga., 5,000 mfg. in Classic model, 500 mfg. in Gold Classic. Both editions feature game scenes, John M. Browning's profile, and other inscriptions, special silver grey finished receiver. Introduced 1984.

* *A-5 Gold Classic Model* - features 4 gold inlays depicting duck hunting scenes, plus head silhouette of John Browning. 500 mfg. beginning 1986 with inventory depleted during 1989.

$9,950	$7,450	$5,200	N/A	N/A	N/A	N/A

Last MSR was $6,500.

* *A-5 Classic Model* - no inlays. Factory inventories were depleted in 1987.

$2,850	$2,000	$1,750	N/A	N/A	N/A	N/A

Last MSR was $1,260.

FN CENTENARY EDITION - 12 or 16 ga., limited production mfg. 1989 to commemorate the 100th anniversary of FN, available for worldwide FN sales and not limited to Browning.

* *FN Centenary Edition 12 ga.* - 2 3/4 in. chamber, 28 in. VR barrel, Mod. choke, more engraving than a standard A-5, gold relief FN logo on left side of receiver, high grade French walnut flat knob pistol grip stock, 20 LPI checkering, ser. no. CENT 211 001 - 100, 100 mfg.

$2,900	$2,200	$1,500	N/A	N/A	N/A	N/A

Last MSR was $2,100.

* *FN Centenary Edition 16 ga.* - 2 3/4 in. chamber, 26 in. VR barrel, Mod. choke, ornate engraving with gold relief inlay (24 Kt.), commemorative FN medallion on left side of receiver, high grade French walnut flat knob pistol grip stock, 25 LPI checkering, ser. no. CENT 221 001 - 010, 10 mfg.

$8,000	$6,250	$4,750	N/A	N/A	N/A	N/A

Last MSR was $6,855.

A-5 BCA COMMEMORATIVE - 12 ga., 3 in. Mag., round knob, Belgian mfg., 1984 issue price was $595.

$1,550	$1,275	$1,000	N/A	N/A	N/A	N/A

A-5 DU 50TH ANNIVERSARY

* *A-5 DU Light 12* - 12 ga. only, 5,500 mfg. in 1987 only for Ducks Unlimited chapters throughout North America.

$2,100	$1,700	$1,200	N/A	N/A	N/A	N/A

* *A-5 DU Sweet 16* - 16 ga. only, companion 1988-89 DU auction gun, 4,500 mfg. 1988 only.

$2,450	$2,050	$1,350	N/A	N/A	N/A	N/A

SHOTGUNS: SEMI-AUTO, DOUBLE AUTO MODELS

MSR	100%	98%	95%	90%	80%	70%	60%

* ***A-5 DU Light 20*** – 20 ga. only, companion 1990 DU auction gun, 4,500 mfg. 1990 only.

	$2,200	$1,800	$1,350	N/A	N/A	N/A	N/A

A-5 FINAL TRIBUTE – 12 ga. only, limited edition of 1,000 guns, features elaborate engraving on white receiver, the last of the A-5 semi-autos. Mfg. 1999 only, sellout occurred during 2000.

	$3,200	$2,700	$2,300	N/A	N/A	N/A	N/A

Last MSR was $1,330.

A5 HUNTER – 12 ga. only, 3 in. chamber, recoil operated humpback design with fixed barrel featuring Kinematic Drive System, aluminum receiver, bi-tone black anodized finish, 26, 28, or 30 in. VR barrel with 3 Invector-DS choke tubes, checkered gloss finish walnut stock with Inflex II recoil pad and forearm, speed loading/unloading, ergonomic bolt latch, includes extra stock spacers and ABS case, approx. 6 3/4 lbs. New 2012.

MSR $1,560	$1,375	$1,150	$925	$800	$675	$550	$495

A5 STALKER – 12 ga., similar to A5 Hunter, except has Dura-Touch armor coated black composite stock and forearm with textured gripping surfaces, matte black metal finish, approx. 7 1/4 lbs. New 2012.

MSR $1,400	$1,225	$1,025	$875	$750	$650	$550	$450

A5 CAMO – 12 ga., similar to A5 Stalker, except has 100% Mossy Oak Duck Blind (disc. 2012), Mossy Oak Break-Up Infinity, or Mossy Oak Shadow Grass Blades (new 2013) camo coverage, approx. 7 1/4 lbs. New 2012.

MSR $1,560	$1,375	$1,150	$925	$800	$675	$550	$495

SHOTGUNS: SEMI-AUTO, DOUBLE AUTO MODELS

Add 10% for NIB condition on the following models.

STANDARD DOUBLE AUTO – 12 ga. only, 2 shot, 26, 28, or 30 in. barrel, various chokes, checkered pistol grip stock and forearm, blued steel receiver, approx. 7 1/2 lbs. Mfg. 1952-1960.

	$825	$725	$550	$475	$375	$325	$300
Vent. or Raised Rib	$975	$850	$675	$600	$475	$375	$325

LIGHTWEIGHT DOUBLE AUTO – similar to Standard Model, except has hiduminum (aircraft alloy) frame, anodized in velvet grey, dragon black, autumn brown, or forest green, approx. 6 3/4 lbs. Approx. 67,000 (all variations) mfg. 1952-1956.

	$875	$750	$550	$475	$375	$325	$275
Vent. or Raised Rib	$1,000	$875	$675	$600	$475	$375	$325

Add 25% for autumn brown or forest green receiver.
Add 100%+ for all other colors (rare, only a few mfg.).

MSR	100%	98%	95%	90%	80%	70%	60%

TWELVETTE DOUBLE AUTO – similar to Lightweight model, except has "Twelvette" stamped above loading port. Mfg. 1957-1971.

	$875	$750	$550	$475	$375	$325	$275
Vent. or Raised Rib	$1,000	$875	$675	$600	$425	$375	$325

Add 25% for autumn brown or forest green receiver.
Add 100%+ for all other colors (rare, only a few mfg.).

TWENTYWEIGHT DOUBLE AUTO – similar to Twelvette, but 3/4 pound lighter, jet black finish with engraving accented with gold foil, "Twentyweight" stamped above loading port, 26 1/2 in. barrel only. Mfg. 1957-1971.

	$950	$825	$625	$550	$450	$400	$300
Vent. Rib	$1,050	$925	$725	$650	$525	$475	$400

SHOTGUNS: SEMI-AUTO, MISC. - RECENT MFG.

BROWNING CHOKES AND THEIR CODES (ON REAR LEFT-SIDE OF BARREL)

* designates full choke (F).

*- designates improved modified choke (IM).

** designates modified choke (M).

**- designates improved cylinder choke (IC).

**$ designates skeet (SK).

*** designates cylinder bore (CYL).

Add $195-$375 per additional barrel, depending on the condition and configuration.

B/2000 STANDARD – 12 or 20 ga. (new 1975), 2 3/4 in. chamber, 26, 28, or 30 in. VR barrel, various chokes, gas operated, checkered pistol grip stock, Belgian manufactured but assembled in Portugal, approx. 115,000 imported (approx. 95,000 in 12 ga., and 20,000 in 20 ga.) into the U.S. between 1974-1983.

$495	$425	$375	$350	$325	$300	$275

Last MSR was $475.

Add 20% for 20 ga.

This model could be converted to accept 3 in. Mag. shotshells by simply installing a barrel chambered for 3 in. shells. Even though production on this model ceased in 1979, assembly and sales were not discontinued until 1983.

B/2000 MAGNUM – similar to B/2000 Auto Shotgun, except with 3 in. chambered barrel (all receivers were the same), recoil pad, vent. rib.

$495	$425	$375	$350	$325	$300	$275

B/2000 SKEET – similar to Standard, with 26 in. skeet bored barrel, floating vent. rib, skeet stock, pad.

$450	$395	$350	$325	$300	$275	$250

SHOTGUNS: SEMI-AUTO, MISC. - RECENT MFG.

MSR	100%	98%	95%	90%	80%	70%	60%

B/2000 TRAP – similar to Standard, with 30 or 32 in. barrel bored F or IM, floating rib, Monte Carlo trap stock.

	$450	$395	$350	$325	$300	$275	$250

B/2000 BUCK SPECIAL – 12 or 20 ga., rifle sights on 24 in. barrel.

	$450	$395	$350	$325	$300	$275	$250

1976 CANADIAN OLYMPICS B2000 – 12 ga., 100 manufactured in 1976 for Canadian sales only, high polish blue with multiple gold inlays including Olympic crest, 30 in. barrel, cased. Issue price was $1,295.

	$1,495	$1,095	$850	N/A	N/A	N/A	N/A

MODEL B-80 – 12 or 20 ga., offers 2 3/4 or 3 in. capability by changing barrel, gas operation, 4 shot, hunting models use choice of steel or aluminum receiver, anodized aluminum was used in the Superlight (12 ga. mfg. 1984 only), 6 to 8 lbs. 1 oz. Buck special disc. 1984. Components manufactured by Beretta of Italy and finished and assembled at FN's plant in Portugal. Mfg. 1981-late 1988, final inventory was sold in 1991. Invector chokes became standard in 1985.

	$450	$375	$325	$295	$275	$250	$230

Last MSR was $562.

Add 10% for Invector chokes.

Steel frames were reintroduced into production again in 1988.

* ***Model B-80 Upland Special*** – 12 or 20 ga., 2 3/4 in. chamber, 22 in. vent. rib barrel, straight grip stock, Invector chokes. Mfg. 1986-88.

	$525	$450	$395	$350	$325	$300	$275

Last MSR was $562.

MODEL B 80 DU COMMEMORATIVE – mfg. for American DU Chapters (The Plains and others), price fluctuates greatly as collector support is sometimes limited. Unless new, this model's values approximate those of the regular Model B-80. If NIB, values recently have been in the $795-$995 range.

A-500 (R) HUNTING – 12 ga. only, 3 in. chamber, new design utilizing short recoil system with a four-lug rotary bolt design, capable of shooting all 12 gauge loads interchangeably, magazine cut-off, 26, 28, or 30 in. VR barrel with Invector chokes standard, 24 in. barrel on Buck Special (fixed choke), high polished blue finish with red accents on receiver sides, gold trigger, checkered semi-pistol grip walnut stock with vent recoil pad, 7 lbs. 11 oz. - 8 lbs. 1 oz. Mfg. 1987-1993.

	$525	$450	$395	$350	$325	$300	$275

Last MSR was $56

Add $33 for Buck Special variation (Invector chokes).

This model features fewer moving parts than many other semi-auto shotguns due to the short recoil operating system. From 1987-90 this model was the Model A-500 - R suffix was added in 1991.

SHOTGUNS: SEMI-AUTO, MISC. - RECENT MFG.

MSR	100%	98%	95%	90%	80%	70%	60%

A-500G HUNTING – similar to A-500, except is gas operated, distinguishable by "A-500G" in gold accents on receiver, capable of shooting all 2 3/4 or 3 in. shells interchangeably, approx. 8 lbs. Mfg. 1990-93.

$575 $495 $425 $375 $340 $325 $295

Last MSR was $653.

A Buck Special variation was mfg. until 1992. No premiums currently exist.

* ***A-500G Sporting Clays*** – 12 ga. only, Sporting Clays variation with 30 in. VR barrel, 8 lbs. 2 oz. Mfg. 1992-93.

$575 $495 $425 $375 $340 $325 $295

Last MSR was $653.

GOLD 3 IN. HUNTER – 12 or 20 ga., 3 in. chamber, self-cleaning piston rod gas action with self-regulation, alloy receiver with non-glare black finish and "Gold Hunter" on receiver side, 26, 28, or 30 (12 ga. only, disc. 2001) in. VR Invector Plus (12 ga. only) or Invector (20 ga. only) choked barrel with high polish bluing, cross-bolt safety, gloss finish checkered walnut stock and forearm with recoil pad (vent on 12 ga.), includes 3 choke tubes, 6 lbs. 12 oz. - 7 lbs. 10 oz. Parts mfg. in Belgium and final assembly in Portugal. Mfg. 1994-2005.

$825 $575 $450 $375 $300 $275 $250

Last MSR was $1,025.

Do not use 12 ga. 3 1/2 in. chambered barrels on either a 2 3/4 or 3 in. receiver, or vice versa.

* ***Gold Superlite Hunter*** – 12 or 20 ga., similar to Gold 3 in. Hunter, except has new alloy magazine, "Gold SL" on receiver sides, 6 lbs. 7 oz. - 7 lbs., 15 oz. Mfg. 2006-2008.

$975 $750 $535 $425 $325 $275 $250

Last MSR was $1,161.

GOLD 3 1/2 IN. HUNTER – 12 ga., 3 1/2 in. chamber, 24 (mfg. 2002-2003), 26, 28, or 30 (disc. 2003) in. VR barrel with Invector Plus choking, otherwise similar to Gold Hunter, 3-4 shot mag., approx. 7 3/4 lbs. Mfg. 1998-2005.

$985 $725 $600 $550 $450 $375 $335

Last MSR was $1,190.

* ***Gold 3 1/2 In. Superlite Hunter*** – 12 ga., similar to Gold 3 1/2 in. Hunter, except has new alloy magazine, "Gold SL" engraved on receiver sides, approx. 7 1/4 lbs. Mfg. 2006-2007.

$1,075 $900 $700 $525 $425 $350 $300

Last MSR was $1,279.

* ***Gold 3 1/2 In. Turkey/Waterfowl Hunter*** – similar to Gold 3 1/2 in. Hunter, full coverage (including barrel) Mossy Oak Break-Up camo finish, 24 in. VR barrel with extra full choke tube, 7 1/4 lbs. Mfg. 1999-2000.

$875 $695 $600 $500 $425 $375 $335

Last MSR was $1,038.

MSR	100%	98%	95%	90%	80%	70%	60%

* **Gold 3 1/2 In. NWTF Mossy Oak Break-Up** – 12 ga. only, 3 1/2 in. chamber, 24 in. VR barrel with 4 choke tubes and Hi-Viz sight, full coverage Mossy Oak Break-Up camo pattern, Dura-Touch armor coating became standard 2003, 7 1/4 lbs. Mfg. 2001-2002.

    $875 $695 $600 $525 $450 $385 $335

    Last MSR was $1,221.

* **Gold 3 1/2 In. Mossy Oak New Break-Up/New Shadow Grass** – similar to Gold 3 1/2 in. Hunter, choice of full coverage (including barrel) Mossy Oak Break-Up, New Break-Up (standard beginning 2004) or Shadow Grass camo finish, 24 (Mossy Oak Break-Up only, disc. 2001), 26 (Mossy Oak Shadow Grass only), or 28 (Mossy Oak Shadow Grass only) in. VR back-bored barrel with Invector Plus choke tubes, Dura-Touch armor coating became standard 2003, approx. 7 1/2 lbs. Mfg. 1999-2007.

    $900 $750 $650 $600 $500 $400 $350

    Last MSR was $1,359.

* **Gold 3 1/2 In. Mossy Oak Duck Blind** – 12 ga. only, similar to Gold Mossy Oak New Break-Up, except has Mossy Oak Duck Blind camo coverage. Mfg. 2007.

    $900 $750 $650 $600 $500 $400 $350

    Last MSR was $1,359.

* **Gold 3 1/2 In. NWTF Ultimate Turkey Gun** – 12 ga. only, similar to Gold NWTF Mossy Oak New Break-Up, except has extended full strut turkey choke tube and neoprene sling, 7 1/4 lbs. Mfg. 2003-2007.

    $1,100 $900 $725 $675 $600 $500 $450

    Last MSR was $1,469.

GOLD FIELD HUNTER (CLASSIC) – similar to Gold Hunter, except has semi-hump back receiver design, magazine cutoff, adj. comb, and satin finished wood, 26 or 28 in. VR barrel. Mfg. 1999-2005.

$800 $575 $450 $375 $300 $275 $250

Last MSR was $1,025.

This model was available through Full-line and Medallion dealers only.

* **Gold Superlite Field Hunter** – 12 or 20 ga., similar to Gold 3 in. Superlite Hunter, except is semi-humpback design, approx. 6 1/2 - 7 lbs. Mfg. 2006-2007.

    $1,025 $725 $525 $400 $300 $275 $250

    Last MSR was $1,105.

* **Gold Turkey/Waterfowl Hunter Camo** – similar to Gold Hunter, full coverage (including barrel) Mossy Oak Break-Up camo finish, 24 in. VR barrel with Hi-Viz sights and extra full choke tube, 7 lbs. Mfg. 1999-2000.

    $750 $500 $400 $350 $295 $275 $250

    Last MSR was $867.

SHOTGUNS: SEMI-AUTO, MISC. - RECENT MFG.

MSR	100%	98%	95%	90%	80%	70%	60%

* *Gold Mossy Oak New Break-Up/Shadow Grass* – 12 ga., similar to Gold 3 in. Hunter, choice of full coverage (including barrel) Mossy Oak New Break-Up or New Shadow Grass camo finish (New became standard in 2004), 24 (Mossy Oak Break-Up only, disc. 2004), 26, or 28 in. VR back-bored barrel with Invector Plus choke tubes, Dura-Touch armor coating became standard 2003, approx. 7 1/2 - 7 3/4 lbs. Mfg. 1999-2007.

$850 $700 $525 $450 $325 $285 $250

Last MSR was $1,150.

* *Gold Mossy Oak Duck Blind* – 12 ga. only, similar to Gold Mossy Oak New Break-Up, except has Mossy Oak Duck Blind camo coverage. Mfg. 2007.

$850 $700 $525 $450 $325 $285 $250

Last MSR was $1,150.

* *Gold NWTF Mossy Oak New Break-Up* – 12 ga. only, 3 in. chamber, drilled and tapped receiver, 24 in. VR barrel with 4 choke tubes and Hi-Viz sight, full coverage Mossy Oak New Break-up camo pattern, Dura-Touch armor coating became standard 2003, 7 lbs. Mfg. 2001-2007.

$850 $700 $575 $450 $375 $300 $250

Last MSR was $1,226.

* *Gold Classic High Grade Hunter* – 12 (disc. 2001) or 20 ga. (new 2002), similar to Gold Classic Hunter, except has satin nickel finished receiver featuring multiple gold inlays with ducks, pheasants, and dogs (12 ga.) or doves and quail (20 ga.) and light scroll engraving, deluxe checkered gloss finished walnut stock and forearm, 28 in. barrel only, 6 lbs. 14 oz. Mfg. 1999-2004.

$1,575 $1,250 $1,050 $875 $725 $625 $550

Last MSR was $1,838.

This model was available through Full-line and Medallion dealers only.

GOLD MICRO – 20 ga. only, 3 in. chamber, 24 (new 2002) or 26 in. VR barrel, features shorter stock (13 7/8 LOP) and lighter weight, 6 lbs., 10 oz. Mfg. 2001-2005.

$775 $575 $450 $375 $300 $275 $250

Last MSR was $1,025.

* *Gold Superlite Micro* – 20 ga. only, 3 in. chamber, 26 in. VR barrel, features shorter stock (13 7/8 LOP) and lighter weight, 6 lbs., 3 oz. Mfg. 2006-2007.

$850 $650 $525 $400 $300 $275 $250

Last MSR was $1,105.

GOLD UPLAND SPECIAL – 12 or 20 ga., 3 in. chamber, 24 or 26 (20 ga. only) in. VR barrel, checkered satin finished straight grip stock, 6 3/4 (20 ga.) or 7 lbs. Mfg. 2001-2005.

$775 $575 $450 $375 $300 $275 $250

Last MSR was $1,025.

SHOTGUNS: SEMI-AUTO, MISC. - RECENT MFG.

MSR	100%	98%	95%	90%	80%	70%	60%

GOLD FUSION – 12 or 20 (new 2002) ga., 3 in. chamber, 26, 28, or 30 (12 ga. only, new 2002) in. wide profile lightweight VR barrel with 5 Invector Plus chokes and Hi-Viz Pro-Comp sight system, checkered oil finished Turkish walnut stock and forearm, shim adj. stock system, alloy mag. tube, includes hardshell case, 6.25 - 7 lbs. Mfg. 2001-2007.

$900 $650 $550 $400 $350 $295 $260

Last MSR was $1,152.

* *Gold Fusion High Grade* – 12 or 20 ga., 3 in. chamber, silver nitride receiver with engraving and gold inlays (mallards and lab on 12 ga., quail and pointer on 20 ga.), 26, 28, or 30 in. barrel with five interchangeable Invector Plus chokes, high grade Turkish walnut stock and forearm, shim adj. stock system with 1/4 in. adj. range, Hi-Viz TriComp sight system, includes hard case, 6 lbs., 6 oz. - 7 lbs. Mfg. 2005-2007.

$1,825 $1,300 $1,125 $950 $850 $725 $625

Last MSR was $2,137

GOLD EVOLVE – 12 ga. only, 3 in. chamber, features updated engraved receiver, magazine cap, and canted VR design, 26, 28, or 30 in. barrel, includes shim adj. stock system, newly designed checkered satin finished walnut stock and forearm, alloy mag. tube, Hi-Viz Pro-Comp sight system, approx. 7 lbs. Mfg. 2004-2007.

$900 $650 $525 $425 $335 $285 $250

Last MSR was $1,220

* *Gold Evolve Sporting* – 12 ga. only, similar to Gold Evolve, except has 2 3/4 in. chamber, 28 or 30 in. ported barrel, gold receiver accents, includes case, approx. 7 lbs. Mfg. 2006-2007.

$950 $700 $550 $450 $350 $300 $250

Last MSR was $1,287

Subtract 10% for 28 in. barrel on used guns.

GOLD DEER HUNTER – 12 or 20 (new 2001) ga., 3 in. chamber, 22 in. barrel with choice of 5 in. rifled Invector choke (disc. 1998) or rifled plain barrel, checkered satin finished stock and forearm, cantilevered scope mount, sling swivels, 6 3/4 (20 ga.) or 7 3/4 lbs. Mfg. 1997-2007.

$900 $650 $525 $400 $325 $285 $250

Last MSR was $1,15

Subtract approx. 10% for rifled choke tube (disc. 1998).

* *Gold Deer Hunter with Mossy Oak Break-Up Camo* – 12 ga., similar to Gold Deer Hunter, except has full Mossy Oak Break-Up or New Break Up (standard 2004) camo coverage, rifled barrel standard. Mfg. 1999-2007.

$950 $750 $625 $550 $450 $365 $335

Last MSR was $1,24

MSR	100%	98%	95%	90%	80%	70%	60%

GOLD 3 IN. STALKER – 12 ga., similar to Gold Hunter (3 in. chamber), except has checkered black composite stock and forearm with sling swivels, approx. 7 3/8 lbs. Mfg. 1998-2007.

	$800	$625	$475	$375	$300	$275	$250

Last MSR was $1,001.

* *Gold 3 In. Stalker Field (Classic)* – similar to Gold Stalker, except has semi-hump back receiver design, magazine cutoff and adj. comb, 26 or 28 in. VR barrel. Mfg. 1999-2007.

	$800	$625	$475	$375	$300	$275	$250

Last MSR was $1,001.

This model was available through Full-line and Medallion dealers only.

* *Gold 3 In. Turkey/Waterfowl Stalker* – similar to Gold Stalker, except has 24 in. VR barrel with extra full choke tube, Hi-Viz sights, matte non-glare wood and finish, 7 lbs. Mfg. 1999-2000.

	$650	$500	$400	$350	$300	$275	$250

Last MSR was $850.

* *Gold 3 In. NWTF Stalker* – 12 ga. only, 3 in. chamber, 24 in. VR barrel with 3 choke tubes and Hi-Viz sight, 7 lbs. Mfg. 2001-2002.

	$635	$475	$415	$350	$300	$275	$250

Last MSR was $744.

* *Gold 3 In. Rifled Deer Stalker* – 12 ga. only, 22 in. rifled barrel, cantilevered scope mount, sling swivels, 7 3/4 lbs. Mfg. 1997-2007.

	$850	$625	$475	$400	$340	$300	$265

Last MSR was $1,108.

GOLD 3 1/2 IN. STALKER – 12 ga., 3 1/2 in. chamber, 26, 28, or 30 (disc. 2002) in. VR barrel with Invector Plus choking, otherwise similar to Gold Stalker, 3-4 shot mag., approx. 7 lbs. 10 oz. Mfg. 1998-2007.

	$985	$725	$625	$525	$425	$375	$335

Last MSR was $1,171.

* *Gold 3 1/2 In. Turkey/Waterfowl Stalker* – similar to Gold 3 1/2 Stalker, except has 24 in. VR barrel with extra full choke tube, matte non-glare wood and finish, 7 1/4 lbs. Mfg. 1999-2000.

	$800	$650	$595	$500	$420	$375	$335

Last MSR was $1,022.

GOLD SPORTING CLAYS – 12 ga. only, similar specs as the Gold Hunter, except has 2 3/4 in. chamber, 28 or 30 in. ported barrel with Invector Plus choking, gloss finished walnut stock and forearm, adj. stock shims, Hi-Viz front sight, approx. 7 3/4 lbs. Mfg. 1996-2008.

	$1,000	$850	$700	$600	$500	$400	$350

Last MSR was $1,184.

This model was supplied standard with 2 interchangeable gas pistons for light or heavy loads.

MSR	100%	98%	95%	90%	80%	70%	60%

* ***Gold Golden Clays*** – 12 ga. only, 2 3/4 in. chamber, engraved coin finished alloy receiver with gold accents and game birds, new scroll motif was introduced during 2005, deluxe satin finished checkered walnut stock and forearm, 28 or 30 in. VR ported barrel with Hi-Viz Tri-Comp front sight and mid-bead, approx. 7 3/4 lbs. Mfg. 1999-2008.

$1,650 $1,225 $950 $850 $750 $650 $550

Last MSR was $1,941

Subtract approx. 10% if with older engraving motif (non-scroll, disc. 2004).

* ***Gold Sporting Ladies/Youth*** – similar to Gold Sporting Clays, except has shorter 13 1/2 in. LOP stock, 28 in. barrel only, approx. 7 1/2 lbs. Mfg. 1999-2008.

$1,000 $850 $700 $600 $500 $400 $350

Last MSR was $1,184

» ***Gold Golden Clays Ladies/Youth*** – similar to Gold Sporting Ladies/Youth, except features coin finished receiver with "golden clays" rose motif and gold enhancements, satin finished select walnut stock and forearm. Mfg. 2005-2007.

$1,575 $1,175 $925 $850 $750 $650 $550

Last MSR was $1,848

GOLD NRA SPORTING – 12 ga. only, 2 3/4 in. chamber, similar to Gold Sporting Clays, except has NRA logo/banner on left side of receiver, approx. 7 3/4 lbs. Mfg. 2006-2007.

$950 $800 $650 $550 $450 $400 $350

Last MSR was $1,16

This model was supplied standard with 2 interchangeable gas pistons for light or heavy loads.

BSA 10 – while advertised, this gun had its model nomenclature changed to the Gold 10 Ga. before mfg. started.

GOLD LIGHT 10 GA. 3 1/2 IN. HUNTER/STALKER – 10 ga. Mag., 1/2 in. chamber, short stroke self-cleaning gas action, 4 shot mag, steel (disc. 2000) or aluminum (new 2001) receiver, choice of high polish (Hunter Model, disc. 2000), dull finish (Stalker Model, disc. 199, reintroduced 2000) bluing, 24 (NWTF Model only with Break-Up, new 2001), 26, 28, or 30 (disc. 2001) in. VR standard Invector choke barrel available with either high-gloss checkered walnut (Hunter, disc. 200 stock/forearm, matte black fiberglass (Stalker, disc. 1998, reintroduced 2000-2003) stock/forearm, or choice of 100% camo treatment Shadow Grass (disc. 2003), Break-Up (mfg. 2001-2003), New Shadow Grass (mfg. 2005-2008), Mossy Oak Duck Blind (new 2007), New Break-Up (mfg. 2004-2009), Break-Up Infinity (new 2010), or Mossy Oak Shadow Grass Blades (new 2013), vent. recoil pad, Dura-Tou armor coating became standard for camo finishes during 2003, appro

SHOTGUNS: SEMI-AUTO, MISC. - RECENT MFG.

MSR	100%	98%	95%	90%	80%	70%	60%

9 1/2 lbs. (aluminum receiver) or 10 lbs. 10 oz. (steel receiver, disc. 2000), mfg. by Miroku, Japan. New 1994.

MSR $1,740 $1,425 $1,050 $875 $775 $675 $575 $500

Add $130 for the NWTF Model with Mossy Oak New Break-Up.
Add 10% for extra 24 in. turkey barrel.
Subtract approx. 10% for matte black fiberglass stock and forearm.
Subtract 15% for steel receiver.

During 1999-2001, this model was packaged to include an extra 24 in. turkey barrel.

SILVER HUNTER – 12 or 20 ga., 3 in. chamber, semi-humpback design, silver finished aluminum alloy receiver, gas operating system similar to Gold Hunter, 26, 28, or 30 in. VR barrel with three Invector-Plus choke tubes, checkered satin finished stock and forearm with vent. recoil pad, includes three choke tubes, approx. 6 1/4 - 7 1/2 lbs. New 2006.

MSR $1,180 $1,025 $825 $650 $575 $495 $425 $375

SILVER HUNTER MICRO MIDAS – 12 or 20 ga., similar to Silver Hunter, except has 24 or 26 in. VR barrel and 13 in. LOP, approx. 6 - 7 3/8 lbs. New 2011.

MSR $1,180 $1,025 $825 $650 $575 $495 $425 $375

SILVER MICRO – 20 ga., 3 in. chamber, 26 in. VR barrel, lightweight aluminum alloy receiver, semi-humpback design, satin finished walnut stock and forearm, compact dimensions for smaller shooters, three Invector Plus choke tubes, 6 lbs., 3 oz. New 2008.

MSR $1,180 $1,025 $825 $650 $575 $495 $425 $375

SILVER SPORTING – 12 ga. only, 2 3/4 in. chamber, 28 or 30 in. ported barrel with flush choke tubes, adj. satin finished walnut stock with Pachmayr Decelerator recoil pad, 7 1/2 lbs. New 2009.

MSR $1,300 $1,100 $925 $775 $675 $575 $475 $425

SILVER SPORTING MICRO – 12 ga., 2 3/4 in. chamber, 28 in. VR ported barrel, lightweight aluminum alloy receiver, semi-humpback design, satin finished walnut stock and forearm, features 13 3/4 in. LOP adj. in 1/4 in. increments using three included adj. spacers, premium Pachmayr Decelerator pad, three Invector Plus chokes, 7 lbs. New 2008.

MSR $1,300 $1,100 $925 $775 $675 $575 $475 $425

SILVER LIGHTNING – 12 ga., 3 in. chamber, 26 or 28 in. VR barrel, silver finished aluminum alloy receiver, semi-humpback design, gloss finished Lightning style walnut stock, three Invector Plus choke tubes, approx. 7 1/2 lbs. New 2008.

MSR $1,180 $1,025 $825 $650 $575 $495 $425 $375

This model is available only through Browning Full Line and Medallion dealers.

MSR	100%	98%	95%	90%	80%	70%	60%

SILVER NWTF MOSSY OAK CAMO – 12 ga., 3 in. chamber, 24 in. VR barrel, aluminum alloy receiver, composite stock and forearm with Dura-Touch Armor coating and 100% Mossy Oak New Break-Up (disc. 2009) or Break Up Infinity (new 2010) camo treatment, NWTF logo, Hi-Viz 4 in 1 fiber optic sight, three Invector Plus choke tubes, 7 lbs. Mfg. 2008-2012.

$1,175 $1,000 $850 $675 $550 $500 $450

Last MSR was $1,360.

SILVER RIFLED DEER MOSSY OAK CAMO – 12 or 20 (new 2009) ga., 3 in. chamber, 22 in. rifled deer barrel, aluminum alloy receiver, composite stock and forearm with Dura-Touch Armor coating and 100% Mossy Oak New Break-Up (disc. 2009) or Break-Up Infinity (new 2009) camo treatment, cantilever scope mount, 7 lbs., 12 oz. New 2008.

MSR $1,420 $1,220 $1,040 $885 $750 $600 $500 $400

SILVER RIFLED DEER STALKER/SATIN – 12 or 20 ga., 3 in. chamber, 22 in. rifled deer barrel, choice of non-glare matte black finish composite stock and forearm (Stalker) or satin finished walnut stock with Dura-Touch Armor coating, cantilever scope mount, 7 lbs. 12 oz. New 2008.

MSR $1,280 $1,100 $875 $750 $650 $525 $475 $425

Add $60 for satin finished walnut stock and forearm with matte grey finished receiver (20 ga.).

SILVER 3 1/2 IN. HUNTER/STALKER – 12 ga. only, 26 or 28 in. VR barrel, semi-humpback design, choice of silver metal (Silver Hunter) or matte black (Silver Stalker) metal finish, choice of wood (Silver Hunter) or black composite (Silver Stalker) stock and forearm, includes three choke tubes, approx. 7 1/2 lbs. New 2006.

MSR $1,200 $1,050 $850 $725 $625 $525 $475 $425

Add $140 for satin finished walnut stock and forearm (Silver Hunter).

* *Silver 3 1/2 In. Camo* – 12 ga. only, similar to Silver 3 1/2 In. Hunter/Stalker, except has choice of 100% Mossy Oak New Break-Up (disc 2009), Break-Up Infinity (new 2010), Mossy Oak Duck Blind (mfg. 2007-disc.), New Shadowgrass (mfg. 2006 only), Mossy Oak Shadow Grass Blades (new 2013) camo finish, 26 or 28 in. VR barrel with 3 Invector Plus chokes, 7 1/2 lbs. New 2006.

MSR $1,340 $1,150 $950 $825 $725 $625 $495 $425

SILVER 3 1/2 IN. LIGHTNING – 12 ga., similar to Silver Lightning 3 In. except has 3 1/2 in. chamber., 26 or 28 in. VR barrel with 3 Invector Plus choke tubes. New 2008.

MSR $1,360 $1,125 $850 $750 $625 $550 $500 $450

This model is available only through Browning Full Line and Medallion dealers.

SILVER 3 1/2 IN. NWTF MOSSY OAK CAMO – 12 ga., 3 1/2 in. chamber, 24 in. barrel, aluminum alloy receiver, composite stock and forearm

MSR	100%	98%	95%	90%	80%	70%	60%

with Dura-Touch Armor coating and 100% Mossy Oak New Break-Up or Break-Up Infinity (new 2009) camo treatment, NWTF logo, Hi-Viz 4 in 1 fiber optic sight, three Invector Plus choke tubes, 7 1/4 lbs. New 2008.

| MSR $1,540 | $1,325 | $1,125 | $950 | $800 | $675 | $500 | $425 |

MAXUS HUNTER 3 IN. – 12 ga., 3 in. chamber, 26, 28, or 30 in. VR barrel with Vector Pro lengthened forcing cone, similar to Maxus Stalker, except has satin nickel finished receiver with laser engraved duck and pheasant, checkered walnut stock with Inflex Technology recoil pad and forearm, removeable Lightning trigger and turnkey magazine plug and speed lock forearm, includes shims and spacers, approx. 7 lbs. New mid-2010.

| MSR $1,500 | $1,295 | $1,100 | $925 | $800 | $675 | $500 | $425 |

* *Maxus Hunter 3 1/2 In.* – 12 ga., 3 1/2 in. chamber, otherwise similar to Maxus Hunter 3 in. except is also available with Mossy Oak Break-Up Infinity camo finish, approx. 7 lbs. New mid-2010.

| MSR $1,640 | $1,395 | $1,025 | $875 | $750 | $625 | $525 | $450 |

Add $40 for Mossy Oak Break-Up Infinity camo finish.

MAXUS MOSSY OAK DUCK BLIND – 12 ga., similar to Maxus Stalker, except has Mossy Oak Duck Blind camo finish. Mfg. 2009-2012.

| | $1,200 | $1,025 | $875 | $750 | $625 | $525 | $450 |

Last MSR was $1,400.

* *Maxus 3 1/2 In. Mossy Oak Duck Blind* – similar to Maxus Mossy Oak Duck Blind, except has 3 1/2 in. chamber. Mfg. 2009-2012.

| | | $1,350 | $975 | $850 | $725 | $600 | $525 | $475 |

Last MSR was $1,600.

MAXUS MOSSY OAK SHADOW GRASS BLADES – 12 ga., 3 in. chamber, similar to Maxus Stalker, except has 100% Mossy Oak Shadow Grass Blades camo coverage, approx. 7 lbs. New 2013.

| MSR $1,470 | $1,225 | $900 | $800 | $700 | $600 | $500 | $450 |

* *Maxus 3 1/2 In. Mossy Oak Shadow Grass Blades* – 12 ga., similar to Maxus Mossy Oak Shadow Grass Blades, except has 3 1/2 in. chamber. New 2013.

| MSR $1,600 | $1,350 | $1,025 | $875 | $750 | $650 | $550 | $475 |

MAXUS STALKER – 12 ga., 3 or 3 1/2 in. chamber, 26 or 28 in. VR barrel with three Invector Plus choke tubes, Vector Pro forcing cone became standard 2010, aluminum alloy receiver, gas operated with new Power Drive gas system (reduces recoil), matte black composite pistol grip stock with speedlock forearm and Dura-Touch Armor coating, turnkey magazine plug, Inflex recoil pad, approx. 6 lbs. 15 oz. New 2009.

| MSR $1,340 | $1,150 | $950 | $800 | $700 | $600 | $500 | $425 |

MSR	100%	98%	95%	90%	80%	70%	60%

* ***Maxus 3 1/2 In. Stalker*** – similar to Maxus Stalker, except has 3 1/2 in. chamber. New 2009.

MSR $1,500 $1,250 $925 $825 $725 $625 $525 $450

MAXUS ULTIMATE – 12 ga., 3 in. chamber, gas operated, engine turned bolt, 26, 28, or 30 in. flat VR barrel with three Invector Plus choke tubes, laser engraved featuring pheasant on right side, and mallard on left, checkered gloss oil finish Grade III walnut stock and forearm, Inflex Technology recoil pad, magazine cutoff includes spacers and hardshell ABS case, brass front bead sight, approx. 7 1/4 lbs. New 2013.

MSR $1,870 $1,550 $1,325 $1,100 $925 $800 $675 $575

MAXUS RIFLED DEER CAMO – 12 ga., 3 in. chamber, 22 in. fully rifled barrel with cantilever sight base and w/o sights, 100% Mossy Oak Break-Up Infinity camo coverage, includes extra shims and spacer, approx. 7 1/4 lbs. New 2011.

MSR $1,590 $1,370 $1,150 $975 $825 $700 $600 $500

MAXUS RIFLED DEER STALKER – 12 ga., 3 in. chamber, 22 in. fully rifled barrel with cantilever sight base and no sights, black composite stock and speed lock forearm, black metal finish, approx. 7 1/4 lbs. New 2011.

MSR $1,470 $1,275 $1,085 $925 $785 $675 $525 $425

MAXUS SPORTING – 12 ga., 3 in. chamber, 28 or 30 in. VR barrel with Vector Pro lengthened forcing cone, includes 5 Invector Plus choke tubes, satin finished aluminum receiver with laser etched game birds transformed into clay birds, high grade gloss finish, walnut stock and speed lock forearm, HiViz front sight, Inflex Technology recoil pad, approx. 7 lbs. New 2011.

MSR $1,700 $1,475 $1,250 $1,050 $895 $750 $600 $500

MAXUS SPORTING GOLDEN CLAYS – 12 ga., 3 in. chamber, 26, 28 or 30 in. VR barrel with three Invector Plus choke tubes, features satin nickel finished receiver with gold enhanced game birds transforming into a clay target on receiver sides, checkered gloss finished Grade III walnut stock and forearm with Inflex Technology recoil pad, engine turned bolt, includes ABS case, 7 1/4 lbs. New 2013.

MSR $2,000 $1,675 $1,450 $1,200 $1,000 $850 $750 $575

MAXUS SPORTING CARBON FIBER – 12 ga., 3 in. chamber, 28 or 30 in. barrel, similar to Maxus Stalker, except has two-tone carbon fiber receiver finish and barrel, Dura-Touch armor coating, five Invector Plus choke tubes, approx. 7 lbs. New mid-2010.

MSR $1,500 $1,290 $1,095 $950 $800 $675 $550 $425

SHOTGUNS: SINGLE BARREL, BT-99 & BT-100

During 2010, the Vector Pro lengthened 2 1/2 inch forcing cone became standard on the following current models.

SHOTGUNS: SINGLE BARREL, BT-99 & BT-100

MSR	100%	98%	95%	90%	80%	70%	60%

BT-99 STANDARD TRAP GUN – 12 ga., 32 or 34 in. vent. rib barrel, mod., imp. mod., or full choke, boxlock, auto ejector, checkered pistol grip with Monte Carlo or conventional style stock, beavertail forearm. Invector chokes became standard in 1986 and ported barrel with Invector Plus chokes and back boring became standard in 1992. Values below assume Invector Plus choking with ported barrel. Mfg. 1968-94 by Miroku.

	$900	$800	$700	$600	$550	$500	$450

Last MSR was $1,288.

Subtract $125 without Invector chokes or ported barrels.

* *BT-99 2 Barrel Set* – 12 ga., without Invector choking or barrel porting. Disc. 1983.

	$1,150	$995	$850	$750	$700	$650	$600

* *BT-99 Stainless* – 12 ga., features all stainless construction with Invector Plus ported 32 or 34 in. black VR barrel. Mfg. 1993-1994.

	$1,500	$1,200	$1,000	$700	$575	$495	$450

Last MSR was $1,738.

* *BT-99 Current Mfg.* – 12 ga., choice of 32 or 34 in. back bored unported barrel with 11/32 in. high post rib and one full Invector Plus choke tube, satin finished conventional or adj. comb stock, beavertail forearm, ejector only, 8 lbs. 5 oz. New 2001.

MSR $1,430	$1,230	$1,050	$900	$750	$600	$525	$450

Add $250 for factory adj. comb stock.

* *BT-99 Micro* – 12 ga., 30 or 32 in. high post VR barrel, similar to BT-99, except has shortened 13 3/4 LOP, approx. 7 3/4 lbs. New 2004.

MSR $1,430	$1,075	$900	$775	$675	$600	$525	$450

* *BT-99 Micro Midas* – 12 ga., 2 3/4 in. chambers, 28 or 30 in. VR barrel with one Invector-Plus choke tube, compact variation with 13 in. LOP, blued finish, extractor, satin finished walnut stock, beavertail forearm, recoil pad, approx. 7 3/4 lbs. New 2013.

MSR $1,430	$1,075	$900	$775	$675	$600	$525	$450

* *BT-99 Pigeon Grade* – 12 ga., features higher grade walnut and gold receiver accents, Invector chokes and ported barrels. Mfg. 1993-1994.

1978-1985 mfg.	$1,700	$1,500	$1,200	$1,100	$650	$575	$525
1986-1994 mfg.	$1,395	$1,150	$875	$600	$525	$495	$450

Last MSR was $1,505.

Older Pigeon Grade guns featured a satin grey receiver with deep relief, engraved pigeons in a fleur-de-lis background.

* *BT-99 Signature Painted* – 12 ga., features painted red/black stock with Browning logos on stock and forearm, Invector Plus ported barrels. Mfg. 1993-1994.

	$1,250	$1,050	$900	$700	$600	$500	$330

Last MSR was $1,323.

SHOTGUNS: SINGLE BARREL, BT-99 & BT-100

MSR	100%	98%	95%	90%	80%	70%	60%

BT-99 GRADE III – 12 ga., similar to BT-99, except has silver nitride receiver finished with gold accents, gloss finished Grade III/IV Monte Carlo stock with beavertail forearm, 32 or 34 in. ported barrel, approx. 8 1/2 lbs. New 2008.

MSR $2,540 $2,440 $2,075 $1,750 $1,485 $1,175 $950 $750

Add $290 for adj. comb.

* **BT-99 Golden Clays** – 12 ga., features gloss finished Grade V/Grade VI wood and gold outline receiver and inlays depicting a transitional hunting to clay pigeon scene, current mfg. includes 32 or 34 in. ported barrel, adj. comb and LOP, and GraCoil recoil reduction, approx. 9 lbs. Mfg. 1994, reintroduced 2003.

MSR $4,340 $3,740 $3,180 $2,700 $2,300 $1,850 $1,475 $1,185

Subtract 15% for older mfg. w/o current features.

BT-99 PLUS GRADE I – similar to BT-99, except has adj. rib to control point of impact and new recoil reduction system that reduces felt recoil by 50%, stock has adj. comb and buttplate (recoil pad), back-bored barrel, Invector chokes, 8 3/4 lbs. Mfg. 1989-94.

$1,775 $1,525 $1,275 $1,100 $1,000 $800 $700

Last MSR was $1,835.

Add 5% for ported barrel.

In 1990, the Grade I designation was added to this model. In 1991, this model was supplied with a travel vault gun case as standard equipment. Older mfg. will not have these cases as an original accessory.

Beginning 1991, a Micro Plus Model was introduced that incorporates smaller dimensions (shorter stock and choice of shorter barrel). Values are the same as listed.

* **BT-99 Plus Stainless Grade I** – features all stainless construction with Invector Plus ported 32 or 34 in. black VR barrel. Mfg. 1993-94.

$1,950 $1,725 $1,425 $1,255 $1,020 $885 $715

Last MSR was $2,240.

Beginning 1991, a Micro Plus Model was introduced that incorporates smaller dimensions (shorter stock and choice of shorter barrel). Values are the same as listed.

* **BT-99 Plus Pigeon Grade Grade I** – 12 ga., features higher grade walnut and gold receiver accents, Invector chokes and ported barrels. Mfg. 1993-disc.

$1,875 $1,600 $1,250 $1,100 $895 $785 $630

Last MSR was $2,065

Beginning 1991, a Micro Plus Model was introduced that incorporates smaller dimensions (shorter stock and choice of shorter barrel) Values are the same.

| MSR | 100% | 98% | 95% | 90% | 80% | 70% | 60% |

* ***BT-99 Plus Signature Painted Grade I*** – features painted red/black stock with Browning logos on stock and forearm, Invector Plus ported barrels. Mfg. 1993-94.

$1,750 $1,525 $1,250 $1,100 $895 $785 $630

Last MSR was $1,890.

Beginning 1991, a Micro Plus Model was introduced that incorporates smaller dimensions (shorter stock and choice of shorter barrel). Values are the same.

* ***BT-99 Plus Golden Clays Grade I*** – features high-grade wood and gold outline receiver and inlays depicting a transitional hunting to clay pigeon scene. Mfg. 1994 only.

$2,700 $2,350 $2,050 $1,850 $1,700 $1,550 $1,395

Last MSR was $3,205.

Beginning 1991, a Micro Plus Model was introduced that incorporates smaller dimensions (shorter stock and choice of shorter barrel). Values are the same.

BT-99 MAX – 12 ga. only, choice of blue steel with engraving or stainless steel barrel, receiver, and trigger guard, 32 or 34 in. high post VR ported barrel, thin forearm with finger grooves, select walnut pistol grip stock (regular or Monte Carlo) with high gloss finish, ejector/extractor selector, no safety, approx. 8 lbs. 10 oz. Mfg. 1995-96.

$1,300 $1,000 $800 $600 $525 $495 $450

Last MSR was $1,496.

Add $400 for stainless steel.

BT-100 STANDARD TRAP GUN – 12 ga. only, 32 or 34 in. steel high-post ported Invector Plus or fixed choked (F) barrel, without safety, choice of blue or stainless steel receiver, removable trigger assembly, ejector selector (either ejects or extracts) adj. comb and thumbhole stock (disc. 1999) are optional, approx. 8 lbs. 10 oz. Mfg. 1995-2002.

$1,900 $1,600 $1,300 $795 $575 $495 $450

Last MSR was $2,266.

Subtract approx. 10% for fixed choke.
Add $100 for adj. comb.
Add $558 for replacement trigger assembly (blue or stainless).

* ***BT-100 Stainless*** – features stainless steel barrel, receiver, trigger guard and top lever. Disc. 2002.

$2,210 $1,800 $1,600 $1,000 $815 $695 $580

Last MSR was $2,742.

Subtract approx. 10% for fixed choke.
Add $100 for adj. comb.
Add $558 for replacement trigger assembly (blue or stainless).

| MSR | 100% | 98% | 95% | 90% | 80% | 70% | 60% |

BT-100 SATIN (LOW LUSTER) – features 32 or 34 in. Invector Plus barrel, satin/low luster metal/wood finish, conventional type stock without Monte Carlo, quick removable trigger with adj. trigger pull, 8 lbs. 10 oz. Mfg. 1998-2000.

$1,400 $1,200 $1,000 $775 $650 $575 $495

Last MSR was $1,684.

SHOTGUNS: SINGLE BARREL, RECOILLESS TRAP

RECOILLESS SINGLE BARREL TRAP – 12 ga., special bolt action design that eliminates 72% of felt recoil, 27 (also available in Micro Model) or 30 in. high-post vent. rib Invector Plus choked back-bored barrel, rib adjusts for 3 points of impact (3, 6, or 9 in.), stock has adj. pull (2 sizes) and comb height, anodized receiver, no safety, approx. 8 1/2 lbs. Mfg. 1994-96.

$995 $850 $750 $650 $525 $500 $450

Last MSR was $1,995.

The Micro Model featured a 27 in. barrel and shorter length of pull.

* ***Recoilless Single Barrel Trap Signature Painted*** – features painted red/black stock with Browning logos on stock and forearm, Invector Plus ported barrels. Mfg. 1994 only.

$995 $850 $750 $650 $525 $500 $450

Last MSR was $1,900.

SHOTGUNS: SLIDE ACTION

Do not use BPS barrels chambered for 3 1/2 in. shotshells on a BPS 3 in. receiver or vice versa.

BPS HUNTER/FIELD MODEL – 12, 16 (new 2008), 20, 28 (new 1994) ga., or .410 bore (new 2000), 2 3/4 (28 ga. only) or 3 in. chamber, bottom ejection, double action bars, top tang safety, 5 shot capacity, vent. rib, all steel receiver with variety of finishes, receiver engraving became standard 1991 and was disc. during 1998, 20 and 28 ga. are approx. 1/2 lb. lighter than 12 ga. Field Models, Invector or Invector Plus (new 1994 in 20 ga.) choking, various barrel lengths, Invector Plus choking became standard 1995 (except 28 ga.), back bored barrels on 12 and 20 ga. BPS Models (except Game guns) became standard during 2003, 7 - 7 3/4 lbs. Mfg. by Miroku. New 1977.

MSR $650 $565 $450 $350 $275 $230 $195 $175

Add $40 for 16, 28 ga., or .410 bore.
Subtract 10% if without Invector Plus choke tubes.

* ***BPS Stalker Model*** – 12 ga. only, 3 in. chamber, all metal parts have a dull matte finish, non-glare black synthetic composite stock and forearm, 24 (mfg. 1999-2000), 26, 28, or 30 in. VR barrel, approx. 8 lbs. New 1987.

MSR $650 $565 $450 $350 $275 $230 $195 $175

SHOTGUNS: SLIDE ACTION

MSR	100%	98%	95%	90%	80%	70%	60%

* ***BPS Camouflage*** – 12 or 20 (disc. 2006) ga., 3 in. chamber, features Mossy Oak Shadow Grass (disc. 2006), Mossy Oak Duck Blind (new 2007), Mossy Oak Break-Up (mfg. 2000-2003), Break-Up Infinity (new 2010), New Break-Up (mfg. 2004-2009), Mossy Oak Shadow Grass Blades (new 2013) full camo treatment, 24 (standard model disc., or NWTF Model with Mossy Oak Break-Up camo - new 2001), 26, or 28 in. barrel, Dura-Touch armor coating became standard during 2003, approx. 8 lbs. New 1999.

MSR $780 $650 $550 $425 $350 $300 $275 $250

Add $120 for NWTF Model with 24 in. barrel.

* ***BPS Pigeon Grade*** – 12 ga. only, 3 in. chamber, features high grade walnut and gold trimmed receiver, 26 or 28 in. VR barrel with Invector chokes, 7 lbs. 10 oz. Mfg. 1992-98.

$550 $465 $395 $350 $310 $290 $275

Last MSR was $603.

* ***BPS Upland Special*** – 12, 16 (new 2008), or 20 ga., 2 3/4 (16 ga.) or 3 in. chamber, 22 (12 and 20 ga.), 24, or 26 in. VR barrel, straight grip satin finished stock and forearm, Invector (pre-1994) or Invector Plus (new 1994, standard 1995) choking, 6 3/4 or 7 1/2 lbs. New 1985.

MSR $650 $595 $500 $400 $325 $230 $195 $175

Add $50 for 16 ga.
Subtract 10% if without Invector Plus choke tubes.

* ***BPS Turkey Special*** – 12 ga. only, 3 in. chamber, 20 1/2 in. lightened barrel, non-glare walnut stock, matte finished barrel and receiver, receiver is drilled and tapped for scope base, rifle-style stock dimensions, sling swivels, new extra-full Invector choke tube, 7 lbs. 8 oz. Mfg. 1992-2001.

$400 $340 $275 $240 $215 $190 $175

Last MSR was $500.

* ***BPS Micro*** – 20 ga. only, 22 in. vent. rib barrel, pistol grip stock (13 1/4 in. LOP), Invector Plus choking (includes 3 chokes), 6 3/4 lbs. New 2001.

MSR $650 $565 $480 $385 $300 $230 $195 $175

* ***BPS Micro Midas*** – 12, 20, 28 ga., or .410 bore, 24 or 26 in. VR barrel with three standard Invector choke tubes, checkered satin finished walnut stock and forearm includes two stock spacers, 13 in. LOP, 7-7 1/2 lbs. New 2013.

MSR $650 $565 $480 $385 $300 $230 $195 $175

Add $40 for 28 ga. or .410 bore.

* ***BPS Micro - Youth and Ladies Model*** – 20 ga. only, 22 in. vent. rib barrel, straight grip shortened stock (13 1/4 in. LOP), Invector (pre-1994) or Invector Plus (new 1994, standard 1995) choking, 6 3/4 lbs. Mfg. 1986-2002.

$385 $300 $260 $225 $200 $185 $170

Last MSR was $473.

Subtract 10% if without Invector Plus choke tubes.

SHOTGUNS: SLIDE ACTION

MSR	100%	98%	95%	90%	80%	70%	60%

* **BPS Deer Hunter/Special (DG, DS or DH)** – 12 or 20 (new 2007) ga., 3 in. chamber, 20 1/2 (disc. 2000) or 22 in. barrel with 5 in. rifled choke tube or rifled barrel (DH, cantilever scope mount with satin finish only, new 1997), iron sights, scope mount base, choice of gloss (DG, disc. 1997) or satin (DS, disc. 2000) finish checkered stock with recoil pad and forearm, sling swivels, polished or matte finished metal, approx. 7 1/2 lbs. New 1992.

  MSR $780 $680 $580 $465 $375 $295 $200 $175

  Subtract approx. 10% for rifled choke tube. Add $20 for 20 ga. (new 2007).

* **BPS Deer Camo** – 12 or 20 ga., 3 in. chamber, 22 in. rifled barrel with cantilever scope mount, 100% Mossy Oak New Break-Up (disc. 2009) or Mossy Oak Break-Up Infinity (new 2010) camo coverage, approx. 7 1/2 lbs. New 2007.

  MSR $830 $715 $600 $485 $390 $300 $200 $175

  Add $100 for 20 ga.

* **BPS Buck Special** – 12 or 20 (disc. 1984) ga., 3 in. chamber, 24 in. cyl. bore barrel, iron sights, 7 lbs. 10 oz. Reintroduced 1988-disc. 1998.

            $335 $275 $230 $200 $185 $175 $160

  Last MSR was $409.

BPS MAGNUM HUNTER/STALKER 12 GA. 3 1/2 IN. – 12 ga., 3 1/2 in. chamber, 24 (disc. 1997, reintroduced 1999-2000 - Stalker only), 26, 28, or 30 (disc. 1997) in. barrel with Invector chokes and vent. rib, 4 shot mag., 7 3/4 lbs. Hunter 3 1/2 in. Model disc. 2002.

  MSR $750 $645 $500 $425 $365 $310 $275 $250

In 1990, the back-bored Invector Plus choke tube system became standard in 12 ga. 3 1/2 in. chamber only.

* **BPS Camo Magnum Hunter** – 12 ga., similar to Magnum Hunter or Stalker 12 ga., features Mossy Oak Shadow Grass (disc. 2006), Mossy Oak Duck Blind (mfg. 2007-2012), Mossy Oak Break-Up Infinity (new 2010), Mossy Oak Break-Up (mfg. 2000-2009), or Mossy Oak Shadow Grass Blades (new 2013) full camo treatment, 24 (standard model disc., or NWTF Model with Mossy Oak Break-Up camo - new 2001), 26 or 28 in. VR barrel, Dura-Touch armor coating became standard during 2003, approx. 7 3/4 - 9 1/4 lbs. New 1999.

  MSR $900 $775 $625 $550 $450 $375 $315 $275

  Add $80 for NWTF Model with 24 in. barrel (12 ga., available in Mossy Oak Break-Up from 2000-2009, Break Up Infinity beginning 2010).

* **BPS Magnum Hunting Waterfowl** – 10 ga., 3 1/2 in. Mag. with choice of 28 or 30 in. matte finished VR barrel with standard Invector choking, features higher grade walnut and gold trimmed receiver with Waterfowl outlined, approx. 9 lbs. 6 oz. Mfg. 1993-98.

            $615 $500 $400 $375 $350 $315 $285

  Last MSR was $75

SHOTGUNS: SLIDE ACTION

MSR	100%	98%	95%	90%	80%	70%	60%

* ***BPS Magnum 3 1/2 In. Buck Special*** – 10 or 12 (disc. 1994) ga., 3 1/2 in. chambers, 24 in. cyl. bore barrel, 7 lbs. 10 oz. Mfg. 1990-1997.

$500 $450 $400 $370 $335 $310 $290

Last MSR was $677.

BPS MAGNUM HUNTER/STALKER 10 GA. – 10 ga., 3 1/2 in. chamber, 26 or 28 in. barrel with three standard Invector choke tubes, currently available in either Stalker (black synthetic stock and forearm), or camo - choice of Mossy Oak New Break-Up (disc. 2009), Mossy Oak Break-Up Infinity (new 2010), Mossy Oak Duck Blind (mfg. 2007-2012), New Shadowgrass (disc. 2006), or Mossy Oak Shadow Grass Blades (new 2013) - with Dura-Touch coating configuration, no longer available in Hunter Model, 10 1/2 lbs. Disc. 2001, reintroduced 2004.

MSR $750 $645 $500 $425 $365 $310 $275 $250

Add $150 for 100% camo coverage.

* ***BPS 10 ga. NWTF*** – features 24 in. VR barrel with HiViz TriViz fiber optic sights and extra full XF extended turkey choke tube, 100% Mossy Oak New Break-Up (disc. 2009) or Break-Up Infinity (new 2010) camo coverage, NWTF logo on synthetic stock, 10 lbs. 3 oz.

MSR $980 $815 $600 $500 $400 $350 $300 $275

BPS TRAP MODEL – 12 ga., 30 in. barrel. Disc. 1984 but trap barrels were available separately for several years.

$360 $300 $270 $230 $210 $190 $170

BPS TRAP (CURRENT MFG.) – 12 ga. only, 2 3/4 in. chamber, features dark grey receiver with full coverage engraving, 30 in. VR barrel with HiViz front sight, checkered satin finished Monte Carlo walnut stock and forearm, magazine cutoff, approx. 8 1/2 lbs. New 2007.

MSR $800 $695 $595 $475 $375 $300 $275 $225

* ***BPS Micro Trap*** – 12 ga. only, similar to BPS Trap, except has 28 in. VR barrel and 13 3/4 in. LOP, approx. 8 lbs. New 2007.

MSR $800 $695 $595 $475 $375 $300 $275 $225

BPS WILD TURKEY FEDERATION COMMEMORATIVE – only 500 manufactured. Disc. 1991.

$495 $395 $325   N/A   N/A   N/A   N/A

BPS PACIFIC EDITION DU – limited mfg., DU serialization, cased.

$595 $475 $350 $285 $250 $215 $185

BPS COASTAL DU – limited mfg., DU serialization, cased.

$595 $475 $350 $285 $250 $215 $185

BPS WATERFOWL DELUXE – 12 ga. Mag., gold trigger and etching, Invector chokes, limited mfg.

$625 $525 $450 $385 $335 $280 $235

MSR	100%	98%	95%	90%	80%	70%	60%

MODEL 12 LIMITED EDITION SERIES

* *Model 12 Limited Edition Grade I 20 Ga.* – 20 ga. only, 2 3/4 in. chamber only, reproduction of the famous Winchester Model 12 with slight design improvements, 26 in. VR barrel bored modified, 5 shot mag., high post floating rib, walnut stock and forearm with semi-gloss finish, take down, serialization format similar to 28 ga., 7 lbs. 1 oz. 8,000 mfg. in 1988 with inventory depleted 1990.

$775 $650 $525 N/A N/A N/A N/A

Last MSR was $735.

* *Model 12 Limited Edition Grade V 20 Ga.* – similar specifications to Grade I, except has select walnut checkered 22 lines per inch with high gloss finish, extensive game scene engraving including multiple gold inlays serialization format similar to 28 ga. 4,000 mfg. 1988 only.

$1,350 $1,125 $900 N/A N/A N/A N/A

Last MSR was $1,187.

* *Model 12 Limited Edition Grade I 28 Ga.* – 28 ga. only, similar to Grade I 20 Ga., except in 28 ga., 26 in. VR modified choke barrel, 5 digit ser. no. with NM872 suffix. 7,000 mfg. 1991-92.

$1,050 $875 $700 N/A N/A N/A N/A

Last MSR was $772.

* *Model 12 Limited Edition Grade V 28 ga.* – 28 ga. only, similar to Grade V 20 ga., except in 28 ga., 26 in. VR modified choke barrel, 5 digit ser. no. with NM972 suffix. 5,000 mfg. 1991-92.

$1,675 $1,350 $1,000 N/A N/A N/A N/A

Last MSR was $1,246.

MODEL 42 LIMITED EDITION

* *Model 42 Limited Edition Grade I* – .410 bore, 3 in. chamber, reproduction of the Winchester Model 42 with slight design improvements, 26 in. VR full choke barrel, select walnut stock, 5 digit ser. no. with NZ882 suffix, 6 lbs. 12 oz. 6,000 mfg. late 1991-1993.

$895 $775 $550 N/A N/A N/A N/A

Last MSR was $800.

* *Model 42 Limited Edition Grade V* – .410 bore, engraving and embellishments similar to the Model 12 Grade V, 5 digit ser. no. with NZ982 suffix, 6,000 mfg. late 1991-1993.

$1,495 $1,225 $925 N/A N/A N/A N/A

Last MSR was $1,360.

SPECIAL EDITIONS, COMMEMORATIVES, & LIMITED MFG.

Please refer to the *Blue Book of Modern Black Powder Arms* by John Allen (now online also) for more information and prices on Browning black powder rifles.

SPECIAL EDITIONS, COMMEMORATIVES, & LIMITED MFG.

MSR	100%	98%	95%	90%	80%	70%	60%

BICENTENNIAL 1876-1976 SET – .45-70 Govt. cal., Model 78 rifle with specially engraved receiver, silver finish, fancy wood, cased, with engraved knife and medallion, 1,000 sets mfg. in 1976. Issue price - $1,500.

	$1,975	$1,550	$1,200	N/A	N/A	N/A	N/A

CENTENNIAL O/U RIFLE/SHOTGUN – 20 ga. O/U shotgun w/extra set of .30-06 O/U rifle barrels. Shotgun barrels are 26 1/2 in., rifle barrels are 24 in., SST, ejectors, elaborate scroll engraved receiver with 2 gold inlays, straight grip special oil finished walnut stock and forearm, deluxe walnut full-length case. 500 mfg. 1978 only.

	$6,750	$6,250	$5,250	N/A	N/A	N/A	N/A

Last MSR was $7,000.

CENTENNIAL SET – complete Browning set mfg. in 1978, includes the Centennial O/U rifle/shotgun, 9mm Hi-Power, B92 .44 Mag., Mountain Rifle, and a set of three knives.

	$8,750	$7,750	$6,250	N/A	N/A	N/A	N/A

1 OF 50 BICENTENNIAL RIFLE – .30-06 cal., Model 78 single shot with 26 in. octagon barrel, includes special engraving by Neil Hartliep (non-factory), extra fine walnut, 4X wide angle scope, special luggage case. 50 mfg. (one for each state) during 1976 only and sold by silent mail order bidding (minimum bid was $3,100 in 1976).

As very few specimens are bought or sold each year, pricing is rather unpredictable. A few specimens have been sold in the $6,000 range recently. Remember, this is not a "factory edition" as the work on this gun was subcontracted by Centennial Guns (division of Frigon Guns located in Clay Center, KS).

BUCK MARK COMMEMORATIVE PISTOL – features 6 3/4 in. Challenger style tapered barrel, white bonded ivory grips with scrimshaw style patterning including "1 of 1,000 Commemorative Model" on sides, matte blue finish, gold trigger, 30 1/2 oz. 1,000 mfg. 2001-2002.

	$335	$275	$225	N/A	N/A	N/A	N/A

Last MSR was $437.

NOTES

FABRIQUE NATIONALE

Current manufacturer located in Herstal, near Liege, Belgium. The current company name is "Group Herstal", however, the company is better known by "Fabrique Nationale" or "Fabrique Nationale d'Armes de Guerre". FN entered into their first contract with John M. Browning in 1897 for the manufacture of their first pistol, the FN 1899 Model. Additional contracts were signed and the relationship further blossomed with the manufacture of the A-5 shotgun. FN was acquired by GIAT of France in 1992. In late 1997, the company was purchased by the Walloon government of Belgium. Additional production facilities are located in Portugal, Japan, and the U.S.

Also see: Browning Arms under Rifles, Shotguns, and Pistols, and FNH USA for current offerings in the U.S.

The author would like to express his sincere thanks to Anthony Vanderlinden from the Browning Collector's Association for making FN contributions to this edition.

PISTOLS: SEMI-AUTO

For FN Models 1899, 1900, 1903, 1905, 1910, 1922 (10/22), Baby Model, Model 10/71, and BAC marked Hi-Powers (post 1954 mfg.), please refer to the Browning Pistol section in this text.

MSR	100%	98%	95%	90%	80%	70%	60%

PISTOLS: SEMI-AUTO, HI-POWER VARIATIONS

The F.N. Hi-Power (also known as P-35) was John Browning's last pistol design. A 9mm Para., single action, semi-auto pistol, it was the first to incorporate a staggered high capacity magazine. It has a 4 2/3 in. barrel, 13 shot mag., hammer and mag. safeties, a wide variety of finishes and sight options. It's probably the most widely used military pistol in the world.

For information on post-WWII BAC marked Hi-Powers, including model codes and identification, please refer to the Browning section under Serialization.

PRE-WAR COMMERCIAL AND MILITARY HP – 9mm Para. cal., single action, blue, wood grips, slotted for stock with tangent rear sight (fixed rear sight with unslotted rear grip strap not encountered in this model), 13 shot mag., commercial pistols display Liege proofs only, Belgian military pistols display Liege proofs and Belgian military acceptance markings. Mfg. 1935-1940.

Tangent sight & slotted	$2,750	$2,200	$1,700	$1,250	$950	$750	$650

Add $1,200 for original pre-war flat board stock with attached holster, commercial stocks are most often not numbered. Beware of post-war reproductions!

Add $1,400 for original prewar Belgian military flat board stock w/o attached holster. Check stock for small Belgian military acceptance marking.

Add $1,000 for correct Belgian military combination shoulder-stock - pistol holster.

PISTOLS: SEMI-AUTO, HI-POWER VARIATIONS

MSR	100%	98%	95%	90%	80%	70%	60%

PRE-WAR FOREIGN MILITARY CONTRACTS – mfg. under military contract for various countries.

Lithuanian Crest	N/A	$3,600	$2,950	$1,900	$1,350	$1,000	$900
Estonian Contract ("E.V." or "K.L.")	N/A	$3,700	$3,100	$2,500	$1,800	$1,350	$1,000
Finnish Contract ("SA" marked)	N/A	$2,800	$2,300	$1,900	$1,600	$1,100	$800
Paraguayan crest	N/A	$3,750	$3,000	$2,500	$2,250	$1,900	$1,750
Chinese, original finish	N/A	$2,400	$1,850	$1,500	$1,000	$850	$750

Add $1,200 for original (Finnish contract) pre-war flat board stock with attached holster.

Add $1,000 for original Finnish contract stock (ser. no. 11,000-15,000) with removed holster.

Add $200 for period Chinese inventory marking on Chinese contract pistols.

Subtract 50% for refinished Chinese contract pistols or reworks with Inglis parts.

Note: Finnish contract guns can be identified by the "SA" marking on frame, and/or slide, and/or mag. 2,400 pistols were shipped to Finland in 1940, all are in ser. no. range: 11,000 - 15,000.

Most Chinese contract pistols were refinished or reworked to include Inglis parts. Chinese contract pistols fall in the 6,000 - 11,000 and 20,000 - 21,000 ser. no. range.

Paraguayan contract guns are rare in the U.S. Numerous counterfeits have surfaced - check crest and slide markings for originality. Check bluing carefully, as most were refinished. Beware of matching numbered shoulder stocks as most are counterfeits or recently renumbered.

WWII PRODUCTION: WAFFENAMT PROOFED

There is a range of finishes during Nazi production that varies from the excellent pre-war commercial finish on early guns assembled from captured parts to the roughly milled, poorly finished specimen mfg. late in the war. Values listed assume all major parts (slide, barrel, and frame) are matching with original magazine.

In recent years, some Nazi production Hi-Powers have had the rear grip strap milled out and slotted to accept a shoulder stock. Careful observation is advised before purchasing a "rare" (and expensive) slotted and tangent sight specimen. Many HPs have been restored since the restoration is easily accomplished by professionals.

* **WWII Production: Waffenampt Proofed Type I** – tangent slights, slotted, taken from existing pre-war Belgian production, quality is excellent, correct ser. range is quite limited, approx. 42,000-46,000+. Ser. range for production under German occupation is 50,001-52,500. All are proofed WaA 613.

N/A	$5,200	$4,400	$3,700	$2,900	$2,450	$2,250

MSR	100%	98%	95%	90%	80%	70%	60%

Beware of fakes and restorations. A large percentage of WaA613 pistols in the U.S. are counterfeits.

* *WWII Production: Waffenampt Proofed Type II* – tangent sights, not slotted, approx. 90,000 mfg. with last ser. no. approx. 145,000, generally good quality finish, pistols are proofed WaA613, WaA103, some are WaA140.

N/A	$2,250	$1,650	$1,250	$1,000	$900	$800

Add 25% if pistol is marked WaA613.
Add 15% if pistol is marked WaA103.

* *WWII Production: Waffenampt Proofed Type III Standard Fixed Sights* – not slotted, most common HP pistol produced during the war.

$1,200	$950	$700	$600	$500	$450	$400

Add 15% for late war Bakelite/synthetic grips.
Add 20% for eagle N proof instead of WaA140 proof, or for no WaA140 proof.

POST-OCCUPATION PRODUCTION – commercial assembly began September 1944 from wartime parts. Complete manufacturing from raw materials started in 1946. First imported with BAC markings in 1954 (see Browning HP section). Early (1944-1945) models are identifiable by an "A" serial number prefix and are not fitted with a magazine safety. Starting in 1947, the rear slide bushing was hardened by a new heat treatment process. Other design modifications were added in 1950. Many thousands manufactured for various government contracts.

Add $200-$2,000 for military pistols with crests, depending on condition and variation.

* *Post-Occupation Production Tangent sight only*

$1,300	$1,100	$900	$700	$650	$550	$500

Add $100 for "T" prefix.

* *Post-Occupation Production Tangent sight* – slotted for stock, military or commercial mfg.

$1,500	$1,350	$1,100	$900	$750	$600	$500

Add $150 for "T" prefix.
Add $50 for internal extractor.

* *Post-Occupation Production Fixed sight* – most common variation.

$650	$525	$450	$400	$350	$325	$300

Add $100 for ring hammer.
Add 40% for "A" prefix, but only in 98%+ condition.

SULTAN OF MUSCAT AND OMAN CONTRACT

* *Sultan Of Muscat And Oman Contract First Model* – matte finish, reverse crest, scarce.

$4,500	$3,500	$2,500	$2,200	$2,000	$1,600	$1,300

* *Sultan Of Muscat And Oman Contract Second Model* – high polish finish, standard crest.

$4,000	$2,950	$1,750	$1,540	$1,265	$1,055	$875

| MSR | 100% | 98% | 95% | 90% | 80% | 70% | 60% |

REVOLVERS

BARRACUDA – .357 Mag./9mm Para. cal., 4 in. barrel, blue finish, includes two cylinders chambered for .357 Mag. and 9mm Para. cal. Very limited importation.

$875 $775 $675 $600 $525 $450 $375

Add $175 for original styrofoam box, moon clips and documents.
Subtract $250 if sold with only one cylinder.

RIFLES: BOLT ACTION

FN MAUSER SPORTER DE LUXE – available in popular American and European calibers, 24 in. barrel, checkered pistol grip stock. Sold in the U.S. 1947-1963. Sold in the U.S. without rear sight installed or with a choice of Armstrong sights. No engraving. Note that barreled actions were also sold in the U.S.

$900 $750 $500 $450 $400 $350 $300

Add $100 for original FN box.
Prices assume original FN rifles with FN stock and FN buttplate, prices do not apply to FN barreled actions assembled by independent gunsmiths.

FN MAUSER SPORTER DE LUXE SCROLL ENGRAVED – available in popular American and European calibers, 24 in. barrel, checkered pistol grip stock. Introduced shortly after the standard De Luxe model. Sold in the U.S. without rear sight installed or with a choice of Armstrong sights. FN scroll engraving in floral motif on receiver, buttplate and triggerguard. Note that scroll engraved barreled actions were also sold in the U.S.

$2,000 $1,500 $1,000 $750 $500 $450 $350

Prices assume original FN rifles with FN stock and FN buttplate, prices do not apply to scroll engraved FN barreled actions assembled by independent gunsmiths.
Add $100 for original FN box
Subtract $350 (95% or better) if the top of the engraved receiver is drilled and tapped for a scope.

FN MAUSER SPORTER (DE LUXE) PRESENTATION RIFLE – 30.06 or .270 Win. cal., other calibers only available on special order, 24 in. barrel, checkered pistol grip stock, rear sight installed on barrel, elaborate FN presentation grade engraving with dragon motifs on receiver, buttplate, triggerguard and barrel, engraved receiver and triggerguard are polished white and not blued, engraving design created and first executed by FN's Master Engraver Felix Funken. Note that presentation grade barreled actions were also sold in the U.S. Introduced 1954.

$3,800 $3,200 $2,300 $1,250 $900 $800 $700

Prices assume original FN rifles with FN stock and FN buttplate, prices do not apply to presentation grade FN barreled actions assembled by independent gunsmiths.
Add $100 for original FN box
Subtract $1,000 (95% or better) if the top of the engraved receiver is drilled and tapped for a scope.

MSR	100%	98%	95%	90%	80%	70%	60%

FN SUPREME – .243 Win., .270 Win., 7mm Rem. Mag., .308 Win. or .30-06 cal., 24 in. barrel, peep sight, checkered pistol grip stock. Sold in the U.S. 1957-1975.

	$850	$725	$500	$450	$400	$350	$300

FN SUPREME MAGNUM – .264 Win. Mag., 7mm Rem. Mag., .300 Win. Mag., or .375 H&H cal. Mfg. beginning circa 1957.

	$975	$850	$700	$550	$475	$425	$375
.375 H&H cal.	$1,950	$1,700	$1,400	$1,100	$950	$850	$750

FN SNIPER RIFLE (MODEL 30) – .308 Win. cal., this model was a Mauser actioned Sniper Rifle equipped with 20 in. extra heavy barrel, flash hider, separate removable diopter sights, Hensoldt 4x scope, hardcase, bipod, and sling. 51 complete factory sets were imported into the U.S., with additional surplus rifles that were privately imported.

	$4,750	$4,250	$4,000	$3,500	$3,000	$2,750	$2,500

Subtract 15% if removable diopter sights or bipod is missing.
Subtract 10% if scope is not marked with F.N. logo.

Values assume complete factory outfit with all accessories.

RIFLES: SEMI-AUTO

BROWNING PATENT 1900 – .35 Rem. cal. only, usually features matted rib barrel and checkered stock and forearm, similar to Remington Model 8 auto-loading rifle. 4,913 mfg. 1910-1929 by FN, and not officially exported to the U.S.

	N/A	$3,500	$3,250	$3,000	$2,500	$2,000	$1,500

Add 15% if rifle has plain barrel with tangent leaf rear sight.
Factory engraved rifles are very rare and will command substantial premiums.

MODEL 1949 – 7x57mm Mauser, 7.65mm Mauser, 7.92mm Mauser, or .30-06 cal., (.308 Win. cal. for Argentine conversion rifles), gas operated, 10 shot box mag. (20 round detachable mag. for Argentine conversions), 23 in. barrel, military rifle, tangent rear sight.

Columbia	$1,700	$1,400	$1,150	$1,000	$900	$750	$700
Luxembourg	$1,500	$1,250	$1,000	$900	$800	$650	$600
Venezuela	$1,350	$1,100	$900	$850	$700	$600	$550
Argentina	N/A	$1,250	$1,100	$950	$850	$750	$650
Egyptian	$1,600	$1,350	$1,100	$995	$895	$725	$675

Add $100 for detachable grenade launcher.
Subtract 30% for U.S. rebuilt, non-matching rifles with reproduction stocks.
Original FN-49 sniper rifles are extremely rare and may add $2,500+.

Beware of U.S. assembled "sniper" configurations, and Belgian military "ABL" scopes mounted on other contract rifles and sold as original sniper configurations.

FN-49 contract rifles not listed above are very rare in the U.S. and will demand a premium.

Carefully inspect black paint finish for factory originality, as all FN-49s were factory painted.

RIFLES: SEMI-AUTO, FAL/LAR/CAL/FNC SERIES

After tremendous price increases between 1985-88, Fabrique Nationale decided in 1988 to discontinue this series completely. Not only are these rifles not exported to the U.S. any longer, but all production has ceased in Belgium as well. The only way FN will produce these models again is if they are given a large military contract - in which case a "side order" of commercial guns may be built. 1989 Federal legislation regarding this type of paramilitary design also helped push up prices to their current level. FAL rifles were also mfg. in Israel by I.M.I.

F.N. FAL – semi-auto, French designation for the F.N. L.A.R. (light automatic rifle), otherwise similar to the L.A.R.

MSR	100%	98%	95%	90%	80%	70%	60%
	$4,175	$3,950	$3,750	$3,475	$3,150	$3,100	$2,750

* **F.N. FAL G**

	100%	98%	95%	90%	80%	70%	60%
Standard	$4,800	$4,000	$3,500	$2,950	$2,450	$2,150	$2,000
Paratrooper	$5,200	$4,400	$3,900	$3,350	$2,850	$2,550	$2,400
Heavy Barrel	$6,800	$6,250	$4,950	$4,400	$3,750	$3,250	$2,750
Lightweight	$5,200	$4,250	$3,750	$3,100	$2,600	$2,350	$2,100

Values listed assume inclusion of factory bipod.

The Standard G Series was supplied with a wooden stock and wood or nylon forearm. The Heavy Barrel variant had all wood furniture and was supplied with a bipod. The Lightweight Model had an aluminum lower receiver, piston tube and magazine.

G Series FALs were imported between 1959-1962 by Browning Arms Co. This rifle was declared illegal by the GCA of 1968, and was exempted 5 years later. Total numbers exempted are: Standard - 1,822, Heavy Barrel - 21, and Paratrooper - 5.

F.N. L.A.R. COMPETITION (50.00, LIGHT AUTOMATIC RIFLE) – .308 Win. (7.62x51mm) cal., semi-auto, competition rifle with match flash hider, 21 in. barrel, adj. 4 position fire selector on automatic models, wood stock, aperture rear sight adj. from 100-600 meters, 9.4 lbs. Mfg. 1981-83.

$4,250	$4,025	$3,850	$3,625	$3,450	$3,175	$2,950

This model was designated by the factory as the 50.00 Model.

Mid-1987 retail on this model was $1,258. The last MSR was $3,179 (this price reflected the last exchange rate and special order status of this model).

* **FN L.A.R. Competition Heavy barrel rifle (50.41 & 50.42)** – barrel is twice as heavy as standard L.A.R., includes wood or synthetic stock, short wood forearm, and bipod, 12.2 lbs. Importation disc. 1988.

$4,495	$4,275	$4,150	$4,000	$3,675	$3,500	$3,250

Add $500 for walnut stock.
Add $350 for match sights.

MSR	100%	98%	95%	90%	80%	70%	60%

There were 2 variations of this model. The Model 50.41 had a synthetic buttstock while the Model 50.42 had a wood buttstock with steel buttplate incorporating a top extension used for either shoulder resting or inverted grenade launching.

Mid-1987 retail on this model was $1,497 (Model 50.41) or $1,654 (Model 50.42). The last MSR was $3,776 (this price reflected the last exchange rate and special order status of this model).

* **FN L.A.R. *Competition Paratrooper rifle* (50.63 & 50.64)** – similar to L.A.R. model, except has folding stock, 8.3 lbs. Mfg. 1950-88.

$4,275 $3,700 $3,300 $3,000 $2,550 $2,300 $2,150

There were 2 variations of the Paratrooper L.A.R. Model. The Model 50.63 had a stationary aperture rear sight and 18 in. barrel. The Model 50.64 was supplied with a 21 in. barrel and had a rear sight calibrated for either 150 or 200 meters. Both models retailed for the same price.

Mid-1987 retail on this model was $1,310 (both the Model 50.63 and 50.64). The last MSR was $3,239 (this price reflected the last exchange rate and special order status of this model).

CAL – originally imported in 1980, FN's .223 CAL military rifle succeeded the .308 FAL and preceeded the .223 FNC, at first declared illegal but later given amnesty, only 20 imported by Browning.

$7,800 $7,000 $6,250 $5,500 $4,750 $4,100 $3,600

FNC MODEL – .223 Rem. (5.56mm) cal., lightweight combat carbine, 16 or 18 1/2 in. barrel, NATO approved, 30 shot mag., 8.4 lbs. Disc. 1987.

$2,950 $2,700 $2,550 $2,100 $1,900 $1,650 $1,500

Add $350 for Paratrooper model (16 or 18 1/2 in. barrel).

While rarer, the 16 in. barrel model incorporated a flash hider that did not perform as well as the flash hider used on the standard 18 1/2 in. barrel.

Mid-1987 retail on this model was $749 (Standard Model) and $782 (Paratrooper Model). The last MSR was $2,204 (Standard Model) and $2,322 (Paratrooper Model) - these prices reflected the last exchange rate and special order status of these models.

SHOTGUNS: SxS

FN ANSON STANDARD GRADE – 12 or 16 ga., 26, 28, or 30 (most common) in. barrels, boxlock action, with or w/o ejectors, DT, checkered walnut stock, Greener style crossbolt, FN legend roll engraved on bottom of boxlock, minor engraving on and around screws. Mfg. circa 1910-1940.

$1,500 $1,300 $950 $625 $550 $375 $325

Add $150 for factory checkered stock options or semi-pistol grip option.
Add $200+ for more elaborate engraving. FN offered six luxury engraving styles.

MSR	100%	98%	95%	90%	80%	70%	60%

Subtract $50-$100 if w/o ejectors.

Subtract approx. $250 for replacement buttplate (not original), if in 95%+ original condition.

FN NEW ANSON STANDARD GRADE – 12 or 16 ga., 26, 28, or 30 (most common) in. barrels, boxlock action, with or w/o ejectors, DT, checkered walnut stock, FN legend hand engraved on top of the barrels, minor engraving on and around screws. Mfg. circa 1930-1968.

$1,400 $1,150 $850 $550 $475 $350 $300

Add $150 for factory checkered stock options or semi-pistol grip option.

Add $200+ for more elaborate engraving. FN offered six luxury engraving styles.

Subtract approx. $250 for replacement buttplate (not original), if in 95%+ original condition.

FN SIDELOCK STANDARD GRADE – 12 or 16 ga., 26, 28, or 30 (most common) in. barrels, sidelock action, ejectors, DT, checkered walnut stock, minor engraving on sideplates Mfg. 1921-1950. Improved in 1930, and often referred to as the Model 1930.

$1,500 $1,300 $950 $625 $550 $375 $325

Add $200+ for more elaborate engraving. FN offered six luxury engraving styles.

Subtract approx. $250 for replacement buttplate (not original), if in 95%+ original condition.

FNH USA

Current manufacturer and importer established in 1998, and located in McLean, VA. Dealer and distributor sales.

In the U.S., FN (Fabrique Nationale) is represented by two entities - FNH USA, which is responsible for sales, marketing, and business development, and FNM, which stands for FN Manufacturing, which handles manufacturing. FNH USA has two separate divisions - commercial/law enforcement, and military operations. FN Manufacturing is located in Columbia, SC. Design, research and development are conducted under the authority of FN Herstal S.A. Some of the firearms that FNM currently produces for the U.S. government are M16 rifles, M249 light machine guns, and M240 medium machine guns. FNM also produces the FNP line of handguns for the commercial, military, and law enforcement marketplaces. FNM is one of only three small arms manufacturers designated by the U.S. government as an industry base for small arms production. In November 2004, the FN model was chosen by the U.S. Special Operations Command (USSOCOM) for the new SCAR paramilitary rifle.

MSR	100%	98%	95%	90%	80%	70%	60%

CARBINES/RIFLES: SEMI-AUTO

PS90 – 5.7x28mm cal., blowback operation, bullpup configuration, 16 in. barrel, 10 or 30 shot box mag. runs horizontally along the top, empty cases are ejected downward, integrated muzzle brake, olive drab or black finish, configurations include PS90 RD with reflex sight module (mfg. 2009), PS90 USG with non-magnifying black reticle optical sight, and the PS90 TR with three M-1913 rails for optional optics, 6.3 lbs. Disc. 2011.

$1,925 $1,675 $1,450 $1,295 $1,075 $925 $800

Last MSR was $2,199.

* **PS90 Standard** – 5.7x28mm cal., similar to PS90, except no optical sights, 10 (new 2012) or 30 shot mag, black, OD Green, or olive drab (disc.) finish. New 2010.

MSR $1,695 $1,550 $1,325 $1,100 $975 $850 $725 $650

FS2000 STANDARD/TACTICAL – .223 Rem. cal., bullpup configuration, 17.4 in. barrel, gas operated with rotating bolt, 10 or 30 shot AR-15 style mag., empty cases are ejected through a forward port, includes 1.6x optical sighting package on Standard Model (disc. 2010), Tactical Model features emergency back up folding sights, CQB model features lower accessory rail, ambidextrous polymer stock, top mounted M-1913 rail, olive drab green or black finish, 7.6 lbs.

MSR $2,779 $2,425 $2,100 $1,825 $1,675 $1,450 $1,250 $995

MSR	100%	98%	95%	90%	80%	70%	60%

SCAR 16S – .223 Rem. cal., semi-auto only version of U.S. SOCOM's newest service rifle, gas operated short stroke piston system, free floating 16 1/4 in. barrel with hard chrome bore, 10 or 30 shot detachable box mag., folding open sights, fully ambidextrous operating controls, three optical rails, side folding polymer stock, fully adj. comb and LOP, black or Flat Dark Earth finish on receiver and stock, 7 1/4 lbs. New 2009.

| MSR $2,995 | $2,695 | $2,375 | $2,050 | $1,850 | $1,575 | $1,275 | $1,050 |

SCAR 17S – .308 Win. cal., 10 or 20 shot mag., otherwise similar to SCAR 16S, 8 lbs. New 2009.

| MSR $3,349 | $2,925 | $2,550 | $2,175 | $1,900 | $1,575 | $1,275 | $1,050 |

FNAR STANDARD – .308 Win. cal., 16 (new 2010) or 20 in. light or heavy fluted contoured barrel, 10 or 20 shot detachable box mag., one-piece M-1913 optical rail, three accessory rails attached to forearm, matte black synthetic pistol grip stock with soft cheekpiece, adj. comb, ambidextrous mag. release, 8.8 - 9 lbs. New 2009.

| MSR $1,699 | $1,550 | $1,325 | $1,100 | $975 | $850 | $725 | $650 |

PISTOLS: SEMI-AUTO

In addition to the models listed, FNH USA also imported the HP-SA ($800 last MSR), and the HP-SFS until 2006.

All FNP guns come standard with three magazines and a lockable hard case.

FNP-9 – 9mm Para. cal., 4 in. barrel, 10 or 16 (disc. 2010) shot mag., polymer frame, matte black or matte stainless steel slide, DA/SA, matte black or flat Dark Earth (mfg. 2010 only) finish, ambidextrous frame mounted decocker, underframe rail, interchangeable backstrap inserts, 25.2 oz. Disc. 2011.

| | | $575 | $495 | $435 | $380 | $340 | $300 | $275 |

Last MSR was $649.

Add $125 for night sights (disc. 2009).

Add $50 for USG operation (DA/SA, ambidextrous frame mounted decocker/manual safety), disc. 2010.

FNP-9M – 9mm Para. cal., 3.8 in. barrel, 10 or 15 shot mag., polymer frame, similar to the FNP-9, except is smaller frame, 24.8 oz. Disc. 2008.

| | | $525 | $450 | $400 | $365 | $335 | $300 | $275 |

Last MSR was $593.

Add $118 for night sights.

FNP-357 – .357 SIG cal., similar to FNP-9, black finish only, 14 shot mag., 27.2 oz. Mfg. 2009.

| | | $565 | $475 | $425 | $375 | $335 | $300 | $275 |

Last MSR was $629.

Add $65 for USG operation (features ambidextrous frame mounted decocker/manual safety levers).

PISTOLS: SEMI-AUTO 137

MSR	100%	98%	95%	90%	80%	70%	60%

FNP-40 – .40 S&W cal., 4 in. barrel, 10 or 14 (disc. 2010) shot mag., DA/SA, black or flat Dark Earth (mfg. 2010 only) polymer frame, optional stainless steel slide, underframe rail, interchangeable backstrap, external hammer, 25.2 or 26.7 oz. Disc. 2011.

$575 $495 $435 $380 $340 $300 $275

Last MSR was $649.

Add $125 for night sights (disc. 2009).

Add $50 for USG operation (features ambidextrous frame mounted decocker/manual safety levers), disc. 2010.

FNP-45 – .45 ACP cal., 4 1/2 in. barrel, DA/SA, 10 (disc. 2011), 14, or 15 (new 2011) shot mag., polymer frame, matte black finish with optional stainless steel slide, or flat Dark Earth (new 2010) finish, external extractor, underframe rail, interchangeable backstraps, 33.2 oz.

MSR $795 $725 $625 $575 $525 $450 $400 $350

Add $125 for night sights (disc.).

Subtract approx. 5% if without USG operation (features ambidextrous frame mounted decocker/manual safety levers).

Add approx. $186 for pistol package, which include three mags., molded polymer holster, double mag. pouch, and training barrel (mfg. 2009 only).

* **FNP-45 *Competition*** – .45 ACP cal., DA/SA, matte black finish, 15 shot mag., lower accessory rail, interchangable arched and flat backstrap inserts with lanyard holes, 33.2 oz. New 2011.

MSR $1,239 $1,075 $925 $825 $725 $625 $550 $475

* **FNP-45 *Tactical*** – .45 ACP cal., 5.3 in. threaded barrel, 15 shot mag., DA/SA, polymer frame with MIL-STD 1913 mounting rail and interchangeable backstraps with lanyard eyelets, serrated trigger guard, ambidextrous mag. release, manual safety, and slide stop, fixed combat sights, Black or Flat Dark Earth finish, stainless steel slide, includes fitted soft case. New 2010.

MSR $1,395 $1,200 $1,025 $875 $775 $675 $575 $495

FNS-9/FNS-40 – 9mm Para. or .40 S&W cal., DA, matte black or stainless steel slide, black polymer frame, 14 or 17 shot mag., fixed 3-dot night sights, loaded chamber indicator, front and rear cocking serrations, lower accessory rail, interchangeable backstrap inserts, serrated triggerguard, ambidextrous safety, 25.2 - 27 1/2 oz. New 2012.

MSR $699 $625 $525 $450 $395 $350 $300 $275

FNX-9/FNX-40 – 9mm Para. or .40 S&W cal., 4 in. barrel, 10 (new 2012), 14 (.40 S&W) or 17 (9mm Para.) shot mag., DA/SA, matte black or matte black with stainless steel slide, front and rear cocking serrations, MIL-STD mounting rail, deep V fixed combat sights, serrated trigger guard, ambidextrous mag. release and manual safety, four interchangeable backstrap inserts, 21.9-24.4 oz. New 2010.

MSR $699 $625 $525 $450 $395 $350 $300 $275

MSR	100%	98%	95%	90%	80%	70%	60%

FNX-45/FNX-45 COMPACT – .45 ACP cal., DA/SA, Black or Flat Dark Earth finish, 10, 12, or 15 shot mag., matte black or stainless steel slide, low profile fixed 3-dot sights, matte black polymer frame, front and rear cocking serrations, four interchangeable backstrap inserts, lower accessory rail, ambidextrous decocking levers, ring style external hammers, approx. 32 oz. New 2012.

MSR $809	$725	$650	$575	$500	$425	$350	$295

* *FNX-45 Tactical* – .45 ACP cal., similar to FNX-45, except has threaded barrel, 15 shot mag., high profile night sights, includes fitted Cordura nylon soft case, 33.6 oz. New 2012.

MSR $1,399	$1,200	$1,025	$875	$775	$675	$575	$495

FIVE-SEVEN/USG – 5.7x28mm cal., 4 3/4 in. barrel, USG or standard action, 10 or 20 shot mag., reversible mag. release, textured grip, black, OD Green (disc. 2011) or Flat Dark Earth finish, polymer frame, MIL-STD mounting, choice of fixed 3-dot (standard mfg.), adj. (USG model), C-More fixed (disc.), or C-More fixed night sights (disc.), underframe rail, includes three mags., hard case and cleaning kit, 20.8 oz.

MSR $1,299	$1,125	$975	$850	$750	$650	$575	$495

Add 10% for early mfg. that incorporated a larger trigger guard than current mfg.

RIFLES: BOLT ACTION

FNH USA imports a wide range of tactical rifle systems for military and law enforcement only. FNH USA also imported a line of modular system rifles, including the Ultima Ratio Intervention, the Ultima Ratio Commando II, and the .338 Lapua Model. Please contact the company directly for more information, including availability and pricing (see Contact Information).

PBR (PATROL BOLT RIFLE) – .300 WSM (XP Model) or .308 Win. cal., 22 in. heavy free floating barrel standard, stippled black Hogue overmolded stock, Picatinny rail, four shot fixed or removable box mag., some models may be marked "FN Herstal", later production marked "FNH", approx. 9 1/2 lbs.

	$1,075	$925	$825	$750	$625	$500	$425

Last MSR was $1,075.

Add $170 for XP Model in .300 WSM cal.

SPR A3 G (SPECIAL POLICE RIFLE) – .308 Win. cal., 24 in. fluted barrel with hard chromed bore, hinged floorplate, one-piece steel MIL-STD 1913 optical rail, A3 fiberglass tactical stock with adj. comb and LOP, steel sling studs, designed to achieve 1/2 MOA accuracy standard, 14.3 lbs.

MSR $3,395	$3,100	$2,710	$2,325	$2,110	$1,705	$1,395	$1,085

SPR A1/A1a – .308 Win. cal., 20 in. fluted (A1a) or 24 in. non-fluted barrel, 4 shot detachable box mag., pre-'64 Model 70 action, external claw extractor, matte black McMillan fiberglass stock with adj. comb and LOP, textured gripping surfaces, 12.4 lbs.

MSR $2,095	$1,875	$1,625	$1,400	$1,250	$1,025	$825	$725

Add $379 for SPR A1a with 20 in. fluted barrel.

RIFLES: BOLT ACTION

MSR	100%	98%	95%	90%	80%	70%	60%

SPR A2 – .308 Win. cal., similar to A1, 20 in. fluted or 24 in. non-fluted barrel, 11.6 or 12.2 lbs. Disc. 2009.

$2,500 $2,185 $1,875 $1,700 $1,375 $1,125 $875

Last MSR was $2,745.

SPR A5 M – .308 Win. or .300 WSM cal., 20 in. fluted (.308 Win. cal. only) or 24 in. non-fluted barrel, 3 or 4 shot mag., black synthetic tactical stock, 11.6 or 12.2 lbs.

MSR $2,895 $2,650 $2,325 $1,975 $1,750 $1,475 $1,250 $950

Add $100 for traditional hinged floorplate in .300 WSM cal. or $200 for hinged floorplate .308 Win. cal.

Add $200 for TBM (tactical box mag.) with 20 or 24 in. fluted barrel (new 2011).

PSR I – .308 Win. cal., 20 in. fluted or 24 in. non-fluted barrel, 3, 4, or 5 shot internal mag., FN tactical sport trigger system, hinged floorplate, matte black McMillan sporter style fiberglass stock, raised comb, recoil pad, steel sling studs, 7.7 or 8.7 lbs. Disc. 2009.

$2,000 $1,750 $1,500 $1,360 $1,100 $900 $700

Last MSR was $2,253.

PSR II/III – .308 Win. or .300 WSM (PSR II) cal., 22 in. fluted or 24 in. non-fluted barrel, 3, 4 (PSR III), or 5 shot internal or detachable box mag., FN tactical sport trigger system, matte olive drab McMillan sporter style fiberglass stock, raised comb, recoil pad, steel sling studs, 8.7 - 9.8 lbs. Disc. 2009.

$2,000 $1,750 $1,500 $1,360 $1,100 $900 $700

Last MSR was $2,253.

TSR XP/XP USA (TACTICAL SPORT RIFLES) – .223 Rem. (XP USA), 7.62x39mm (XP USA, disc. 2009), .300 WSM, or .308 Win. cal., Model 70 short (XP) or ultra short (XP USA) action, 20 in. fluted (disc. 2010), 20 or 24 in. non-fluted barrel, 3, 4 (detachable box mag., XP Model only), 5, or 6 shot mag., one-piece steel MIL-STD 1913 optical rail, full aluminum bedding block molded into FN/Hogue synthetic stock, olive drab overmolded surface, recoil pad, steel sling studs, 8.7 - 10.1 lbs.

MSR $1,199 $1,050 $925 $800 $700 $600 $500 $400

Add $100 for .300 WSM cal. with floorplate.

SHOTGUNS

FNH USA manufactured tactical style shotguns, including the FN Police Shotgun ($500 last MSR) and the FN Tactical Police Shotgun (with or w/o fixed stock, $923 last MSR).

MODEL SLP (SELF LOADING POLICE) – 12 ga., 18 (SLP Standard), or 22 in. standard cantilever Invector choked (Mark I/Tactical) or rifled (Mark I Rifled) barrel, 6 or 8 shot mag., adj. rear sight, black synthetic stock with half or full pistol grip, rail mounted adj. ghost ring rear sight, two gas pistons for heavy and light loads, 7.7 - 8.2 lbs.

MSR $1,299 $1,025 $975 $850 $725 $625 $525 $425

Add $50 for 18 in. barrel (SLP Standard) with adj. rear sight.

MSR	100%	98%	95%	90%	80%	70%	60%

Add $50 SLP MK1 Competition Model with 22 in. cantilever barrel.

Add $100 for 22 in. Cantilever barrel (SLP MK1 Tactical) with pistol grip stock, rifle sight.

Add $150 for Tactical Model with pistol grip, 18 in. barrel and adj. rifle sights (6 shot mag.).

MODEL SC1 O/U – 12 ga., 2 3/4 in. chambers, 28 in. VR barrel with invector plus choking, silver receiver, blue/gray adj. comb laminate stock with recoil pad. New 2011.

MSR $2,199	$1,950	$1,725	$1,575	$1,375	$1,150	$1,000	$875

NOTES

ABBREVIATIONS

*	Banned due to 1994-2004 Crime Bill (may be current again)	**BR**	Bench Rest
		BT	Beavertail
		BT	Browning Trap shotgun
5R	Five (groove) Rifling	**BUIS**	Back-Up Iron Sight(s)
A	Standard Grade Walnut	**c.**	Circa
A.R.M.S.	Atlantic Research Marketing Systems	**C/B 1994**	Introduced Because of 1994 Crime Bill
A2	AR-15 Style/Configuration w/ fixed carry handle	**CAD**	Computer Assisted Design
		cal.	Caliber
A3	AR-15 Style/Configuration w/ detachable carry handle	**CAR**	Colt Automatic Rifle or Carbine
		CAWS	Close Assault Weapons System
AA	Extra Grade Walnut		
AAA	Best Quality Walnut	**CB**	Crescent Buttplate
ACB	Advanced Combat Bolt (LWRC)	**CC**	Case Colors
ACP	Automatic Colt Pistol	**CCA**	Colt Collectors Association
ACR	Adaptive Combat Rifle	**CF**	Centerfire
ACS	MAGPUL Adaptable Carbine/ Storage (stock)	**CFR**	Code of Federal Regulations
		CH	Cross Hair
adj.	Adjustable	**CLMR**	Colt Lightning Magazine Rifle
AE	Automatic Ejectors or Action Express	**CMV**	Chrome Moly Vanadium Steel
AECA	Arms Export Control Act	**CNC**	Computer Numeric Controlled (machining/machinery)
AFG	MAGPUL Angled Fore Grip		
AK	Avtomat Kalashnikova rifle	**COMM.**	Commemorative
AMU	Army Marksman Unit	**COMP**	Compensated/Competition
AOW	Any Other Weapon (NFA)	**CQB**	Close Quarter Battle
appts.	Appointments	**CQC**	Close Quarter Combat
AR	Armalite Rifle	**C-R**	Curio-Relic
ASAP	MAGPUL Ambi Sling Attachment Point	**CRF**	Controlled Round Feed
		CRPF	Controlled Round Push Feed
ATR	All Terrain Rifle (Mossberg)	**CSAT**	Combat Shooting & Tactics (accessories)
ATS	All Terrain Shotgun (Mossberg)	**CTF**	Copper/Tin Frangible (bullet)
AWB	Assault Weapons Ban	**CTG/CTGE**	Cartridge
AWR	Alaskan/African Wilderness Rifle	**CTR**	MAGPUL Compact/Type Restricted (stock)
B	Blue	**CYL/C**	Cylinder
BAC	Browning Arms Company	**DA**	Double Action
BAD	MAGPUL Battery Assist Device (bolt catch lever)	**DAK**	Double Action Kellerman Trigger (SIG)
BAN/CRIME BILL ERA	Mfg. between Nov. 1989 - Sept. 12, 2004	**DAO**	Double Action Only
		DB	Double Barrel
BAR	Browning Automatic Rifle	**DBM**	Detachable Box Magazine
		DCM	Director of Civilian Marksmanship
BASR	Bolt Action Sniper Rifle (H&K)		
BB	Brass Backstrap	**DI**	Direct Impingement Gas System, see Glossary online
BBL	Barrel		
BLR	Browning Lever Rifle	**DIGS**	Delayed Impingement Gas System, see Glossary online
BMG	Browning Machine Gun		
BOSS	Ballistic Optimizing Shooting System	**DISC or disc.**	Discontinued
		DMR	Designated Marksman Rifle (U.S Army, LWRC)
BOSS-CR	BOSS w/o Muzzle Brake		
BP	Buttplate or Black Powder	**DPMS**	Defense Procurement Manufacturing Services
BPE	Black Power Express		
BPS	Browning Pump Shotgun	**DSL**	Detachable Side Locks
		DST	Double Set Triggers

ABBREVIATIONS

DT	Double Triggers	**IAR**	Infantry Automatic Rifle (LWRC)
DWM	DeutscheWaffen and Munitions Fabriken	**IC**	Improved Cylinder
EGLM	Enhanced Grenade Launcher Module (FNH)	**ILS**	Integral Locking System (North American Arms)
EJT	Ejector or Ejectors	**IM**	Improved Modified
EMAG	MAGPUL Export MAGazine	**IMI**	Israel Military Industries
EMP	Enhanced Micro Pistol (Springfield Inc.)	**in.**	Inch
EXC	Excellent	**intro.**	Introduced
EXT	Extractor or Extractors	**IOM**	Individual Officer Model (FNH model suffix)
F	Full Choke	**IPSC**	International Practical Shooting Confederation
F&M	Full & Modified		
FA	Forearm	**ISSF**	International Shooting Sports Federation
FAL	Fusil Automatique Leger		
FBT	Full Beavertail Forearm	**ITAR**	International Traffic (in) Arms Regulation
FDE	Flat Dark Earth (finish color)		
FDL	Fleur-de-lis	**IVT**	Italian Value-Added Tax
FE	Forend/Fore End	**JCP**	Joint Combat Pistol
FFL	Federal Firearms License	**KAC**	Knight's Armament Co.
FIRSH	Free Floating Integrated Rail System Handguard	**KMC**	Knight's Manufacturing Co.
		KSG	Kel Tec Shotgun
FK	Flat Knob	**L**	Long
FKLT	Flat Knob Long Tang	**LBA**	Lightning Bolt Action (Mossberg)
FM	Full Mag		
FMJ	Full Metal Jacket	**LBC**	Les Baer Custom (Inc.)
FN CAL	FN Carabine Automatique Leger	**lbs.**	Pounds
		LC	Long Colt
FN GP	FN Grande Puissance (pistol)	**LCW**	Lauer Custom Weaponry
FN LAR	Fabrique Nationale Light Automatique Rifle	**LDA**	Light Double Action (PARA USA INC.)
FN	Fabrique Nationale	**LEM**	Law Enforcement Model or Modification
FNAR	FN Automatic Rifle		
FNC	Fabrique Nationale Carabine	**LEO**	Law Enforcement Only
FNH USA	Fabrique Nationale Herstal (U.S. sales and marketing)	**LMT**	Lewis Machine and Tool (Company)
FNH	Fabrique Nationale Herstal	**LOP**	Length of Pull
FPS	Feet Per Second	**LPA**	Lightning Pump Action (Mossberg)
g.	Gram		
ga.	Gauge	**LPI**	Lines Per Inch
GCA	Gun Control Act	**LR**	Long Rifle
G-LAD	Green Laser Aiming Device	**LT**	Long Tang or Light
GOVT	Government	**LTR**	Light Tactical Rifle (Rem.)
gr.	Grain	**LTRK**	Long Tang Round Knob
H&H	Holland & Holland	**LWRC**	Land Warfare Resources Corporation
HB	Heavy Barrel		
H-BAR	H(eavy)-BARrel, AR-15/M16	**LWRC**	Leitner-Wise Rifle Company, Inc.
HC	Hard Case		
HK	Heckler und Koch	**M (MOD.)**	Modified Choke
HMR	Hornady Magnum Rimfire	**M&P**	Military & Police
HP	High Power (FN/Browning pistol)	**M-4**	Newer AR-15/M16 Carbine Style/Configuration
		Mag.	Magnum Caliber
HP	Hollow Point	**mag.**	Magazine
HPJ	High Performance Jacket	**MARS**	Modular Accessory Rail System
I	Improved	**MBUS**	MAGPUL Back-Up Sight

ABBREVIATIONS

MC	Monte Carlo
MCS	Modular Combat System (Rem.)
MFG or Mfg.	Manufactured/manufacture
MIAD	MAGPUL Mission Adaptable (grip, other)
mil	see Glossary online
mil-dot	See Glossary online
MIL SPEC	Mfg. to Military Specifications
MK	Mark
mm	Millimeter
MOA	Minute of Angle
MOE	MAGPUL Original Equipment
MOUT	Military Operations (on) Urbanized Terrain
MR	Matted Rib
MS2	MAGPUL Multi Mission Sling System
MSR	Manufacturer's Suggested Retail
MVG	MAGPUL MOE Vertical Grip
MWS	Modular Weapons System
N	Nickel
N/A	Not Applicable or Not Available
NATO	North Atlantic Treaty Org.
NE	Nitro Express
NFA	National Firearms Act (U.S. 1934)
NIB	New in Box
NM	National Match
no.	Number
NP	New Police
NP3/NP3 Plus	Nickel-Phosphorus (firearm coating)
NSST	Non Selective Single Trigger
NVD	Night Vision Device
O/U	Over and Under
OA	Overall
OAL	Overall Length
OB	Octagon Barrel
OBFM	Octagon Barrel w/full mag.
OBO	Or Best Offer
OCT	Octagon
ODG	Olive Drab Green (finish color)
ORC	Optics Ready Carbine
oz.	Ounce
P	Police (Rem. rifle/shotgun)
P99AS	Pistol 99 Anti Stress (trigger, Walther)
PAD	Personal Anti-recoil Device (Savage)
Para.	Parabellum
PBR	Patrol Bolt Rifle (FNH)
PDA	Personal Defense Assistant (PARA USA INC.)
PFFR	Percentage of factory finish remaining
PG	Pistol Grip
PK	Pistol Kompact (Walther)
PMAG	MAGPUL Polymer MAGazine
POR/P.O.R.	Price on Request
POST-'89	Paramilitary mfg. after Federal legislation in Nov. 1989
POST-BAN	Refers to production after Sept. 12, 2004
PPC	Pindell Palmisano Cartridge
PPD	Post Paid
PPK	Police Pistol Kriminal (Walther 1931 design)
PPKs	Police Pistol Kriminal (Walther 1968 design)
PPQ	Police Pistol Quick (defense trigger, Walther)
PRE-'89	Paramilitary mfg. before Federal legislation in Nov. 1989
PRE-BAN	Mfg. before September 13, 1994 per C/B or before Nov. 1989.
PRS/PRS2	MAGPUL Precision Rifle/Sniper (stock)
PSD	Personal Security Detail rifle (LWRC)
PSG	PrazisionSchutzenGewehr (H&K rifle)
PSR	Precision Shooting Rifle (FNH)
PXT	Power Extractor Technology (PARA USA INC.)
QD	Quick Detachable
RACS	Remington Arms Chassis System
RAS	Rail Adapter System
RB	Round Barrel/Round Butt
RCM	Ruger Compact Magnum
RCMP	Royal Canadian Mounted Police
RDS	Rapid Deployment Stock
REC	Receiver
REM	Remington
REM. MAG.	Remington Magnum
REPR	Rapid Engagement Precision Rifle (LWRC)
RF	Rimfire
RFB	Rifle Forward (ejection) Bullpup
RFM	Rim Fire Magnum
RIS	Rail Interface system
RK	Round Knob
RKLT	Round Knob Long Tang
RKST	Round Knob Short Tang
RMEF	Rocky Mt. Elk. Foundation

ABBREVIATIONS

RMR	Rimfire Magnum Rifle (Kel Tec)
RPD	Ruchnoy Pulemyot Degtyaryova (machine gun)
RR	Red Ramp
RSA	MAGPUL Rail Sling Attachment
RSUM	Remington Short-Action Ultra Magnum
RUM	Remington Ultra Magnum
RVG	MAGPUL Rail Vertical Grip
S	Short
S&W	Smith & Wesson
S/N	Serial Number
SA	Single Action
SAA	Single Action Army
SAAMI	Sporting Arms and Ammunition Manufacturers' Institute
SABR	Sniper/Assaulter Battle Rifle (LWRC)
SAE	Selective Automatic Ejectors
SAS	SIG Anti Snag (pistol models)
SASS	Single Action Shooting Society or (U.S. Army) Semi Automatic Sniper System
SAUM	Short Action Ultra Magnum
SAW	Semiautomatic Assault Weapon
SAW	Squad Automatic Weapon
SB	Shotgun butt or Steel backstrap
SBR	Short Barrel Rifle
SCAR	Special (Operations Forces) Combat Assault Rifle (FNH)
SCW	Sub Compact Weapon (Colt)
SDT	Super Dynamic Technology (PARA USA INC.)
ser.	serial
SG	Straight Grip
SIG	Schweizerische Industriegesellschaft
SIM	Special Impact Munition
SK	Skeet
SLP	Self Loading Police (FNH shotgun)
SMG	Submachine Gun
SMLE	Short Magazine Lee Enfield Rifle
SNT	Single Non-Selective Trigger
SOCOM	Special Operations Command
SOPMOD	Special Operations Peculiar Modification
SP	Special Purpose
SPC	Special Purpose Cartridge
SPEC	Special
SPEC-OPS	Special Operations
SPG	Semi-Pistol Grip
Spl.	Special
SPLLAT	Special Purpose Low Lethality Anti Terrorist (Munition)
SPR	Special Police Rifle (FNH), Special Purpose Rifle
SPS	Special Purpose Synthetic (Remington)
SPS	Superalloy Piston System (LWRC)
sq.	Square
SR	Solid Rib
SRC	Saddle Ring Carbine
SRT	Short Reset Trigger
SS	Single Shot or Stainless Steel
SSA	Super Short Action
SSR	Sniper Support Rifle (FNH)
SST	Single Selective Trigger
ST	Single Trigger
SUR	Sport Utility Rifle - see Glossary online
SWAT	Special Weapons Assault Team
SWAT	Special Weapons and Tactics
SxS	Side by Side
TB	Threaded Barrel
TBA	To be Announced
TBM	Tactical Box Magazine
TD	Take Down
TDR	Target Deployment Rifle (Rem.)
TGT	Target
TH	Target Hammer
TIR	Target Interdiction Rifle (Rem.)
TPS	Tactical Police Shotgun (FNH)
TRP	Tactical Response Pistol (Springfield Inc.)
TRPAFD	Take Red Pen Away From Dave!
TS	Target Stocks
TSOB	Scope Mount Rail Weaver Type
TSR XP USA	Tactical Sport Rifle - Extreme Performance Ultra Short Action (FNH)
TSR XP	Tactical Sport Rifle - Extreme Performance (FNH)
TT	Target Trigger
TTR	Tactical Target Rifle (PARA USA INC.)
TWS	Tactical Weapons System (Rem.)
UBR	MAGPUL Utility/Battle Rifle (stock)
UCIW	Ultra Compact Individual Weapon (LWRC)
UCP	Universal Combat Pistol (H&K)
UIT	Union Internationale de Tir

ABBREVIATIONS

UMC	Union Metallic Cartridge Co.	**WC**	Wad Cutter
UMP	Universal Machine Pistol (H&K)	**WCF**	Winchester Center Fire
USA	Ultra Safety Assurance (Springfield Inc.)	**WD**	Wood
		WFF	Watch For Fakes
USAMU	U.S. Army Marksmanship Unit	**WIN**	Winchester
USC	Universal Self-Loading Carbine (H&K)	**WMR**	Winchester Magnum Rimfire
		WO	White Outline
USG	United States Government (FNH model suffix)	**WRA**	Winchester Repeating Arms Co.
USP	Universal Self-Loading Pistol (H&K)	**WRF**	Winchester Rim Fire
		WRM	Winchester Rimfire Magnum
USPSA	United States Practical Shooting Association	**WSL**	Winchester Self-Loading
		WSM	Winchester Short Magnum
USR	Urban Sniper Rifle (Rem.)	**WSSM**	Winchester Super Short Magnum
USSOCOM	U.S. Special Operations Command	**WW**	World War
		X (1X)	1X Wood Upgrade or Extra Full Choke Tube
VAT	Value Added Tax		
Vent.	Ventilated	**XD**	Extreme Duty (Springfield Inc.)
VG	Very Good		
VR	Ventilated Rib	**XDM**	Extreme Duty M Factor (Springfield Inc.)
VTAC	Viking Tactics, Inc. (accessories)		
VTR	Varmint Triangular Profile Barrel (Remington)	**XX (2X)**	2X Wood Upgrade or Extra Extra Full Choke Tube
		XXX (3x)	3X Wood Upgrade
w/	With	**YHM**	Yankee Hill Machine
w/o	Without		
WBY	Weatherby		

CONTACT INFORMATION

BROWNING

Administrative Headquarters
One Browning Place
Morgan, UT 84050-9326
Phone No.: 801-876-2711
Product Service: 800-333-3288
Fax No.: 801-876-3331
Website: www.browning.com
Website: www.browningint.com

Custom Shop U.S. Representative
Mr. Ron McGhie
Email: ronm@browning.com

Browning Parts and Service
3005 Arnold Tenbrook Rd.
Arnold, MO 63010-9406
Phone No.: 800-322-4626
Fax No.: 636-287-9751

Historical Research (Browning Arms Co. marked guns only)
Browning Historian
One Browning Place
Morgan, UT 84050-9326
Fax No.: 801-876-3331
Website: www.browning.com

FABRIQUE NATIONALE

Factory - Browning S.A.
Fabrique Nationale Herstal SA
Parc Industriel des Hauts Sarts
3me Ave. 25
B-4040 Herstal, BELGIUM
Fax No.: 011-32-42-40-5212

FNH USA
P.O. Box 697
McLean, VA 22101
Phone No.: 703-288-1292
Fax No.: 703-288-1730
Website: www.fnhusa.com
Email: info@fnhusa.com

NOTES

BROWNING SERIALIZATION
SERIALIZATION PRE-1975

Since 1968-1969 was a transition period in Browning serialization, firearms may be serialized with either 1968 or 1969 style markings.

A-5 (AUTOMATIC 5) SHOTGUN -12 ga.

YEAR	SER. # START	SER. # END
1903	1	4121
1904	4122	15300
1905	15301	19920
1906	19921	22320
1907	22321	26970
1908	26971	30446
1909	30447	33431
1910	33432	35630
1911	35631	35925
1912	35926	38988
1913	38989	44250
1914	44251	47298
1915-1918 No Production		
1919	47719	47950
1920	47299	47718
1921	48951	53500
1922	53501	58150
1923	58151	62600
1924	62601	69300
1925	69301	79150
1926	79151	88000
1927	88001	106250
1928	106251	127650
1929	127651	154500
1930	154501	177100
1931	177101	182300
1932	182301	182788
1933	182789	183152
1934	183153	185560
1935	185561	191604
1936	191605	194535
1937	194536	199200

A-5 (AUTOMATIC 5) SHOTGUN -12 ga., cont.

YEAR	SER. # START	SER. # END
1938	199201	208400
1939	208401	218808
1940	218809	224596
1941-1943 No Production		
1944 Production limited to servicemen		
1945 Production limited to servicemen		
1946	228729	240950
1947	240951	256500
1948	256501	274100
1949	274101	288550
1950	288551	316750
1951	316751	352050
1952	352051	387499
1953	387500	437400
1954	437401	447750
1955	447751	454700
1956	454701	459900
1957	459901	463700

In 1953 Browning added an alpha prefix to the serial number to differentiate between Lightweight and Standardweight guns.

YEAR	STD.12	LT.WT. 12
1953	H1-H6600	L1-L4450
1954	H6601-H39700	L4451-L45250
1955	H39701-H83450	L45251-L83600
1956	H83451-H100000	L83601-L99877
1956	M1-M35250	G1-G35450
1957	M35251-M86300	G35451-G85950
1958	M86301-M99999	G85951-G99663

BROWNING SERIALIZATION

1958-1976 Ser. No. sequence changed to include a one or two digit numeral followed by an alpha character.

YEAR	STD. WT.	LT. WT.	MAGNUM
1958	8M	8G	8V
1959	9M	9G	9V
1960	0M	0G	0V
1961	1M	1G	1V
1962	2M	2G	2V
1963	3M	3G	3V
1965	5M	5G	5V
1966	6M	6G	6V
1964	4M	4G	4V
1967	7M	7G	7V
1968	8M	8G	8V
1969	69M	69G	69V
1970	Disc.	70G	70V
1971	Disc.	71G	71V
1972	Disc.	72G	72V
1973	Disc.	73G	73V
1974	Disc.	74G	74V
1975	Disc.	75G	75V
1976	Disc.	76G	76V

A-5 (AUTOMATIC 5) SHOTGUN -16 ga.

YEAR	SER. # START	SER. # END
1909	1	3200
1910-1912	3201	15000
1913	15001	19000
1914-1918	No Production	
1919	19671	20500
1920	20501	22237
1921	22238	24050
1922	24051	26000
1923	26001	28400
1924	28401	35650
1925	35651	40010
1926	40011	51600
1927	51599	57900
1928	57901	65100
1929	65101	82750

A-5 (AUTOMATIC 5) SHOTGUN -16 ga., cont.

YEAR	SER. # START	SER. # END
1930	82751	90500
1931	90501	94000
1932	94001	96072
1933	96073	96143
1934	96144	99500
1935	99501	103500
1936	103501	105850
1937	105851	111000
1938	111001	118200
1939	118201	126123
1940	126123	126175
1941-1943	No Production	
1944	Production limited to servicemen	
1945	Production limited to servicemen	
1946	128117	128646
1947	128647	130616
1947	X1001	X13666
1948	X13667	X23501
1949	X23502	X34600
1950	X34601	X43700
1951	X43701	X59400
1952	X59401	X77700
1953	X77701	X99999

In 1953 Browning changed the Ser. No. alphabetic character to differentiate between Lightweight (Sweet 16) & Standard weight guns.

YEAR	STD.16	SWEET 16
1953	R1-R3100	S1-S3700
1954	R3100-R20800	S3701-S24850
1955	R20801-R48750	S24851-S49350
1956	R48751-R74700	S49350-S72300
1957	R74701-R99999	S72301-S99908

1957-58 Prefix "T" for Standardweight and Prefix "A" for Sweet 16 numbers mixed, but range from 1-10900.

1958-1976 Ser. No. sequence changed to include a one or two digit numeral followed by an alpha character.

YEAR	STD.16	SWEET 16
1958	8R	8S
1959	9R	9S
1960	0R	0S
1961	1R	1S
1962	2R	2S
1963	3R	3S
1964	Disc.	4S
1965	Disc.	5S
1966	Disc.	6S
1967	Disc.	7S
1968	Disc.	8S
1969	Disc.	69S
1970	Disc.	70S
1971	Disc.	71S
1972	Disc.	72S
1973	Disc.	73S
1974	Disc.	74S
1975	Disc.	75S
1976	Disc.	Disc.

A-5 SHOTGUN - 20 ga.

YEAR	LT.WT. 20	MAGNUM 20
1958	8Z	Introduced in 1967
1959	9Z	
1960	0Z	
1961	1Z	
1962	2Z	
1963	3Z	
1964	4Z	
1965	5Z	
1966	6Z	
1967	7Z	7X
1968	68Z	68X

A-5 SHOTGUN - 20 ga., cont.

YEAR	LT.WT. 20	MAGNUM 20
1969	69Z	69X
1970	70Z	70X
1971	71Z	71X
1972	72Z	72X
1973	73Z	73X
1974	74Z	74X
1975	75Z	75X
1976	76Z	76X

SUPERPOSED MODEL - O & U - 12 ga.

YEAR	SER. # START	SER. # END
1931	1	2000
1932	2001	4000
1933	4001	6000
1934	6001	8000
1935	8001	10000
1936	10001	12000
1937	12001	14000
1938	14001	16000
1939	16001	17000
1939-1947 NO PRODUCTION		
1948	17001	17200
1949	17201	20000
1950	20001	21000
1951	21001	27000
1952	27001	33000
1953	33001	37000
1954	37001	43000
1955	43001	48000
1956	48001	54000
1957	54001	59000
1958	59001	68500
1959	68501	76500
1960	76501	86500
1961	86501	96500
1962	96501	99999
1962	1	6500

Serial number change to letter and number suffix

BROWNING SERIALIZATION

YEAR	SER. # PREFIX CODE
1962	S2 suffix after Ser. No.
1963	S3 suffix after Ser. No.
1964	S4 suffix after Ser. No.
1965	S5 suffix after Ser. No.
1966	S6 suffix after Ser. No.
1967	S7 suffix after Ser. No.
1968	S8 suffix after Ser. No.
1969	S69 suffix after Ser. No.
1970	S70 suffix after Ser. No.
1971	S71 suffix after Ser. No.
1972	S72 suffix after Ser. No.
1973	S73 suffix after Ser. No.
1974	S74 suffix after Ser. No.
1975	S75 suffix after Ser. No.
1976	S76 suffix after Ser. No.

1976 to 1984"P" or Presentation Models only

YEAR	SER. # PREFIX CODE
1963	V3 suffix after Ser. No.
1964	V4 suffix after Ser. No.
1965	V5 suffix after Ser. No.
1966	V6 suffix after Ser. No.
1967	V7 suffix after Ser. No.
1968	V8 suffix after Ser. No.
1969	V69 suffix after Ser. No.
1970	V70 suffix after Ser. No.
1971	V71 suffix after Ser. No.
1972	V72 suffix after Ser. No.
1973	V73 suffix after Ser. No.
1974	V74 suffix after Ser. No.
1975	V75 suffix after Ser. No.
1976	V76 suffix after Ser. No.

SUPERPOSED MODEL - O & U - 20 ga.

YEAR	SER. # START	SER. # END
1949	201	1700
1950	1701	2800
1951	2801	3200
1952	3201	5300
1953	5301	6700
1954	6701	8400
1955	8401	9400
1956	9401	10500
1957	10501	11500
1958	11501	14180
1959	14181	17060
1960	17061	20640
1961	20641	23820
1962	23821	27300

SUPERPOSED MODEL - O & U - 28 ga. & .410 bore

YEAR	28 GA.	.410 BORE
1960-1962	NOT AVAILABLE	
1963	F3	J3
1964	F4	J4
1965	F5	J5
1966	F6	J6
1967	F7	J7
1968	F8	J8
1969	F69	J69
1970	F70	J70
1971	F71	J71
1972	F72	J72
1973	F73	J73
1974	F74	J74
1975	F75	J75
1976	F76	J76

Serial number change to letter and number suffix.

LIEGE O & U - Approximately 10,000 produced

YEAR	SER. # PREFIX CODE
1973	73J prefix before Ser. No.
1974	74J prefix before Ser. No.
1975	75J prefix before Ser. No.

DOUBLE AUTOMATIC SHOTGUN

YEAR	SER. # START	SER. # END
1952 -	N/A	
1959	N/A	
1960 -	N/A	
1971	N/A	

1st or both digits indicate last 2 digits in year of manufacture (i.e. - OA1947 - 1960 mfg., 70A245671 - 1970 mfg.)

HI-POWER (9mm) PISTOL

YEAR	SER. # START	SER. # END
1945-1954 no data for the annual breakdown		
	1	2250
1955	72251	75000
1956	75001	77250
1957	77251	80000
1958	80001	85267
1959	85268	89687
1960	89688	93027
1961	93028	109145
1962	109146	113548
1963	113549	115822
1964	115823	T136538
1965	T136569	T146372
1966	T146373	T173285
1967	T173286	T213999
1968	T214000	T258000
1969	T258001	T261000

During 1969 the Hi-Power pistol Serial Number code was changed to a two digit year and "C" prefix. Serial Numbers for "T" prefix Hi-Power pistols exceeded T300000 and were shipped into 1970.

YEAR	SER. # PREFIX CODE
1969	69C prefix before Ser. No.
1970	70C prefix before Ser. No.
1971	71C prefix before Ser. No.
1972	72C prefix before Ser. No.
1973	73C prefix before Ser. No.
1974	74C prefix before Ser. No.
1975	75C prefix before Ser. No.
1976	76C prefix before Ser. No.
1977 to date	New style serialization

BROWNING .380 ACP CAL.

YEAR	SER. # START	SER. # END
1955 -	N/A	
1964	N/A	
1965	500000	598804
1966	598805	603890
1967	603891	619474
1968	619475	N/A
1969 -	N/A	

1970 Discontinued due to GCA of 1968. New model has longer barrel, adj. rear sight, modified grip.

YEAR	SER. # PREFIX CODE
1971	71N prefix before Ser. No.
1972	72N prefix before Ser. No.
1973	73N prefix before Ser. No.
1974	74N prefix before Ser. No.
1975	75N prefix before Ser. No.

BROWNING SERIALIZATION

.25 ACP CAL. BABY BROWNING

YEAR	SER. # START	SER. # END
1955-1958	Records not available	
1959	181000	206349
1960	206350	230999
1961	231000	250999
1962	251000	278999
1963	279000	286099
1964	286100	308499
1965	308500	329999
1966	333000	367443
1967	367444	412999
1968	413000	479000

1969 Discontinued because of GCA of 1968

.22 CAL. (Nomad-Challenger-Medalist)

YEAR	NOMAD	CHALLENGER	MEDALIST
1959	P9	U9	T9
1960	P0	U0	T0
1961	P1	U1	T1
1962	P2	U2	T2
1963	P3	U3	T3
1964	P4	U4	T4
1965	P5	U5	T5
1966	P6	U6	T6
1967	P7	U7	T7
1968	P8	U8	T8
1969	P69	U69	T69
1970	P70	U70	T70
1971	P71	U71	T71
1972	P72	U72	T72
1973	P73	U73	T73
1974	Disc.	U74	T74
1975	Disc.	Disc.	Disc.

BOLT ACTION RIFLES
(Safari, Medallion, & Olympian Models)

YEAR	SER. # CODE
1959 -	N/A
1962	No prefix (numeral-letter) before Ser. No. (i.e., only digits)
1963	3-single letter prefix or suffix by Ser. No.
1964	4-single letter prefix or suffix by Ser. No.
1965	5-single letter prefix or suffix by Ser. No.
1966	6-single letter prefix or suffix by Ser. No.
1967	7-single letter prefix or suffix by Ser. No.
1968	8-single letter prefix or suffix by Ser. No.
1969	Single letter (Y, Z, or L) followed by last 2 digits of year of mfg. Prefix only.
1970	"Y70" prefix
1971	"L71" prefix
1972	"Z72" prefix
1973	"Y73" prefix
1974	"Z74" prefix
1975	"L75" prefix

B.A.R.

YEAR	SER. # SUFFIX CODE
1967	"M7" suffix after Ser. No.
1968	"M8" suffix after Ser. No.
1969	"M69" suffix after Ser. No.
1970	"M70" suffix after Ser. No.
1971	"M71" suffix after Ser. No.
1972	"M72" suffix after Ser. No.
1973	"M73" suffix after Ser. No.
1974	"M74" suffix after Ser. No.
1975	"M75" suffix after Ser. No.
1976	"M76" suffix after Ser. No.
1976 to date	New sequence with "RT" appearing in middle of Ser. No.

.22 AUTO RIFLE (Grades I, II, and III)

YEAR	SER. # CODE
1956-Mid. 1961	"T" prefix = LR, "A" prefix = short
Mid. 1961	"A" changed to "E" prefix 5 digits or less.
1961	"1T" or "1A" or "1E" prefix before Ser. No.
1962	"2T" or "2E" prefix before Ser. No.
1963	"3T" or "3E" prefix before Ser. No.
1964	"4T" or "4E" prefix before Ser. No.
1965	"5T" or "5E" prefix before Ser. No.
1966	"6T" or "6E" prefix before Ser. No.
1967	"7T" or "7E" prefix before Ser. No.
1968	"8T" or "8E" prefix before Ser. No.
1969	"69T" or "69E" prefix before Ser. No.
1970	"70T" or "70E" prefix before Ser. No.
1971	"71T" or "71E" prefix before Ser. No.
1972	"72T" or "72E" prefix before Ser. No.
1973	Japan production

T-BOLT RIFLE (T1 and T2)

YEAR	SER. # CODE
1965	"X5" suffix after Ser. No.
1966	"X6" suffix after Ser. No.
1967	"X7" suffix after Ser. No.
1968	"X8" suffix after Ser. No.
1969	"X69" suffix after Ser. No.
1970	"X70" suffix after Ser. No.
1971	"X71" suffix after Ser. No.
1972	"X72" suffix after Ser. No.
1973	"X73" suffix after Ser. No.
1974	"X74" suffix after Ser. No.
1975	"X75" suffix after Ser. No.

BROWNING SERIALIZATION 1975 TO CURRENT

In 1975 Browning began using the two (2) letter code system (located in the middle of the serial number) for determining the year of manufacture. For example "PN" would be "89" indicating 1989.

LETTER	NUMBER
Z	1
Y	2
X	3
W	4
V	5
T	6
R	7
P	8
N	9
M	10

BROWNING MODEL CONFIGURATION CODES

Beginning in 1976 Browning started identifying models and its configuration using a three number (or possibly a combination of letters and numbers) code in the serial number.

Shotguns O/U

Superposed Grade I

CONFIGURATION	CODE
12 Ga. Hunting	214
12 Ga. Superlight	204
20 Ga. Hunting	264
20 Ga. Superlight	224

BROWNING MODEL CONFIGURATION CODES

Superposed Pigeon Grade

CONFIGURATION	CODE
12 Ga. Hunting	314
12 Ga. Superlight	304
20 Ga. Hunting	364
20 Ga. Superlight	324

Superposed Pointer Grade

CONFIGURATION	CODE
12 Ga. Hunting	414
12 Ga. Superlight	404
20 Ga. Hunting	464
20 Ga. Superlight	424

Superposed Diana Grade

CONFIGURATION	CODE
12 Ga. Hunting	514
12 Ga. Superlight	504
20 Ga. Hunting	564
20 Ga. Superlight	524

Superposed Midas Grade

CONFIGURATION	CODE
12 Ga. Hunting	614
12 Ga. Superlight	604
20 Ga. Hunting	664
20 Ga. Superlight	624

Citori Grade I

CONFIGURATION	CODE
12 Ga. 3-1/2	103
12 Ga. Trap Monte Carlo Stock	143
12 Ga. Trap Conventional Stock	N43
12 Ga. Skeet	1B3
12 Ga. Hunting	153
12 Ga. Lightning	753
12 Ga. Superlight	A13
12 Ga. Upland	B13
325 20 Ga. Sporting	C33
20 Ga. Skeet	1C3
20 Ga. Hunting	163
20 Ga. Lightning	763
20 Ga. Micro Lightning	H33
20 Ga. Superlight	A33
20 Ga. Upland	B33
28 Ga. Skeet	1E3
28 Ga. Hunting	173
28 Ga. Lightning	773
28 Ga. Superlight	A73
.410 Bore Skeet	1F3
.410 Bore Hunting	183
.410 Bore Lightning	783
.410 Bore Superlight	A83
Three Barrel Set	1K3
Four Barrel Set	1A3

BROWNING MODEL CONFIGURATION CODES

Citori Grade III

CONFIGURATION	CODE
12 Ga. Trap Monte Carlo Stock	343
12 Ga. Trap Conventional Stock	R43
12 Ga. Skeet	3B3
12 Ga. Hunting	353
12 Ga. Lightning	853
12 Ga. Superlight	M13
20 Ga. Skeet	3C3
20 Ga. Hunting	363
20 Ga. Lightning	863
20 Ga. Superlight	M33
28 Ga. Skeet	3E3
28 Ga. Lightning	873
28 Ga. Superlight	M73
.410 Bore Skeet	3F3
410 Lightning	883
410 Superlight	M83
Three Barrel Set	3K3
Four Barrel Set	3A3

Citori Grade VI

CONFIGURATION	CODE
12 Ga. Trap Monte Carlo Stock	643
12 Ga. Trap Conventional Stock	S43
12 Ga. Skeet	6B3
12 Ga. Hunting	653
12 Ga. Lightning	953
12 Ga. Superlight	F13
20 Ga. Skeet	6C3
20 Ga. Hunting	663
20 Ga. Lightning	963
20 Ga. Superlight	F33

Citori Grade VI, cont.

CONFIGURATION	CODE
28 Ga. Skeet	6E3
28 Ga. Lightning	973
.410 Bore Skeet	6F3
.410 Bore Lightning	983
.410 Bore Superlight	F83
Three Barrel Set	6K3
Four Barrel Set	6A3

Citori Golden Clays

CONFIGURATION	CODE
12 Ga. Trap Monte Carlo Stock	143
12 Ga. Trap Conventional Stock	N43
12 Ga. Skeet	1B3
20 Ga. 325 Sporting	C33
20 Ga. Skeet	6C3
28 Ga. Skeet	6E3
.410 Bore Skeet	6F3
GTI Sporting	P13
325 Sporting	C13
Special Sporting	T13
Lightning Sporting	W53
PLUS Trap	J43
PLUS Combo	1P3
Three Barrel Set	6K3
Four Barrel Set	6A3

Citori Gran Lightning

CONFIGURATION	CODE
12 Ga.	253
20 Ga.	263
28 Ga.	273
.410 Bore	283

BROWNING MODEL CONFIGURATION CODES

Shotguns Semi-Auto

Auto 5

CONFIGURATION	CODE
Magnum 12 Ga.	151
Magnum Stalker 12 Ga.	T51
Light 12 Ga.	211
Light 12 Stalker 12 Ga.	T11
Sweet 16 Ga.	221
Magnum 20 Ga.	161
Light 20 Ga.	231

A-500

CONFIGURATION	CODE
12 Ga. Recoil	751
12 Ga. Gas	351
12 Ga. Gas Sporting Clays	S51

Gold

CONFIGURATION	CODE
10 Ga.	R91
12 Ga.	F51
20 Ga.	F61

Shotguns Slide Action

BPS

CONFIGURATION	CODE
10 Ga.	192
10 Ga. Stalker	T92
12 Ga. 3-1/2	102
12 Ga. 3-1/2" Stalker	T02
12 Ga. Pigeon	P52
12 Ga. Game	152
12 Ga.	152
(includes all hunting & Upland Models)	
12 Ga. Stalker	T52

BPS, cont.

CONFIGURATION	CODE
20 Ga.	162
(includes all hunting & Upland Models)	
28 Ga.	172

Model 42 Limited Edition 410 Bore

CONFIGURATION	CODE
Grade I	882
High Grade	982

Shotguns Side by Side

B-SS

CONFIGURATION	CODE
Sidelock 12 Ga.	918
Sidelock 20 Ga.	938

Rifles

MODEL	CODE
BAR Grade IV	437
BAR 22 Grade I	146
BAR 22 Grade II	246
A-Bolt 22 Grade I	136
A-Bolt 22 Gold Med.	G36
Trombone 22	337
B-92	167

Pistols 1975-1998

MODEL	CODE
Hi-Power 9mm	245
Hi-Power .40 S&W	2W5
Hi-Power Military	215

Pistols 1999-Current

MODEL	CODE
Hi-Power 9mm	510

NOTES

07337NM 972/3

$*$ = Full, $*$ - IM (Emp uum Medit.), $**$ = M, $**$ = IC (EC)

$***$ - SK, xxx = Cyl

SERIALIZATION INDEX

A-5 (AUTOMATIC 5)
SHOTGUN -12 ga.................148

A-5 (AUTOMATIC 5)
SHOTGUN -16 ga.................149

A-5 SHOTGUN - 20 ga...............150

SUPERPOSED MODEL -
O & U - 12 ga.....................150

SUPERPOSED MODEL -
O & U - 20 ga.....................151

SUPERPOSED MODEL -
O & U - 28 ga. & .410 bore ..151

LIEGE O & U 152

DOUBLE AUTOMATIC SHOTGUN..152

HI-POWER (9mm) PISTOL 152

BROWNING .380 ACP CAL..........152

.25 ACP CAL. BABY BROWNING .153

.22 CAL. (Nomad-Challenger-
Medalist) 153

BOLT ACTION RIFLES
(Safari, Medallion, &
Olympian Models)...............153

B.A.R. 153

.22 AUTO RIFLE (Grades I, II, and
III) 154

T-BOLT RIFLE (T1 and T2) 154

**BROWNING SERIALIZATION
1975 TO CURRENT 154**

**BROWNING MODEL
CONFIGURATION CODES .. 154**

Shotguns O/U 154
Superposed Grade I..................154
Superposed Pigeon Grade..........155
Superposed Pointer Grade 155
Superposed Diana Grade 155
Superposed Midas Grade 155
Citori Grade I...........................155
Citori Grade III.........................156
Citori Grade VI 156
Citori Golden Clays 156
Citori Gran Lightning.................156
Shotguns Semi-Auto 157
Auto 5.....................................157
A-500 157
Gold 157
Shotguns Slide Action 157
BPS 157
Model 42
Limited Edition 410 Bore......157
Shotguns Side by Side 157
B-SS.......................................157
Rifles 157
Pistols 1975-1998.....................157
Pistols 1999-Current 157

CATEGORY INDEX

BROWNING 10
- BROWNING HISTORY 10
- BROWNING FACTS 11
- BROWNING VALUES INFORMATION .. 11
- BROWNING SERIALIZATION 11
- BROWNING CUSTOM SHOP 12
- PISTOLS: SEMI-AUTO, CENTERFIRE, F.N. PRODUCTION UNLESS OTHERWISE NOTED 12
- PISTOLS: SEMI-AUTO, .22 CAL. RIMFIRE 21
- RIFLES: BOLT ACTION 27
- RIFLES: BOLT ACTION, CENTERFIRE A-BOLT I SERIES 30
- RIFLES: BOLT ACTION, CENTERFIRE A-BOLT II SERIES 32
- RIFLES: BOLT ACTION, CENTERFIRE X-BOLT SERIES 39
- RIFLES: BOLT ACTION, RIMFIRE A-BOLT SERIES 40
- RIFLES: LEVER ACTION 41
- RIFLES: O/U 47
- RIFLES: SEMI-AUTO, .22 LR 47
- RIFLES: SEMI-AUTO, BAR SERIES 50
- RIFLES: SEMI-AUTO, FAL & CAL SERIES 54
- RIFLES: SINGLE SHOT 54
- RIFLES: SLIDE ACTION 56
- SHOTGUNS: BOLT ACTION, A-BOLT SERIES 57
- SHOTGUNS: O/U, CYNERGY SERIES .. 58
- SHOTGUNS: O/U, CITORI HUNTING SERIES 61
- SHOTGUNS: O/U, CITORI SKEET 69
- SHOTGUNS: O/U, CITORI SPORTING CLAYS 72
- SHOTGUNS: O/U, CITORI TARGET 78
- SHOTGUNS: O/U, CITORI TRAP 78
- SHOTGUNS: O/U, SUPERPOSED GENERAL INFO & CHOKE CODES 81
- SUPERPOSED: 1931-1940 MFG. (PRE-WWII) 81
- SUPERPOSED: 1948-1960 MFG. (POST-WWII) 83
- SUPERPOSED: 1960-1976 MFG. 85
- SHOTGUNS: O/U, SUPERPOSED HIGH GRADES: 1985-PRESENT 94
- Superposed: Custom Shop Current Pricing & Models 95
- SHOTGUNS: SxS 97
- SHOTGUNS: SEMI-AUTO, A-5 1903-1998, 2012-CURRENT MFG. 98
- SHOTGUNS: SEMI-AUTO, DOUBLE AUTO MODELS 104
- SHOTGUNS: SEMI-AUTO, MISC. - RECENT MFG. 105
- SHOTGUNS: SINGLE BARREL, BT-99 & BT-100 116
- SHOTGUNS: SINGLE BARREL, RECOILLESS TRAP 120
- SHOTGUNS: SLIDE ACTION 120
- SPECIAL EDITIONS, COMMEMORATIVES, & LIMITED MFG. 124

FABRIQUE NATIONALE 127
- PISTOLS: SEMI-AUTO 127
- PISTOLS: SEMI-AUTO, HI-POWER VARIATIONS 127
- REVOLVERS 130
- RIFLES: BOLT ACTION 130
- RIFLES: SEMI-AUTO 131
- RIFLES: SEMI-AUTO, FAL/LAR/CAL/FNC SERIES 132
- SHOTGUNS: SxS 133

FNH USA 135
- CARBINES/RIFLES: SEMI-AUTO 135
- PISTOLS: SEMI-AUTO 136
- RIFLES: BOLT ACTION 138
- SHOTGUNS 139